Dualities

Dualities
A Theology of Difference

Michelle Voss Roberts

© 2010 Michelle Voss Roberts

First edition
Published by Westminster John Knox Press
Louisville, Kentucky

All rights reserved. No part of this book may be reproduced or transmitted in any form or by any means, electronic or mechanical, including photocopying, recording, or by any information storage or retrieval system, without permission in writing from the publisher. For information, address Westminster John Knox Press, 100 Witherspoon Street, Louisville, Kentucky 40202-1396. Or contact us online at www.wjkbooks.com.

Excerpts from *Mechthild of Magdeburg, The Flowing Light of the Godhead*, translated and introduced by Frank Tobin. Copyright © 1998 by Frank Tobin. Paulist Press, Inc., New York/Mahwah, NJ. Reprinted by permission of Paulist Press, Inc. www.paulistpress.com.

Excerpts from *To the Other Shore: Lalla's Life and Poetry*, copyright © 1999 by Jaishree Kak Odin. Vitasta, New Delhi. Used by permission of Jaishree Kak Odin.

Excerpts from *Lal Ded: Her Life and Sayings*, copyright © by Utpal Publications, Motiyar/Rainawari/Srinagar/Kashmir. Used by permission of Utpal Publications.

Book design by Sharon Adams
Cover design by designpointinc.com
Cover art © iStockphoto.com

Library of Congress Cataloging-in-Publication Data

Voss Roberts, Michelle.
  Dualities : a theology of difference / Michelle Voss Roberts.
    p. cm.
  Includes bibliographical references and index.
  ISBN 978-0-664-23449-2 (alk. paper)
  1. Dualism (Religion)—Christianity. 2. Mechthild, of Magdeburg, ca. 1212–ca. 1282.
3. Laldyada, 14th cent. 4. Catholic Church—Relations—Kashmir Saivism. 5. Kashmir Saivism—Relations—Catholic Church. I. Title.
  BR128.D82R63 2010
  230—dc22
                                                                                    2010017882

PRINTED IN THE UNITED STATES OF AMERICA

♾ The paper used in this publication meets the minimum requirements of the American National Standard for Information Sciences—Permanence of Paper for Printed Library Materials, ANSI Z39.48-1992.

Westminster John Knox Press advocates the responsible use of our natural resources.
The text paper of this book is made from 30% postconsumer waste.

To Brian

Contents

Foreword by John J. Thatamanil	ix
Acknowledgments	xv
Introduction	xvii
Abbreviations and Translations	xxiii
1. What to Do about Dualism?	1
2. Duality in Union with the Divine	17
3. Coming "Down" to Earth?	55
4. Body: Prison or Partner?	83
5. Flowing Out to Others	115
6. Fluid Relations in a Dichotomous World	147
Notes	163
Bibliography	183
Index of Names	193
Index of Subjects	197

Foreword

John J. Thatamanil

Constructive theology, theological ontology, feminist theology, ecotheology, metaphorical theology, body theology, and postcolonial theory—Michelle Voss Roberts's *Dualities: A Theology of Difference* makes signal contributions to each of these disciplines by way of comparative theology. Voss Roberts makes a robust case for the worth of comparative theology precisely by contributing to such a rich variety of fields. *Dualities* is not an abstruse methodological treatise about the promise of comparative theology; rather, it is a lively and accessible demonstration of that very promise.

Comparative theology, in its contemporary instantiation, remains a relatively new field. Therefore, comparative theologians shoulder multiple burdens that do not customarily fall to systematic theologians, practical theologians, and others. Systematic theologians assume the concrete burden of bringing off the particular argument they wish to advance, but they need not routinely defend their very enterprise as such. Comparative theologians, for the foreseeable future, will be afforded no such luxury. They must show that (1) comparison across traditions widely separated by time and space is possible; (2) such comparison can be accomplished without conceptual violence to the ideas, figures, practices, or traditions under comparison; and (3) comparative theology is constructive theology proper and so is far more than an exercise in comparing theologies. Voss Roberts's book brilliantly accomplishes these tasks and so marks a milestone in comparative theology. Still more, by demonstrating what comparative theology can do, the book is an invitation and a challenge for other theologians to do likewise.

Dualities is at heart a close and careful comparison of the theologies of two women, Mechthild of Magdeburg and the Kashmiri Śaiva theologian Lalleśwarī. Why these two women in particular? For Voss Roberts, the process of selecting figures for comparison is neither trivial nor arbitrary; she mounts a vigorous case that comparative theology must overcome its inattention to women's theological voices. She warns that a comparative theology which confines itself to the usual male suspects like Śaṅkara risks playing into the hands of a colonialist Orientalism in which Indian thinkers are routinely categorized as part of an otherworldly monistic and mystical East. Conversely, comparison that selects from a conventional canon of orthodox Christian figures can perpetuate an Occidentalism in which the whole of "the West" is characterized yet again as dualistic—marked by a stark and impermeable divide between the uncreated and the created, between God and the world. There are, of course, no ideal or natural objects of comparison, but Voss Roberts reminds scholars that they must exercise imagination and discretion in the work of selection.

The question of the permeable and the impermeable is the most exciting feature of *Dualities*. Voss Roberts argues that both Mechthild and Lalleśwarī are thinkers of the fluid and the permeable. For both these theologians, neither God, nor world, nor bodies, nor souls are to be conceived as impermeable substances. Without erasing the distinction between these realities, Voss Roberts urges us not to read these pre-Cartesian thinkers under the spell of a Cartesian substantialist metaphysics. God flows into the soul, body, and world; and the soul, body, and the world flow out from and back into the divine life. The resulting ontologies can neither be characterized as monistic—as the distinction between these realities are real and never utterly undone—nor can they be characterized as dualistic.

But is the common appeal to the metaphor of flow in these two theologians merely epiphenomenal? Put otherwise, would careful analysis show these similarities to be superficial? Voss Roberts does not evade this question.

Instead, by appeal to metaphor theory as developed by George Lakoff and Mark Johnson, she contends that the very nature of human embodiment entails biological constants that lead to and underwrite certain cross-culturally valid metaphorical configurations. Without denying the poststructuralist emphasis on cultural construction of human experience, Voss Roberts asserts, "Physical experience is not so thoroughly 'constructed' by individuals and their societies that we cannot understand one another" (14). Voss Roberts then goes on to claim that "theological metaphors ensure intelligibility by drawing upon (near) universal bodily experiences to express abstract concepts and values. Thus they offer a basis for interreligious (and intergeneric) comparison. Mechthild and Lalleśwarī's metaphors of fluidity are rooted in bodily experience and therefore can speak to one another" (15). Yet Voss Roberts's claims are nuanced and appropriately guarded. In the logic of metaphors, she finds one basis for cross-cultural communication and translatability. But she does not assert that shared metaphors lead to identity of thought, nor does she claim that metaphor theory must henceforth be the basis of comparison in general.

On the basis of these careful claims, Voss Roberts then advances yet another tentative proposal:

> It might not be too much of a stretch to suggest that their theologies correlate to a heightened awareness of women's bodily experiences as notoriously leaky and fluid, for generative cycles involving blood and milk require attention to the permeability and fluidity of the breathing, reproducing, eating/drinking, and excreting body. In any case, their observations of the world around them instruct that every body exists in relation to other bodies and that no self is an island. Their development of fluid metaphors also reflects their desire for relation. They do not attempt to control or shut off the flow of relation but channel it toward life-giving connectivity with divine, human, and material others. (15–16)

Whether the argument—that the translatability of metaphors is grounded in universal bodily experiences and so can serve as the basis for intelligibility and communication across traditions—will stand remains to be seen. I find Voss Roberts's contention plausible and even compelling. Her proposal is, as it happens, a rare and genuinely testable hypothesis. Comparativists can investigate the logic of metaphors and the metaphorical systems to determine whether they prove to be sites of genuine cross-cultural similarity. In any case, Voss Roberts's appeal to metaphor theory is a key methodological contribution for cross-cultural comparison in general and comparative theology in particular.

Voss Roberts appeals to metaphor theory to argue that cross-cultural comparison is indeed possible, but her subtle attention to the different theological ontologies within which the metaphor of flow is inscribed demonstrates that comparison need not lead to conceptual violence or the erasure of difference. Voss Roberts shows that for Mechthild, the world is an overflow of a loving Trinitarian God whereas for Lalleśwarī the world is a flowing manifestation of Śiva's cosmic consciousness. When Śiva opens his eyes, the world comes into being; when he closes them, a cosmic epoch comes to an end. Over several chapters, Voss Roberts names and explores the distinctions between these two kinds of flow with great dexterity. The quest for similarity does not come at an exorbitant cost.

Throughout her book, Voss Roberts is mindful of feminist critiques of dualisms. The dualism of soul and body has come at the expense of the body, which is regarded as impure and so becomes the object of ascetical regimes of self-abnegation. The God-world dualism comes at the expense of the material world, which is regarded as impure and so merely an instrumental reality for human use rather than loving care. It will come as no surprise to readers of feminist philosophy and theology that the losing side in every such pairing is gendered feminine. Patriarchal reflection grounds itself in hierarchical metaphysical dualism.

But the alternative to such dualism is not, for Voss Roberts, an absolute nondualism. Voss Roberts astutely notes that some versions of nondualism can also yield hierarchical dualisms. Śaṅkara's nondualism arrives at a vision in which only *brahman* is understood to be really real—on the definition that only the unchanging can be counted real—and the world of experience, while not utterly illusory, is unreal because it is subject to change and perishing. Voss Roberts is too sophisticated a thinker to draw facile one-to-one connections between particular metaphysical configurations and ethical conclusions. Hence, she is committed to compelling theologians, East and West, to think against and beyond the false options of monism/nondualism versus dualism. She commends instead a theology of fluid dualities:

> A fluid theology overturns unjust hierarchies such as that of the one over the many. Once seen as the natural state of things, rigid hierarchies and intractable dualisms are unmasked as an extremely limited subset of the many possible metaphorical options for understanding difference. (154)

Ontologies of flow can undercut these rigid hierarchies and thereby ensure that dualities—the world of distinction and difference—never become static and fixed.

Because Voss Roberts is widely read in contemporary feminist constructive theology, she knows and explicitly acknowledges the strong resonances between her theology of dualities and the work of several important contemporary theologians. She notes the kinship of her work to Ellen Armour's elemental theology and Catherine Keller's tehomic theology of the fluid deep. Perhaps the most explicit affinity is to be found with Laurel Schneider's theology of multiplicity, which seeks to develop an ontology that is committed to gestures of fluidity and porosity. Voss Roberts not only learns from these exciting voices in contemporary constructive theology but, more important, she gives these theologians grounding in important classical, albeit neglected, sources in Christian and Hindu traditions. The result is that perspectives that might otherwise appear altogether unconventional and perhaps even heterodox are shown to have deep roots in neglected strands of Christian and non-Christian religious traditions. By contributing vital resources to constructive feminist theological projects, Voss Roberts illustrates once more the promise of a comparative theology that attends to subaltern voices.

I must confess that I read Voss Roberts's book with some trepidation. In my writing, I have argued for a nondualist theology that draws explicitly upon Śaṅkara. It hardly needs to be said that a book titled *Dualities* is unlikely to hold immediate appeal to nondualists. But I would urge nondualists to withhold judgment. Voss Roberts's theology of flow is not—to use the technical language of Indian theology—a Dvaita (dualist) theology. As she repeatedly takes care to show, "duality" is not "dualism." Though at first it may be hard to hear and digest her point, a theology of duality is a double rejection of both categories: nondualism understood as strict monism must be discarded because it erases difference, and dualism grounded in a metaphysic of substance must also be rejected because it generates rigid, hierarchical, and asymmetrical divides. Voss Roberts is after a theology of difference that can ground relationality and mutuality.

Such a theology of fluid dualities is entirely compatible with my account of a world-affirming "dynamic nondualism," in which God is understood not as a substance but in process-theology terms as ontological creativity. On my account, God is the creating of the world of dynamic realities, which are themselves event-occasions and not substances, event-occasions that can never be separated dualistically from the underlying creativity that gives rise to them and in which they participate. Voss Roberts's fundamental metaphor of flow strikes me as entirely compatible with process metaphysics. Moreover, the metaphor can counter the aridity that can creep into a theological system that is overly wedded to the technical terminology of Whiteheadian philosophy. Both process and neoprocess theologians have much to learn from this book.

Because of the real and demonstrable goods generated by Voss Roberts's project, several important questions follow: if comparative theology is both possible, counterhegemonic, and theologically productive, does it not follow that monoreligious theological reflection in an multireligious era is a kind of communal solipsism? If it is indeed possible to learn with and from religious others in an age of interreligious intimacy, does it not become incumbent upon responsible theologians to take up such cooperative learning? Can the divide between comparative theology and constructive or systematic theology be sustained as anything other than a somewhat arbitrary division of labor? Comparative theology done well is a dangerous discipline precisely because it raises such provocative questions and threatens to put an end to business-as-usual theology. By these standards, Michelle Voss Roberts's *Dualities* is a fine and dangerous book indeed.

Acknowledgments

Many great tributaries flow into this little stream. Although I cannot pay due tribute to everyone who has in-fluenced the theology that appears in this book, I would like to extend my warmest thanks to the people who played special roles in the course of the book's development. Wendy Farley proved to be a wise and trustworthy director for the ideas that first emerged in my dissertation. Laurie Patton encouraged me to pursue comparative and linguistic studies of Indian religion and saw me through two theses. Mark Jordan consistently posed the right questions at the right time.

I would not have been able to plumb the depths of Lalleśwarī's thought without the kind assistance of my teachers in Delhi. Dr. Omkar N. Kaul of the Indian Institute of Language Studies patiently worked through Lalleśwarī's verses with me during March and April of 2006. Conversations with S. N. Bhatt and S. S. Toshkhani also aided me at key junctures.

My colleagues in the Rhodes College Department of Religious Studies supplied ample encouragement as the book took shape. Special thanks are due to Kenan Padgett and Karen Winterton for their assistance and to the Dean's Office for finding funds to assist with costs related to this project. I have enjoyed the support of colleagues in the Comparative Theology and Hindu-Christian Studies Groups, particularly Francis Clooney and John Thatamanil. David Jensen kindly read drafts of each chapter, and the book is much improved thanks to his theological insight. I also owe a debt of gratitude to my editor at Westminster John Knox Press, Jon Berquist, whose foresight and support of the emerging discipline of comparative theology steered this book through its production.

The intellectual partners whose conversations with me brought this project to life are almost too numerous to name. Discussions with Liberty Hall,

Emily Holmes, Kent Brintnall, Julie Meadows, Shelly Rambo, Wesley Barker, Andrew Radde-Gallwitz, Jennifer Ayres, Luke Whitmore, Michael DeJonge, Yvonne Zimmerman, and Rachel Anderson stand out in many fond memories set in coffee shops scattered across Atlanta and Memphis. Joy Ann McDougall and the Damen Salon read early parts of this project: thanks to Joy, Saralyn Masselink, Beth Sanders, Teresa Ladrigan-Whelpley, Jessie Smith, and especially Gina Weiser for fruitful conversations. The friendship of Laura Wangsness Willemsen, Anne Apple, and Kendra Hotz; the encouragement of my late grandfather, Howard Voss; the ministries of Oakhurst and Idlewild Presbyterian Churches; and the breath of life at Midtown Yoga also have sustained me far beyond the needs of the intellect. I dedicate this book to Brian Roberts, infinitely patient partner and friend.

Introduction

For much of contemporary theology, "dualism" is an enemy tactic, while "difference" has become its rallying cry. The battleground on which dualism operates has been well-trodden. Critical narratives of world-denying, misogynistic dualism cite a parade of the usual suspects. Aristotle leads the dualistic charge with his famous list pitting the good, maleness, light, and unity against the bad, femaleness, darkness, and plurality.[1] Plato and Descartes inevitably make appearances, contrasting the body with the soul and the mind. A phalanx of religious texts and theologians hover in the wings for support. Tertullian declares woman, the eternal associate of the body and lower materiality, to be the "devil's gateway"; Thomas Aquinas espouses Aristotle's "misbegotten male" theory of female conception. Polarities of spirit and matter, mind and body, and self and other spawn further negative assessments of racial, economic, material, and sexual others.[2]

Dualism comes under vigorous attack in feminist, process, and poststructuralist theologies. Feminists eschew any hierarchical binary that supports the subordination of women, denigrates the body, or neglects materiality. Process thinkers mutually implicate God and the world in a process of evolving relation and thus overcome the radical separation of divinity from the world. Poststructuralist thinkers have taught theologians to question or deconstruct their assumptions and to become conscious of the exclusions and unresolved contradictions embedded within layers of tradition. We have all begun to learn that when we allow differences to calcify into hierarchical binaries, we have likely ceased to think carefully—and that when we lapse into either-or thinking, we have likely ceased to discern justly.

But what shall we do about dualism? How might we launch a counter-offensive? Simple awareness of these firmly entrenched patterns of thought begins to loosen their hold on us; but without alternatives, we are likely to fall back into old, well-worn grooves. Unfortunately, critique alone cannot cure gender inequity, environmental destruction, and apartheid. We must find other ways of thinking and living in relation. Ecofeminist theologian Sallie McFague proposes new metaphors for divinity that are more appropriate to our current world situation: if human beings imagine God as radically related to the world, she argues, we will be less likely to destroy our environment or annihilate the earth in a nuclear holocaust. As viable alternatives, McFague offers the models of the world as the body of God, and God as the Mother who gives birth to all things.[3] In another approach, process theologians style divinity as a process of becoming that includes human activity. Other philosophers encounter God in the ineffable spaces of difference between one person and another. Each of these new metaphors for divinity values diversity, troubles hierarchy, and encourages human responsibility.

Many of these accounts are prefaced by a brisk narrative of the depredations of dualism in Western thought. The narrative itself has almost reached the status of a cliché: Christianity is misogynistic, imperialistic—above all, *dualistic*. Some have argued, however, that before we rush off to diversify our theological portfolios with novel philosophies or ancient wisdoms, we should notice that the venerable tradition is not entirely bankrupt. Gillian McCullough goes as far as to rehabilitate dualism as faithful to the best in Christian theology:

> These critiques have overlooked the possibility that the problem is not dualism itself, but rather the distortion of dualism that arose under patriarchal theology and philosophy. As such, there is no inherent reason why a dualist anthropology, epistemology and metaphysic should remain within the normative tradition of the patriarchal spiritual dynamic.[4]

Here McCullough defines dualism as ontological distinction, as in the distinction between God and the world or between God and humanity.[5] I, too, wish to break the seeming inevitability of the link between duality and its patriarchal perversions. I also would like to propose a closer look at the sources that well up in religious traditions, some of which have been overlooked in the crafting of the antidualist narrative. In contrast to McCullough, however, I maintain that the postmodern value of difference cracks the mold of our easy "-isms": not all duality is dual*ism*.

The central thesis of this book is that there are many ways of relating twos. The one, the two, and the many exist in dynamic relational permutations, within which hierarchical dualism is but one possible configuration. This point could be made entirely from within the Christian tradition, but in chapter 1 I wager that it could be made more effectively by stepping back from the categories modernity has used to structure readings of Christian thought: we read *differently* when we extend our conversations about dualism and difference beyond the Christian West. Critics trained in this context have become so skilled at pinpointing symptoms of dualism—such as subordination of women, suppression of the body, oppression of nonelite groups, and environmental rapine—that these systems and symptoms appear to hold sway everywhere. Parallel structures in Hindu traditions, for example, would include cultural commitments to patriarchy and caste, a final "renouncer" stage of life that turns its back on social ties, and a practical dualism between the illusory material world and *brahman*, the ultimate reality.[6] In contrast to this approach, I argue that the polemic of "dualism" in the West masks other ways of theorizing duality (Sanskrit: *dvaitatva*) and veils complex systems of negotiations that cannot be reduced numerically to one or two.

Religious diversity is only beginning to register in these discussions of dualism. John Thatamanil, for example, develops a Christian nondualism in conversation with Advaita Vedānta Hinduism; and Milton Scarborough retrieves Hebraic thought in conversation with Buddhist traditions to recover a "nondualistic root of Western civilization."[7] In contrast to their worthy focus on the viability of nondualism for the West, I would like to attend to some nuances regarding *duality* that have been lost in the dualism critique. My focus, then, is on the *metaphysics of difference* and *differences between metaphysical systems* in the world's religions. Using the methods of comparative theology, I reclaim two particular voices within the Hindu and Christian traditions that have not yet found their way into the larger narrative: Lalleśwarī (pronounced luhl-LESH-war-EE) of Kashmir and Mechthild (MEK-tild) of Magdeburg. A careful reading of these two underappreciated theologians will assist in opening new routes through the discourse surrounding dualism, duality, and relation.

I have chosen a Hindu interlocutor who taps into Indian conversations about duality that predate by far the dualism critique in the modern West. The process of comparative reading can add important nuances and additional perspective to our critical reconstruction of difference in relation. In contrast to a dualism framed by Aristotle's mutually exclusive binaries and their gendered associations, Indian schools of philosophy frame the question in terms of the nature of union between the ultimate reality (*brahman*, Śiva) and contingent beings. They fine-tune a broad spectrum of positions, from interpretations of the Advaita (nondual) Vedānta philosophy that suggest the unreality of difference, to Madhva's Dvaita (dual) Vedānta philosophy and the Śaiva Siddhānta tradition, which posit the eternal distinction between the absolute and the individual self. Some schools are theistic, inviting worshipers to relate to a personal God; others claim that God is a distinction that falls away in the upper reaches of meditation. Gender and other worldly differences are implicated in the various metaphysical configurations, but the very diversity of these configurations indicates that the links between God-world and other dualisms are not as straightforward as Aristotle would have us believe.

Chapter 2 introduces Kashmir Śaivism, a school of Indian religion that names ultimate reality as Śiva (SHI-va), in order to shift the contemporary discourse on dualism in a new direction. Bringing this school of thought into conversation with the medieval Catholic Christianity of Mechthild of Magdeburg challenges the stereotype of Eastern philosophy as "unitive" or "monistic" in contrast to the "dualism" of the West. On the one hand, Lalleśwarī's Śaivism claims that the differences between God and self are real: they are not illusory constructs, as in some readings of Hindu thought. On the other hand, Mechthild's intimate experience of God blurs the sharp distinctions familiar in much of Western Christian theology. The significance of this comparison for the topic of dualism is its ability to destabilize the customary theological binary of God and the soul. We arrive at a multilayered and many-faceted set of categories for describing the nature of the individual's union with and difference from God.

Not only humans but also all contingent beings are implicated in the relation of beings to their ultimate source. Because Indian discussions of twoness tend not to set human beings apart to dominate or subdue the earth, our conversation in chapter 3 moves quite naturally to a reconsideration of the dualism between God and the world. Modern Christian theology often insists on a strict distinction between Creator and creation in order to preserve the uniqueness and sovereignty of God. This dualism has been blamed for underwriting the devaluation of the earth and its subjugation to human industry: if the earth is mere matter and has nothing divine about it, it is available for human use and consumption. Christianity and Śaivism both contain alternative visions of a dynamic relation between God and the cosmos. Reading the two systems side by side enables the theologian to imagine the world as distinct from God yet permeated with divinity. This salutary vision resists the exploitative hierarchies of environmental degradation and envisions a relation of care between human beings and the earth.

The revaluation of materiality in chapter 3 raises the important question of the goodness of the body. Consequently, chapter 4 takes up a favorite target of feminist theology: dualism between the body and the entities variously called mind, soul, or spirit. When René Descartes formulated his dictum, "I think, therefore I am," he summed up a modern trajectory that favors the intellect, spirit, and transcendence over the body, matter, and immanence. Many premodern authorities do not share this bias. Although the distinction between mind/soul/spirit and the body remains meaningful, Lalleśwarī's yoga and Mechthild's spiritual disciplines assume their interrelation. Lalleśwarī's yogic explorations may assist logophilic Christians with a new appreciation of the body's capacities. Mechthild's frustration with the body in its quest to participate in the soul's progress reminds us, however, to be realistic about the body's limitations. The comparative conversation urges us to move beyond dualism, to reach a fuller understanding of the relation of the faculties, and to cultivate their partnership.

According to poststructuralist critiques, the above dualisms fuel systemic social hierarchies such as sexism and racism, dualisms of self and other that select particular differences to dehumanize certain demographics. Self-other dualism may, in fact, be the most fundamental of binaries. Not only does my body, my own skin, separate me from my neighbor, but God, world, and body also often feel external to my true self. Ruptures in these relationships prove how very connected we are, yet they also trigger temptation to retreat into separative modes of selfhood, to assert oneself over another, or to cower in submission. In order to enter this web of self-other relation, chapter 5 traces the ideals and the tragedies of Mechthild and Lalleśwarī's hopes for community. Each woman envisions flexible social hierarchies in which persons simultaneously occupy positions of authority and tutelage. But despite their visions of mutuality, neither woman lives to see the full flourishing of her ideals. The heartbreak of their lived experiences encourages us today to consider the collusion of intersecting hierarchies of race, class, sexuality, age, and ability.

Each chapter, then, redefines one of the central and interlocking dualisms of Western thought: God and self, God and world, self and body, and self and other are not dualisms but dual*ities* in relation. Hierarchy and oppression are possible but not essential to the experience of being two. The meaning of difference (or *différance*, as the French deconstructionists would have it) is deferred; it is not determined by ready-made binaries. Through comparison, a wider relational vista stretches dualism from two dimensions to many.

Our models of difference and relation *matter* in terms of whether we treat the material world with care, whether we can be at home in our bodies, and whether we support repressive or egalitarian social institutions. The actual, lived consequences of our theologies help us to adjudicate between doctrines that are life giving and those that are not. How, then, shall we respond to the dualisms that press the liveliness of difference into deadening molds? If we are ready to feel the breath of something that cannot be contained in these rigid constraints, our comparative exercise yields an answer. Meandering through the texts of both women theologians is another pattern, a fluid economy of relation that courses through all of the relations surveyed here.

Just as rigid separation finds a basis in embodied experiences of solidity, we can locate a more flexible and subversive pattern if we attend to the movement of water and air. These embodied experiences offer a basis not only for comparing Mechthild and Lalleśwarī, but also for shaping a contemporary theology of difference and relation. The final chapter reaps the fruit of the comparative endeavor by exploring the viability of an elemental theology that takes permeability and flux as its starting point. How might we relate differently to others—the environment, other human beings, divinity—if we experienced them as fluid and interconnected entities? What potential does the metaphor hold for the oppressed? Are the waters of relation sufficient to sustain individual selfhood? The hope of this book is that the metaphorical character of divine and human fluidity will open up a more-adequate route for theorizing duality that neither reduces them to literal material substances nor succumbs to the pitfalls of dualism.

Abbreviations and Translations

FL   Quotations from Mechthild of Magdeburg, *The Flowing Light of the Godhead*, translated and introduced by Frank J. Tobin (New York: Paulist Press, 1998), are cited with book and chapter numbers (e.g., *FL* 3.15). References to the Middle High German text follow the critical edition: Mechthild of Magdeburg, *Das fliessende Licht der Gottheit*, edited by Hans Neumann, 2 vols. (Munich: Artemis, 1990–93).

GB   In citing the translations of Sir George Grierson and Lionel D. Barnett, *Lallā-Vākhyāni: The Wise Sayings of Lal Děd, a Mystic Poetess of Ancient Kashmīr* (London: Royal Asiatic Society, 1920), I supply saying numbers (e.g., GB 7).

K   Unless otherwise noted, translations of Lalleśwarī's sayings are from Nil Kanth Kotru, *Lal Ded, Her Life and Sayings* (Srinigar: Utpal Publications, 1989), cited with saying number (e.g., K 47).

O   Translations from Jaishree Kak Odin's *To the Other Shore* (New Delhi: Vitasta, 1999) are cited with saying number (e.g., O 133). Where I refer to Lalleśwarī's Kashmiri vocabulary, I use Odin's transliterations. On the whole, however, and for the benefit of readers familiar with Indian religions but not with the Kashmiri language, I refer to Kashmir Śaiva discourse using the more widely known Sanskrit terminology.

1

What to Do about Dualism?

> It is important to state that mere difference, opposition, polar opposition, or even contradiction . . . do not in the strictest sense constitute dualism. For both the West and Asia, dualism consists of a dichotomy in which the paired terms, concepts, or things have a static substance or fixed essence.
>
> Milton Scarborough[1]

A person need only apply any of the five senses to become aware of the fact of duality. In order for me to see, hear, smell, taste, or touch something, there must be at least two: myself and another. The smell of bread baking, the sound of your voice, and the feel of cotton on my skin are all perceptions *of something*. If there were only one, only a subject without objects of awareness, these simple pleasures could not exist. Nor, for that matter, would pain. Emotional states such as love and anger likewise require objects. The objects of cognition are manifold: the awareness of another quickly becomes the awareness of *others*.

Our lives are richer for the experience of duality, but experiences of others are not always pleasant. The world makes demands; it threatens and harms us. We invent strategies for organizing the welter of stimuli, for handling the other, for putting things in their proper place. For convenience, we categorize so that we will not have to cope with the naked uniqueness of the other. As cultures we adopt some of these coping strategies wholesale. Dualities become binaries (us/them, white/black) that solidify into dualisms, which serve as shorthand for our preferences (pure/impure, good/evil). With time and use, these dualisms become entities in their own right; these well-entrenched thought patterns stand as obstacles to thinking otherwise. As Val

Plumwood aptly puts it, dualism constructs "central cultural concepts and identities so as to make equality and mutuality literally unthinkable."[2]

Plumwood helpfully distinguishes dualism from the distinctions, dichotomies, and hierarchies necessary to human thought and value. Dualistic concepts of difference can be distinguished from these by five features: (1) denial of dependency on that which has been backgrounded (nature, women, the colonized other); (2) categories that exclude continuity; (3) incorporation of the other into the subject's own identity; (4) instrumentalization of the other for one's own benefit; and (5) homogenization of the differences of those classed as other ("they all look alike").[3] Persons on the underside of dualistic structures are usually essential to the functioning of society but are rendered invisible to those who benefit from their contribution. An attempt to dissolve the dualisms that haunt Christian thought must bring these patterns to light.

As much as we might like to redirect our relational train of thought along nonhierarchical or nonoppressive routes, the paths linking dualism's various permutations (heterosexism, racism, exploitation of the earth, and other hierarchical arrangements) have become well-worn tracks. Salutary patterns are not readily separable from their distortions; yet neither are these distortions inevitable. Plumwood calls for a "recognition of a complex, interacting pattern of continuity *and* difference."[4] In place of a "logic of negation" (women are *not men*), she proposes a "relevant logic" that expresses "otherness as nonhierarchical difference": "It is neither a cancellation nor a lack or absence of a specified condition, but another and further condition—a difference—yielding the concept of an other which is not just specified negatively but is independently characterized and with an independent role on its own behalf."[5] Hierarchical negation is not the only way to express difference. We must learn to think again about duality without resorting to dualism.

TRIBUTARIES OF A THEOLOGY OF DIFFERENCE

Penetrating critiques of dualism have emerged from fields as disparate as process philosophy, psychology, environmental spirituality, and feminist and poststructuralist theory, discourses that have begun to shape new ways of recognizing continuity and difference in the modern West.[6] My interreligious approach to thinking continuity and difference together arises at the confluence of these streams, which can help us think about the embodied differences between God, humanity, and material creation in a more relational manner.

The following chapters arc toward ever more concrete considerations, from the mystical union of God and the human soul to the value of the earth, the body, and human differences from one another. But this book also looks outside Western modernity for clues that will unlock dualism's hold. I wager that comparison of Eastern and premodern sources can reveal the "otherness" of the commonplaces of modern Western culture. The West's critiques of its own dualisms can unwittingly perpetuate dualistic categories, but comparison dissipates the givenness of these categories. The additional tributary of comparative theology will, I hope, facilitate constructive, interreligious, theological thinking.

As an uncharted stream in the Western dualism critique, the religious and philosophical traditions of India offer natural conversation partners on the subject of duality. The six orthodox systems of Hinduism include schools that distinguish themselves as dualism (*dvaita*), nondualism (*advaita*), and "qualified" nondualism (*viśiṣṭādvaita*) on the issue of the difference between the ultimate principle and the world.[7] In contrast to the Western tendency to view a variety of dualisms (God-world, mind-body, men-women, etc.) as inevitably linked, the place of dualism in Indian discourse belies this inevitability. For example, God-world dualism is not a prerequisite for the hierarchies of patriarchy and caste, which have flourished in communities holding all three views. Each of the Hindu systems, whether dualist or nondual, has at times fostered world- and body-denying tendencies; but each also offers unique ways of viewing difference.[8] These other ways of thinking about duality, in which metaphysical and practical dualisms are not linked in the same manner, may be of use in rethinking the metaphysical foundations for worldly relation.

COMPARATIVE THEOLOGY

The history of the discipline of comparative theology sounds a cautionary tale as we embark on our comparative endeavor. Comparative studies in religion have evolved significantly over the last century, running the gamut from early impressionistic observations of Christian missionaries and colonizers to contemporary interreligious dialogue.[9] Because earlier comparativists often read Christian presuppositions onto the traditions they studied, a new generation of scholars has responded to this hegemony with renewed care in their descriptions of religious others. J. Z. Smith, a pointed critic of earlier comparative efforts,[10] outlines a brief but useful method for responsible comparison: (1) describe each phenomenon, first locating it "within the rich texture of its social, historical, and cultural environments that invest it with its local significance," and then within its reception history; (2) compare the exempla in light of each other on a focused topic; (3) redescribe the exempla in light of the comparison; and (4) rectify the categories of comparison. Smith cautions that because there is no essential reason to compare one thing to another, scholars must frame and defend their comparisons carefully.[11]

The field of comparative theology has been revitalized in light of such critiques. Francis X. Clooney, for example, goes deep into Hindu traditions in order to accomplish the first comparative task: understanding. He grounds the brilliance of individual thinkers in their commentarial lineages to avoid the careless applications of Christian categories: "the opportunities present in the interreligious situation are most fruitfully appropriated slowly and by way of small and specific examples taken seriously and argued through in their details."[12] For Clooney the truth of comparative theology comes through the prolonged practice of reading the texts of different traditions together. He recommends dwelling in the space of creative tension between two traditions for as long as possible before drawing normative conclusions.[13] The back-and-forth movement between the home tradition and what one is coming to know sets up a cycle of questioning that leads deeper and deeper into understanding.

The chapters that follow engage in this sort of back-and-forth reading, but they also risk a normative gesture. As Smith comments, the "'end' of comparison cannot be the act of comparison itself."[14] Redescription of the exempla and rectification of scholarly (theological) categories go hand in hand with careful comparative reading. From my perspective, the constructive move takes on special urgency in light of the concrete, lived effects of religious symbols: if comparison offers viable alternatives to the hierarchical dualisms that deny justice and care, theologians should consider incorporating these insights into their systematic theologies.

OUTSIDERS WITHIN

The dualism critique launched at the world's religious traditions by process, feminist, and poststructuralist philosophies is often made from *within* the traditions. Sometimes a simple rereading of the major, canonical sources with gender or class issues in mind can resolve longtime misperceptions. Another route, which I pursue here, is to listen to the voices *left out* of the canon as an effect of various dualisms. Patricia Hill Collins develops the category of the "outsider within" with reference to African Americans in the United States. Their subject position is "riddled with contradictions": they "appear to belong" because they possess "formal citizenship rights," yet they do not always enjoy "substantive citizenship rights."[15] Similarly, women participate in religious traditions and bear the names of Christian, Buddhist, Muslim, or Hindu; yet they have not been admitted into authoritative canons of these traditions to the same extent as men. Because the voices of the marginalized offer unique perspectives on the operation of power within communities, in this work I draw upon the insight of two women who speak as "outsiders within" their religious traditions.[16]

To claim insider status for women draws attention to the power operating within religious traditions. To be sure, individual women sometimes do rise to positions of institutional power. We are concerned here with "woman" as a subject on the margins of religious traditions, a subject position that is worth exploring in comparative perspective as we search for a metaphysic conducive to the flourishing of women, men, and the earth. In the chapters that follow, two such subjects will guide us: Mechthild of Magdeburg, a thirteenth-century Christian woman who breaks out of the accepted molds of marriage and the convent, and Lalleśwarī of Kashmir, a fourteenth-century Hindu woman who renounces marriage for an unconventional teaching career.

Despite the critical purchase of outsider-within perspectives for theology, a scan of recent offerings in comparative theology yields a list of the usual suspects for comparison: Thomas Aquinas, Śaṅkara, Buddhaghosa, Mencius. These brilliant figures in the world's religious traditions deserve continued attention; but we must also inquire, from the margins, why so few women appear. One major reason implicit in scholars' choices is the criterion that the subjects of comparative theology should "represent" their religious traditions. For example, Peter Feldmeier introduces Saint John of the Cross and Bhadantacariya Buddhaghosa as "two classical representatives of the Christian and Buddhist traditions" and claims that "while these two representatives cannot speak for the whole of either the Christian or the Theravada Buddhist tradition, they do represent themes, practices, and theological commitments that are broadly agreed upon in their spiritual traditions."[17] Feldmeier thus illustrates how the attempt to be circumspect in claims about one's subject matter sometimes conflicts with the desire to assert its importance. The paucity of women's texts in the recently revitalized field of comparative theology points to androcentric expectations of what qualifies a teacher as a theologian. Scholars rarely expect women's thought and practice to represent their religious traditions as a whole. The denial of women's competence as theologians is maddeningly circular: barred from access to the systems of transmission that define "tradition," women like Mechthild and Lalleśwarī cannot be legitimate representatives of these traditions.

Beyond their gender, these women have an additional mark against them: they are associated with "medieval" religious movements that scholars have interpreted as aberrations from their mainstream theological traditions. The periods in question—roughly the eighth through eighteenth centuries in India, and the fifth through the fifteenth centuries in Europe—begin with the decline of a centralized empire (the Romans) or dynasty (the Guptas) and signify political, economic, cultural, and religious stagnation. In scholarship on Hinduism and Christianity alike, the term "medieval" denotes a corrupt "middle" period degenerated from an original purity that would later be recovered by modern, enlightened minds. The Renaissance in Europe tried to return to classical Greco-Roman culture, and the Protestant Reformation likewise claimed a return to a Christianity purged of the excesses of the medieval Catholic Church. Along the same lines, Indologists depict the proliferation of theistic sects in India during the medieval period as departures from the six orthodox philosophical schools.[18] Both Mechthild and Lalleśwarī have been implicated in characteristically "medieval" movements—Mechthild in the upsurge of women's spirituality known as the beguine movement, and Lalleśwarī in the popular devotional (*bhakti*) movement, both of which I discuss at greater length below.

Medieval degeneration has been linked with the feminine. Ronald Inden explains:

> Indological discourse has represented classical Hinduism rather ambiguously as a decline of the earlier mystical religion and also as a popularization or emotionalization of it.... That ambiguity disappears in their depictions of [the] second, medieval phase. Clearly, the classical, imperial lid is off. The imagination of the Indian Aryan, itself a weak form of reason, is being overcome by the passions. What semblance of unity there was has collapsed into sectarian bickering. Male Aryan spirit is being strangled by the overheated female matter of India.[19]

Beyond the link between medieval dissipation and the feminine in both the European and Indian cases, this historical period witnesses the explosion of vernacular devotional literature, notably by women such as Antal and Mirabai in India, and Hadewijch and Teresa of Avila in Christian Europe. For these reasons, it would seem that choosing two "medieval" women to break down the essential barrier between East and West is a fundamental mistake. If Mechthild and Lalleśwarī resemble one another, the argument might go, it is not because their traditions offer points of contact but because as individuals they *depart* from the essential patterns of their tradition.

Each woman, therefore, illustrates the problem of women's nonrepresentative status within theology. The lives and works of these underappreciated theologians bear several further similarities to one another: Both women stand at unique junctures in their regional languages, religious movements, and theologies. As women, they were excluded from the most extensive education in the intellectual traditions and scholarly languages of their day (Latin and Sanskrit); yet their experiences of divinity and their formation by their respective religious traditions impelled them to compose theological texts. Both were among the first to contribute to religious literature in their vernacular tongues (Middle German and Old Kashmiri), and both aided significantly in the development of those modern languages. Mechthild expanded the German language in her attempt to find vocabulary appropriate to her subject matter; Lalleśwarī has been called "the maker of modern Kashmiri language as well as literature."[20] Each woman's life received little attention in written records of their day. No independent sources remain to corroborate Mechthild's biography: all we know of her life must be gleaned critically from allusions in her writings, which went through a number of editions, translations, and anthologies. Lalleśwarī's verses, which provide little information about her as a historical figure, were passed along orally; and the first written legends about her appear three centuries later.[21]

In the interest of developing a comprehensive understanding of these women's work that will position us to make responsible theological comparisons beyond these surface similarities, we must say a bit more about their particular historical and religious contexts.

MECHTHILD OF MAGDEBURG

Born in 1207 or 1208, Mechthild left home to join a house of beguines in Magdeburg around 1230. Although she describes herself as the "least" among them (*FL* 3.15), she may have become a leader of this community. The term "beguine" describes laywomen who began to devote themselves to a life of chastity in the twelfth century in parts of Germany, France, Belgium, and the Netherlands. Such women were known for their asceticism, poverty, humility, eucharistic piety, care of the sick, visions, and prophecy. Beguines followed no established order or rule: some were solitary and itinerant, while others lived together in houses or cities called beguinages. The name "beguine" eventually came to carry overtones of heresy, possibly due to a spurious connection with the Albigensians in southern France and their unregulated (and thus, from a practical standpoint, unorthodox) way of life.[22]

The beguines worked within the monastic and scholastic contexts of the Christian Middle Ages. For example, many developed trajectories from Bernard of Clairvaux's sermons on the biblical Song of Songs. Bernard amplified the traditional bridal imagery for Christ and the church into an allegory for the relation between God and the soul; the beguines explored the personal and experiential aspects of the love of God the Bridegroom. Some wrote in Latin, but other vernacular writers adapted the courtly style of the troubadour poets. Their reflections on mystical union became unacknowledged influences on theologians such as Meister Eckhart (d. 1328), whose German sermons for both male and female religious audiences posit a radical unity with God in the ground of the soul.[23]

Mechthild's beautiful and variegated book, *The Flowing Light of the Godhead*, exemplifies these trends of beguine writing. The love between God and the soul is the clear focus of her work. The book contains visions of heaven, hell, and purgatory; accounts of personal experiences; admonitions, instructions, and prophecies; as well as dialogues and poems in a number of courtly genres. Her frequent references to the images, manners, and language of the courts of the time suggest a noble upbringing and education.

Mechthild's work also exhibits signs of a difficult political context. In courtly mode, she reports that she received her first divine "greeting" and vision at the age of twelve (*FL* 4.2); but she only began to write at the age of forty-three, at the encouragement of her Dominican confessor and editor, Heinrich of Halle. A Dominican synod in Magdeburg issued a decree critical of beguines in 1261, demanding that they obey their parish priests. While one can only guess the extent to which Mechthild experienced opposition before or after this event, later portions of her text—particularly book 6, written between 1260 and 1269—seem to reflect increasing sensitivity to criticism in matters of orthodoxy. It is possible that Mechthild's choice to enter the Cistercian convent at Helfta around 1270 was precipitated by mounting opposition, although failing health may also have been a factor.[24]

After spending her adult life as a beguine, Mechthild fit somewhat uneasily into convent life. The nuns at Helfta were known for their learning and piety: they knew Latin, and she did not. Frank Tobin writes that they "treated her less as a member of their community than as an object of veneration to whom they looked for spiritual instruction."[25] Although book 7 of Mechthild's work is full of such instructions as well as contributions to the community's liturgy, as an older woman, Mechthild was painfully aware that she lacked the sisters' extensive education and that her spiritual and poetic powers were on the wane.

Although Mechthild's writing resonates with motifs of Scripture and medieval Christian theology, theologians have been late to appreciate her work. Indeed, she lacks the kind of training available to men in the great schools of the day, and she does not cite traditional authorities, follow scholastic methods of exposition and argumentation, or provide commentary on Scripture in the same manner as the scholastic and monastic males of her time.[26] The specter of heresy that haunts beguine writing may be another factor that has inhibited theologians from treating it on par with other theological texts. Although the beguines were initially seen as emblems of holiness and piety, they later earned the censure of the church and dwindled in number. Church officials, threatened by the upsurge of women's authority and the challenges they presented for the administration of confession and the sacraments, issued warnings against women's wandering, living alone, and teaching. The beguines' fall from favor culminated in the burning of Marguerite Porete in 1310 and the

Council of Vienne in 1311–12. The council "called for an inquisitional investigation of beguines and beghards—their male counterparts—in Germany. It also decreed that beguine communities were to be dissolved and that such organizations should be permanently forbidden, but it left open the possibility for truly faithful women to live lives of penance and humility in common."[27] After the Council of Vienne, it became difficult not to associate all previous and subsequent beguines with heresy because the council projected a certain unity of thought and practice upon the loosely organized movement.[28] This stigma is being removed in today's scholarship, but it contributed to centuries of neglect, during which today's canons were formed.

The shape of contemporary concerns with authorship has further obscured the ways female authors *were* included in the canons of religious literature.[29] The original text, which Mechthild wrote in her native tongue of Middle Low German (spoken in northern Germany between 1050 and 1450), was lost; but two lines of transmission kept her book in circulation. A version in the closely related dialect of Middle High German, translated around 1345, survives in its most complete form in the Einsiedeln manuscript (ms. E). This vernacular text was extracted and anthologized for female readers during reform movements of the fourteenth and fifteenth centuries. These manuscripts lack Mechthild's name as an author, for as Sara Poor explains, "in texts meant to foster an internal dialogue with God, earthly authorship had little importance. In an environment where bypassing church authority could prove hazardous, claiming authorship could be dangerous."[30] The second line of transmission was in Latin, beginning with a fourteenth-century edition of books 1–6 called the *Lux divinitatis*. The Dominican translators of the Latin text "toned down Mechthild's criticism of the clergy and some of her erotic imagery" and offered explanations of certain obscure passages, but nonetheless they preserved it.[31] Even though her name and various parts of her work dropped out of circulation at various times, her ideas lived on in the Middle Ages. The complex dynamics surrounding Mechthild's texts thus encourage comparativists to reenvision the qualifications they require of their subjects.

LALLEŚWARĪ OF KASHMIR

Lalleśwarī's verses make only the scantest allusions to her personal history, although many legends sprouted in the oral and, later, textual traditions about her.[32] Sources place Lalleśwarī's birth either at Sempor (a village near Pampore) or at Pandrenthan (near Srinagar) between 1317 and 1320. J. L. Kaul, who narrates a fairly complete register of stories about her, estimates her death at a "fairly advanced age" between 1388 and 1391.[33] The legends agree that Lalleśwarī was born to a Brahmin (upper-caste) family, where she would have participated in religious rites and received some education, and that she came under the influence of Siddha Śrīkantha, a preceptor whom she eventually outstripped in her abilities and insight. When she married, she received the name Padmavatī; but she continued to refer to herself by her maiden name, Lalla. The affectionate title Lal Ded (Mother Lal) attached to her over time; and the name Lalleśwarī, which I use throughout this work, compounds her name with an honorific marker denoting spiritual authority.

In Lalleśwarī's husband's home, she was treated harshly by her mother-in-law, who daily withheld food from her, giving her only a stone covered with a thin layer of rice. She renounced her married life after a famous incident in which her husband accused her of infidelity. She had returned late from fetching water at the river, where she was in the habit of meditating. He struck and broke the pitcher she was carrying and, miraculously, the water remained intact upon her head. She emptied the water into the household vessels and threw the remainder outside. It formed a pond known as Lalla Trag (the Pond of Lalla). With her miraculous powers now evident, she left home. She wandered alone, unconcerned with clothing or outward appearance.

Attempts to classify Lalleśwarī offer a valuable window into the interests of those who argue for her importance today. Lalleśwarī has been called a "prophetess,"[34] "mystic saint-poetess,"[35] "the wise old woman of Kashmiri culture,"[36] and "a goddess, a seer, who had descended upon this earth with a divine message for mankind."[37] Each of these monikers highlights various aspects of her thought, from her prophetic reforming critique of pedestrian religion, to her purported mysticism. Most significantly, legends accruing around her life exhibit patterns of Indian female sainthood that solidified during the *bhakti* movement. This movement was an upsurge in devotional expressions in vernacular languages catalyzed by men and women whose absorption in God led them to reject the boundaries of caste, gender, and religious observance. It began in the far south of India as early as the sixth century CE, spread through the middle and western regions around the twelfth century, and flourished in the north through the seventeenth century. Modern anthologies of women saints perpetuate Lalleśwarī's association with *bhakti* even though she, living in the fourteenth century, would have been at the very forefront of the appearance of the phenomenon in the far north.[38] Despite this diversity in classification, however, all commentators agree in viewing her as a participant in the traditions of Kashmir Śaivism.

Lalleśwarī's theological terminology identifies her as a devotee of Śiva and a practitioner of yoga. Her teaching has the most affinities with the Trika school, the tradition now generally associated with the term "Kashmir Śaivism."[39] In Lalleśwarī's day there was no single way of practicing Kashmir Śaivism. Several different, though mutually influential, textual and ritual schools were in operation, many of which have roots in non-Vedic texts (the Tantras) and practices such as dwelling in cremation grounds and imbibing impure substances. By the fourteenth century these schools had reached a compromise with "orthodox" Vedic traditions, so that Kashmir Śaivas engaged in practices similar to other householders of the Brahmin caste, with some additional ritual obligations.[40]

Lalleśwarī's positioning vis-à-vis Kashmir Śaivism, like that of Mechthild in her tradition, creates difficulties for contemporary readers. Her place in the textual tradition cannot be precisely pinpointed. Lalleśwarī says that she learned some things through books, others through practice (K 47). She likely learned from a guru and continued in this traditional mode by verbally conveying her wisdom to others. As Lance Nelson explains, orality is crucial for the transmission of Śaiva teaching. The tradition

> has never intended that the texts that elaborate its various branches of knowledge (*śāstras*) should function independently of an oral teaching tradition. . . . The notion of mastering a field of knowledge without relying on a preceptorial tradition is unthinkable in a culture still oral in its most genuine expression. . . . In such a setting, the written manuscript functions more as an outline or point of departure than final authority. The latter rested with the *guru*.[41]

The oral nature of Lalleśwarī's teachings both legitimates and masks her place in Kashmir Śaivism. Written commentarial traditions were the foundation for the oral expositions of the guru. At the very least, Lalleśwarī would have been exposed to portions of the Śaiva texts preserved within the memory of adepts whom she met. Which books she knew, and in what form, remains hidden; therefore, one can only speculate about the extent of her contact with the Sanskrit texts of the Tantras.[42] Her aphoristic sayings (*vaakh*s) were transmitted orally in Kashmiri; the precise number of her sayings is now disputed. Jai Lal Kaul arrives at 138 *vaakh*s he believes to be authentic. I follow Nil Kanth Kotru's translations of these 138 verses; but because Lalleśwarī continues to be constructed in a living tradition, I occasionally refer to sayings and legends that may be of more recent origin.[43]

COMPARISON AND OUTSIDERS WITHIN

The above challenges to traditional and contemporary ideals of theological authorship need not disqualify Mechthild and Lalleśwarī from being theological authorities today. Comparativists are interested in difference, including religions' internal diversity. Female, lay, and disenfranchised voices all deserve attention in addition to the wisdom of the elites. Despite lacunae in their religious pedigrees, Mechthild and Lalleśwarī refuse to be dismissed as feminine exceptions to the ordered reason of masculine discourse—or as fuzzy-headed "mystics" rather than "real theologians."[44] These women of spiritual insight are theologians, traditioned (rather than strictly "traditional") thinkers who have much to teach on divine and human relationality.

Removing the "traditional-enough" bar opens the door to outsiders within, subjects who fail to mirror the criteria that have defined "the tradition" as such. The temptation to claim representative status for the figures in this book is blocked by lack of evidence for the women's training, their distance from the "authoritative" texts of their traditions, and their anomalous positions as female teachers. Women appear to fall short as theologians because they deviate from androcentric norms. Just as we should not expect male theologians to be ambassadors for their entire religion or milieu, however, the solution to this problem is not to prove the value of female theologians by virtue of how "traditional" they are. The entry of the outsider within into theological discourse promises to change the degree of *difference* permitted under the umbrella of "tradition."

Darśana, a Sanskrit term signifying point of view or way of seeing, may be an appropriate way of accommodating the perspectives of the outsider within. Usually denoting the six orthodox schools of Hinduism, *darśana* refers to a metaphysical and ethical perspective within a given doctrinal structure, distinguished by its soteriological orientation from more disinterested investigations.[45] Mechthild and Lalleśwarī are conditioned by the orthodoxy of their religious communities without necessarily being initiated into a specific lineage of teachers. They see through the lenses of their religious milieu; but they also offer much in the way of contemplation of the human situation and may speak to a universal audience, both then and now. In this wider point of view, they may be considered to be theologians, those who see (*dṛś*), as they reflect upon God and the world from within particular *darśana*s or traditioned perspectives.[46]

Religious traditions are diverse and polyvalent. We may, therefore, treat theology in a local manner, without expectations of broad representation. This approach solicits a reading of the women in the world's religious traditions as theologians despite definitions of revelation and theology that have disqualified their contributions in the past. As a discourse relating to divinity and revelation, theology should also include women's wisdom in oral, poetic, and devotional modes.

APPLES TO ORANGES?

I have argued that Lalleśwarī and Mechthild deserve attention as theologians; but a number of factors appear to stand in the way of responsible comparison of the works of Mechthild and Lalleśwarī: they write in such diverse genres, their theologies each carry an all-encompassing culture and worldview, and their religious practices of yoga and Eucharist seem to be worlds apart. We may feel as though we are comparing incommensurate things, like apples and oranges. When we approach their work while looking for alternatives to dualism, however, we find deep resonance between their patterns of relational thought. The answer to how to compare them arises out of their answer to dualism in the form of a metaphor that runs throughout their works. Instead of solid dichotomous structures, we find a subtle permeability or connectivity bathed in the imagery of fluids.

Permeating all of her diverse topics and genres is Mechthild's central metaphor of fluidity. Everything flows: the Trinity, creation, the soul. She claims the highest authority for her work when God titles it "a flowing light of my Godhead into all hearts that live free of hypocrisy" (FL 1.0). All relations are caught up in the overflow and return of love: within Godself, between God and the world, and especially in the mutual desire of God and the soul.[47] Interpersonal human relations flow outward from the heart's abundance to those in need. The presence of sin and evil in the world is nothing more than the blockage of this permeating flow of God. In order to convey this systemic permeability, Mechthild employs images of salvific water, light, milk, blood, and air. James Franklin has suggested that Mechthild's imagery originates in popular medieval conceptions of the four elements—earth, air, water, and fire—where water is a transitional substance and air is associated with divinity.[48] Indeed, "real and imagined bodily fluids of all kinds" played an important role in medieval European physiology and spirituality.[49] The motion and dynamism of Mechthild's fluid vision demonstrates an inherently relational approach to duality—a pattern that she shares with Lalleśwarī.

Lalleśwarī, too, deals with the phenomena of duality with the language of fluidity. When duality overwhelms her sense of God, she imagines life as a river or ocean to cross, to reach God on the other shore. As she comes to recognize the dynamic relationality supporting her perception of difference, she shifts her language to that of immersion, mingling, and flow. Her vision of the flowing mutuality of the divine couple, Śiva and Śakti, becomes the foundation for the relations of the world and individual selves to each other and God.

METAPHOR AND EXPERIENCE AS BASIS FOR TEXTUAL COMPARISON

The shared metaphorical domain of fluidity, then, may serve as the basis for comparison between the two women's theologies. Feminist theologians claim to draw upon experiences of the marginalized (particularly marginalized women) as a source for theology alongside Scripture, tradition, and reason. By way of conceptual metaphor theory, I suggest that metaphors of fluidity have an experiential base in bodily existence that is even more basic than what feminists typically intend by "experience." No essential "women's experience" can be identified across time, geography, and culture; but the recurrence of images of air and water in these women's thought may point to a physical intuition of a symbolic pattern that resists notions of the self as a static and self-contained entity.

George Lakoff and Mark Johnson's conceptual metaphor theory demonstrates that such simple constructions as "Good is up" and "Life is a journey" derive from the physical experience of basic motor functions. "Spatialization metaphors are rooted in physical and cultural experience; they are not randomly assigned. A metaphor can serve as a vehicle for understanding a concept only by virtue of its experiential basis."[50] Simple spatial metaphors structure more-complex perceptions of social and power hierarchies such as being "on top" or "down on your luck." Metaphor becomes the basis of systems of beliefs and actions: the metaphors we use in speech and writing are the "metaphors we live by."

What is the role of culture in moving from experience to coherent systems of metaphor? Lakoff and Johnson acknowledge that culture conditions all experience; yet they maintain that given the type of bodies and planet we have, human beings *share* much of the cultural orientation that supplies our most important metaphors. Primary metaphors emerge directly from human embodiment. For example, "*Up* is not understood purely in its own terms but emerges from the collection of constantly performed motor functions having to do with our erect position relative to the gravitational field we live in." In the culture of a "spherical being living outside any gravitational field," the concept *up* would make little sense.[51] More-complex metaphors involve more-particular cultural considerations: "We can still make the important distinction between experiences that are 'more' physical, such as standing up, and those that are 'more' cultural, such as participating in a wedding ceremony."[52] Lakoff, Johnson, and others cite empirical studies that demonstrate the similarity of metaphor systems across cultures. Despite poststructuralist theory to the contrary, physical experience is not so thoroughly "constructed" by individuals and their societies that we cannot understand one another.[53]

In light of the way that poetic metaphors build upon common physical foundations, scholars of religion have proposed that the field of cognitive linguistics provides an embodied link explaining the "similarity in symbol and metaphor across the world's major religions."[54] Because language forms at a very basic level through embodied interaction with the world, the metaphorical structures that appear in all kinds of texts from all kinds of cultures possess a basis for comparison:

> The structure of conceptual metaphors is more general than any individual linguistic sign but also more basic than a theory. . . . If we want to know what people *really* think about concept X, then we need to look at the actual metaphors they use when discussing a concept rather than third-person theoretical accounts of the concept (although, of course, such theoretical accounts will almost inevitably invoke a metaphor in a revealing way).[55]

Theological metaphors ensure intelligibility by drawing upon (near) universal bodily experiences to express abstract concepts and values. Thus they offer a basis for interreligious (and intergeneric) comparison.

Mechthild and Lalleśwarī's metaphors of fluidity are rooted in bodily experience and therefore can speak to one another. The idea that substances can flow in and out of one another is related to what Lakoff and Johnson call the *container* metaphor: The self is a container "bounded and set off from the rest of the world by the surface of our skins."[56] We are discrete bodies with an inside and an outside. We project this in-out orientation upon other container objects (rooms, clearings in the woods, territories) and container substances (*in* the water, *bodies* of water). We feel the flow of air and water around us, into us, and out of us. The primary metaphor of the self as a self-contained object lends itself to models of the self as individual, to whom relation is external; but using their poetic imagination, their experience of fluids, and their desire for divine and human relation, Mechthild and Lalleśwarī experiment with other models of self and society.

In Mechthild and Lalleśwarī, fluidity supplants the container metaphor as the primary expression of their theological insights. Where is the salt in the water? Where does the river end and the ocean begin? What becomes of the water I drink, the rain upon the earth, and the earth washed away by the flood? These theologians allow flowing and dissolving to orient their reality. They observe that despite ideals of continence and control, no body—male or female—is a self-enclosed container. It might not be too much of a stretch to suggest that their theologies correlate to a heightened awareness of women's bodily experiences as notoriously leaky and fluid, for generative cycles involving blood and milk require attention to the permeability and fluidity of the breathing, reproducing, eating/drinking, and excreting body. In any case, their observations of the world around them instruct that every body exists in relation to other bodies and that no self is an island. Their development of fluid metaphors also reflects their desire for relation. They do not try to control or shut off the flow of relation but channel it toward life-giving connectivity with divine, human, and material others.

The fluid relations between self and others gently dissolve the rigid hierarchies set up by Aristotle and his heirs. Their critical purchase is at least twofold: (1) In some cases, the dissolution of dualistic categories reveals that what contemporary critiques have identified as dualism is in fact *not two*. For example, our dualisms of God-world and mind-body are not Mechthild's and Lalleśwarī's terminology. Their texts represent both more and less than the simple binary; their categories are more fluid than our dichotomy implies. (2) At other points—as in our dualisms of self-other and male-female—the duality is real but misrepresented; difference exists but is not an inevitable precursor to dualism or oppression. Metaphors structure the reality we live in, and new (or newly rediscovered) metaphors create new possibilities. Thus Lakoff and Johnson write: "If a new metaphor enters the conceptual system that we base our actions on, it will alter that conceptual system and the perceptions and actions that the system gives rise to."[57] The following chapters offer one such attempt to reimagine our basic theological symbols toward a more just existence, in which unjust hierarchical dualisms are no longer the default mode of relation but only one option among many for experiencing difference. We begin with the metaphysical relationship that is most basic to the human being and from which all others flow: the relation of ourselves to divinity.

2

Duality in Union with the Divine

It is the unrepresentative nature of the "East-West" dichotomy—its failure to relate to the complexities of material reality—which necessitates its active displacement by a "discourse of heterogeneity."

Richard King[1]

What are you made of, Soul, that you ascend so high above all creatures, mingle with the holy Trinity, and yet remain whole in yourself?

Mechthild of Magdeburg (FL 1.22)

From early opponents of the gnostics and Manicheans to contemporary advocates of environmental justice, Christian antidualist polemicists typically assail their competitors' devaluation of the material world. An intense interest in affirming the physical realm unites these allies against any implication that matter is evil or unreal. We shall take up the body and the physical world in future chapters; but if we want to approach the subject of duality through the lens of Indian traditions, we must start elsewhere. We must back up to a more-fundamental level of duality between the one and the many: the duality between God and the soul.

Indian philosophers have long debated the relation of the individual soul (*ātman*) to the ultimate reality (*brahman*). The Upaniṣads and the commentaries of the great eighth-century teacher, Śaṅkara, received much of the attention of missionaries, philologists, and colonial administrators as these debates became familiar in the West. Śaṅkara's Advaita Vedānta school offered Westerners a means to account for India's bewildering variety of religious beliefs and practices. Śaṅkara taught that although persons bound by ignorance at the phenomenal (*vyavahārika*) level are deluded by the world's apparent diversity, from the ultimate (*paramārthika*) perspective, reality is one—or better, not two (*a-dvaita*).[2] This teaching contributed to the received wisdom that Eastern thought is essentially mystical, monistic, or pantheistic.[3] It also allowed the classification of other views, including the multiplicity of deities observed throughout much of India, as corruptions of an essentially nondual religious orientation.

Early nineteenth-century European philosophers and poets hailed the nondualist vision as a primordial wisdom consonant with a Romantic vision of the world. The discovery of the Sanskrit roots of the Indo-European languages offered the hope of recovering the lost origins of the human spirit. The "great sayings" of the Upaniṣads—"*Ātman* is *brahman*, that art thou"—appeared to affirm the endeavor of Romantics such as Goethe and Herder to put the soul in contact with divinity through art and literature.

For others in the West, nondualism came perilously close to conflating divinity with the material world. In contrast to the Romantic drive to break down the divisions that sever humanity from its essential unity with the divine, Christian missionaries were wary of pantheism. The affirmation that "All is God" appears not only to circumscribe the divine, but also to open the door to idolatry. Jewish, Christian, and Muslim insistence on the ontological divide between Creator and creature appears radically incommensurate with the Hindu East. Rudyard Kipling famously penned, "East is East, and West is West, and never the twain shall meet."[4] The Christian commitment to creation ex nihilo (out of nothing) seems completely at odds with the Hindu teaching that this world is, in essence, *brahman*, the only eternal reality. Furthermore, the essential divinity of the Self in nondualist doctrine appears deeply incompatible with doctrines of sin that caution against prideful self-deification, idolatry, and association with the divine.[5]

The convenient foil of an essentially monistic East against the dualism of the West has served not only Western Romanticism and Christian polemics, but Hindu apologetics for the superior spirituality of the East as well, as in Vivekananda's proclamation to the 1893 World Parliament of Religions in Chicago of Hinduism's universal tolerance.

The stark contrasts between the unitive East and dualistic West blurs under scrutiny. Part of the task of the comparative theologian is to view one's own tradition through the categories of the other. This practice enables us to ask new questions and to discover patterns hidden beneath the grooves of well-worn narratives.

The elegance of the spiritual goal of nondual union with God, for example, invites Christian theologians to become newly receptive to voices in the

Christian tradition that articulate similar aims. As it turns out, one need not look far for Christian examples of nondualism. In *The Mirror of Simple Souls*, the thirteenth-century beguine Marguerite Porete delineates how the soul becomes one with the God who is Love. From one perspective, the soul is "annihilated": it first dies to sin, and then its will is completely conformed to God's. From another side, the soul is divinized: it becomes "simple" when it is transformed by grace into divine love. With the eradication of duality, the soul becomes nothing, and so the soul becomes God.[6] Porete's younger contemporary, the German preacher and theologian Meister Eckhart, posits an absence of duality at the heart of God in which even the three persons of the Trinity dissolve into "the simple ground . . . into which distinction never gazed."[7] He teaches that within every person there resides a "little spark" that "is so closely akin to God that it is an undivided simple one, and bears within itself the images of all created things."[8] God gives birth to the Son in the simplicity of this soul; and the soul in turn gives birth to God.

Porete and Eckhart seriously disrupt the notion that nondualism is foreign to Christian thought. Notions of duality—of subject and object, of lover and beloved, of Creator and creature—dissolve in two ways. First, the apophatic tradition in which they participate asserts that God is beyond human speech. God is no thing and therefore is not subject to enumeration. Second, the soul's virtue of humility and God's humility in the incarnation make them "nothing" with respect to one another, and this allows them to become one. In Porete's words, the annihilated "Soul," "thus pure and illumined, sees neither God nor herself, but God sees himself of himself in her, . . . [so] there is nothing except him. And therefore this Soul knows nothing except him, and loves nothing except him, and praises nothing except him, for there is nothing but he."[9] This vision is nondual because of the absence of subject-object distinction when the soul unites with God.

Unsurprisingly, the subtlety and paradox of these teachings invite misunderstanding. Porete testifies that beginners are unlikely to grasp the radical grounding of the soul in God; and despite the fact that her book gained approval by three contemporary theological authorities and continued to circulate among the pious after its later condemnation, she was burned as a relapsed heretic in 1310. Eckhart, too, faced charges of heresy: the bull *In agro dominico* (1329) condemned seventeen of his propositions as heretical and eleven more as dangerous to simple believers. He died before he could defend them fully. Their stories testify to the difficulty of articulating the mystery of union without domesticating it through conventional formulations.

Nondualism's apparent threat to Christian orthodoxy haunts the work of some comparative theologians as well. Rudolf Otto's largely favorable reading of Śaṅkara and Meister Eckhart, for example, exonerates Eckhart (but not Śaṅkara) from the potential pitfalls of pantheism and self-deification. Otto reads his German counterpart through a Lutheran lens. He argues that Eckhart's teaching of the mutual birthing of God and the soul signifies not divinization but "the new obedience of the soul due to the experience of justification."[10] In the face of Śaṅkara's world-denying quietism, Otto's Eckhart offers a this-worldly ethics; and in contrast to Śaṅkara's static *brahman*, Eckhart's divinity eternally creates. For Otto, Eckhart's nondualist teachings can be salvaged because he values the *difference* of the world and the soul from God. God, soul, world, and human relations in Eckhart all retain a value purportedly lost in Eastern monism.

More recent Christian comparativists have been less quick to dismiss the Indian nondualist tradition. John Thatamanil puts Śaṅkara in conversation with Paul Tillich to develop a Christian nondualism that both affirms the union of beings with their source and accounts for the perception of duality. Thatamanil's analysis grapples with two major obstacles to a truly nondual Christian system: free will and the status of the empirical world. For Tillich, despite the creature's ontological rootedness in "the creative ground of being," human freedom creates the possibility of a human rift with the divine source.[11] And although Śaṅkara believes there can never be any real separation between *ātman* and *brahman*, Thatamanil finds that this argument leads him to deny the reality of the world as the illusory work of *māyā*. Thatamanil thus strives for "some way of imagining the relation between being-itself and beings that neither compromises on the reality of the world nor seeks to preserve creaturely freedom at the expense of a tragic and universal separation between God and humanity."[12] His solution invokes process metaphysics alongside Śaṅkara and Tillich to arrive at a vision of creation within God (pan*en*theism) that is both real and facilitates genuine freedom.

While Thatamanil's comparative work fruitfully demonstrates the usefulness and possibility of a nondualist framework, I explore another option. In contrast to approaches that reconcile Christianity with the *nondualism* of the East, I instead ask how Indian thought affirms *duality* (including the reality of the world and the experience of free will) without falling into a world-denying dualism. In contrast to the effort to retrieve nondualist voices from the Christian canon, I look to Hindu traditions for helpful patterns of thinking about difference. I wager that such an investigation can yield a richly textured account of the many facets of Creator-creature union-in-differentiation. How does a soul radically grounded in its divine source retain the integrity to be in relation with that divine source? What new language might we find for difference in union, and for union in relation?

KASHMIR ŚAIVISM

Śaṅkara is hardly the only Indian teacher to consider the relation of the one and the many. His Advaita Vedānta school represents only one branch within one of the six "orthodox" or Vedic schools to ponder this question, not to mention other strands that do not accept the authority of the Vedas such as Buddhism and Tantric traditions. These include dualist (*dvaita*) schools that posit the eternal difference between God and the soul, nondualist (*advaita*) schools that affirm their ultimate identity, and many degrees of relation in between. Because these conversations do not map precisely onto previous or current Christian debates, they can inject new life into current theology.

The theological tradition of Kashmir Śaivism has been underexplored in Christian-Hindu dialogue. This school holds the reality of the created world in tension with the ultimate unity of all things with Śiva, the highest reality. Because its concerns parallel some of those in the Christian evaluation of nondualism, including the status of the world and the individual will, its carefully nuanced metaphysical treatment of the experience of diversity deserves consideration from a comparative angle.

Kashmir Śaivism emerges in dialogue with several philosophical adversaries. Compared to Śaiva Siddhanta, a tradition that affirms three eternally distinct entities, Kashmir Śaivism has been called nondualistic or monistic because it unites all differences in a single source (Śiva).[13] Compared to Śaṅkara's Advaita Vedānta, however, Kashmir Śaivism is not strictly nondualistic. The two metaphysical systems are often confused with one another,[14] but Kashmir Śaiva doctrine differs from Advaita Vedānta in important ways. Whereas Śaṅkara evidently rejects creation as an illusion covering the true nature of *brahman*, Kashmir Śaivas insist on the reality of the world. In an ironic twist, Kashmir Śaivas charge Advaita Vedānta with an unwitting dualism: the Advaita "doctrine of two truths, one absolute and the other relative," sets up a dualism between the real (nonduality) and the illusory (duality).[15]

The shifting nature of these family disputes demonstrates the general unhelpfulness of essentialized "isms" such as "monism," "dualism," and "nondualism" across changing contexts. Rather than rely upon these transhistorical categories, I propose to read particular thinkers for particular patterns of relational thinking.

THE MYSTICAL AND THE FEMININE

I have chosen figures from the two traditions that disrupt not only the dichotomy of the monistic East and the dualistic West, but its gendered undertones as well. Political ramifications of the East-West stereotype include the colonial logic that the feminine, intuitive East required the government of the masculine, reasoned West. Postcolonial scholarship has explored the similarity of colonial and patriarchal logics: just as the colonized appear as women in the symbolic of the colonizer, women are colonized as the "other" of the masculine subject. Edward Said's monumental work, *Orientalism*, elucidates the first half of this syllogism, in which imperial agents "feminize" the colonial subject as impotent, irrational, and in need of Western governance. Recently scholars have also begun to identify how nationalist discourses in India and elsewhere also reinforced this model of masculinity. Yet insofar as "woman" remains a symbol in these conversations, the contributions of actual women disappear, and historical women's voices remain suppressed in the current discourse.[16]

To observe how Mechthild and Lalleśwarī disrupt his dynamic, we must understand that the colonial creation of a monistic and feminine East overlapped with the modern construction of mysticism in the West to such an extent that "the view that mysticism and monism are interlinked was received as truth by almost everyone in post-Kantian philosophy and theology."[17] A general devaluation of mysticism in post-Kantian thought reinforces fears of the East and the feminine: all three inexorably lead to the dissolution of the boundaries between things. Grace Jantzen highlights theological and philosophical suspicion of the mystical tendency to regard the soul as feminine in relation to God. Because "theologians and philosophers, predominantly male," viewed "sexuality precisely in terms of the submergence of the female, her loss of name and self and any power of her own," union with (masculine) divinity implied an unacceptable dissolution of the boundaries of the (masculine) self.[18]

Texts, authors, and ideas coded as feminine disappear from public discourse as a result of this triple feminine-mystical-monistic marginalization. As a political strategy, the association of the East with the mystical bars colonized subjects from the (essentially Western) domains of rationality and government. As Richard King observes, the effect of the "mysticization" and feminization of the East is to exclude India from the realms of history, politics, and public philosophy: the Indian mind speaks primarily to the private sphere, the domain of the spirit.[19]

A similar relegation has occurred with the "women mystics" of the Christian tradition. The scarcity of women such as Mechthild and Lalleśwarī in the theological canons is unsurprising given the links between colonial, gendered, and theological discourses. When Mechthild and Lalleśwarī have received scholarly attention, it has almost always been in the context of a study of mysticism. The poetic style of their teaching seems at odds with the ordered reason of masculine discourse; but Jantzen presses the question: "Is it possible that the consistent identification of mysticism with monism, and the persistent failure to read the mystics properly, is because taking them seriously would radically undermine patriarchal ideas of sexuality and power?"[20] Reading Lalleśwarī and Mechthild as theologians with noteworthy teachings about union, identity, and relation powerfully disrupts these habitual patterns of thinking.

Mechthild and Lalleśwarī each fail to harmonize with modern conceptions of theology in its "Western" and "Eastern" registers. When we reintroduce them into canons formed in light of such distinctions, we break open the canons for reinterpretation and fruitful comparison. When we clear the ground of the constructs that inherently separate East from West, feminine from masculine, and mysticism from "real" theology, we discover affinities that have been hitherto unexplored. We widen the textual sources for theology to include nonscholarly genres, including vernacular and oral traditions. At the same time, however, we narrow the scope of claims the theologian may make based on such exemplars. No single school of thought may stand for the East as a monolithic whole. No convenient category of the feminine may disqualify women's writing from the public sphere.

In what follows, Lalleśwarī's verses offer a closer look at the experience of twoness in Kashmir Śaivism, while Mechthild's writing offers a view of intimate union in the Christian tradition. For these theologians, God and the self are both *dvaita* and *advaita*, dual and nondual. To understand this claim, we must first investigate their views of difference *within* divinity and then work toward the implications regarding the difference between God and the self.

UNITY AND DUALITY IN LALLEŚWARĪ OF KASHMIR

According to legend, Lalleśwarī once stood in an earthen pot with a second pot over her head for the duration of a forty-day fast. As the moon waned, she diminished in size until the pots met. When her teacher looked inside the pots on the day of the new moon, he saw nothing but a mass of quicksilver. As the moon waxed, Lalleśwarī grew again to her normal size. Lalleśwarī's example physically expresses her insight into the nature of unity and duality. She recapitulates Śiva's own expansion and contraction. When Śiva expands, the world comes into being; when he contracts, he withdraws it all back into himself. Difference and union are both moments in the divine life, and the person who has become aware of this truth can experience Śiva in both states.

In her fast, Lalleśwarī demonstrates not only the emergence and withdrawal of the manifest world, but also a space between the solidity of the empirical self and its capacity for absolute dissolution in the true Self that is Śiva.

> [Her] body does not dissolve into the blankness of nothingness, but is turned into vibrant quicksilver. . . . The image presents the immanence and transcendence in tension, leading to the experience of the third space which goes beyond the binary dualism. . . . Transgressing the distinctions between the inside and outside, the subject and object[,] leads to the opening up of an entirely new space which refuses to be contained in any dualistic framework.[21]

Jaishree Kak Odin calls upon Luce Irigaray's metaphor of touch to describe the dynamism represented by the two pots. The vessels rest together, touching, at the most unified moment. Although composed of the same earthen substance, they remain two. Exploring this "third space" between monism and dualism will help us to move beyond the unhelpful East-West dichotomy.

"IMPURITIES"

For Lalleśwarī, the fundamental conundrum is to discover why human beings perceive difference so clearly but fail to realize their fundamental identity with Śiva. Indeed, most phases of consciousness exhibit degrees of duality. Just as God experiences differentiation, first as the masculine Śiva and the feminine Śakti, and then in the creation of the cosmos, the individual person experiences difference in thought, language, and perception. For the human being, unlike for God, the inability to perceive the unity of all things results in deep alienation from our true selves. Lalleśwarī bemoans this problem:

> My soul, why have you become fond of the not-self?
> Why have you mistaken the false for the true?
> It is ignorance that has bound you to the alien path
> and subjected you to the ordeal of coming and going, birth and death.
>
> *(K 14)*

The mistaken conclusions that human beings draw from the diversity of worldly experience keep them mired in a self-perpetuating case of mistaken identity in the round of rebirth. However, knowledge that human identity is rooted in divine consciousness provides both the diagnosis and the remedy for this malaise.

In Lalleśwarī's philosophical tradition, consciousness is the most salient feature of both ultimate reality and the human being. Śiva's awareness creates objects for itself; he not only perceives all things as they come into being but in fact *perceives them into being*. When he opens his eyes, as it were, creation begins; and when he closes them, the universe dissolves. Śiva is the power of consciousness in the universe. Human beings participate in that consciousness on two levels: they arise from Śiva-consciousness, and in turn they exhibit the powers of consciousness. In other words, human beings are at the same time *objects for divine consciousness* and *centers of consciousness* to which other objects present themselves.

The contraction of Śiva's unlimited powers into personal centers of thought and action obscures the connection between universal consciousness and individual consciousness. Human ignorance results from three particular limitations of consciousness: Śiva's power of intentionality condenses into the individual (*āṇava*) will, his omniscience becomes subject to illusion (*māyā*), and his universal action becomes bound to the limited action of individual selves (*karma*). These three limitations are known as the *mala*s, or "impurities," which obscure consciousness and prevent a person from realizing one's true nature. The powers of the embodied human being become restricted within individual mental processes, senses, and actions, all of which reinforce a sense of separateness between self and others and between self and the true Self, Śiva.[22]

Lalleśwarī reflects upon the power of each of the three *mala*s to block spiritual realization. The first, *āṇavamala*, is the projection of consciousness from its universal source onto an individual (*āṇava*) center of consciousness. It endows beings with differentiated perceptions so that they experience themselves as separate individuals. The *mala*s are smudges on the mirror of identity; they prevent the self from seeing the Self within. Lalleśwarī says,

> When my mind like
> dust from a mirror got purged of all impurities;
> ... the knowledge came
> to me that He was everything and I nothing.
> (K 100)

Identification with the embodied personality is "nothing" compared to the all-encompassing "everything" of the universal subject. Liberation comes when we cease to identify ourselves in a limited manner.

A second *mala*, *māyīyamala*, is evident in the diversity of the phenomenal world; it is the aspect of creation (*māyā*) that obscures the perception of unity. Unlike some schools of Indian thought, Kashmir Śaivism vigorously affirms the reality of creation. *Māyā* is not illusion; the world really exists. *Māyā* does, however, impede the human mind from seeing beyond worldly diversity to its source.

> Gently and gently shall I weep for you, O Mind.
> You have been caught under the spell of delusion.
> Even the shadow of worldly possessions will not stand by you.
> Alas, you have lost your own identity!
> (K 2)

Individuals forget their essential nature because *māyā* spins out five "coverings" that limit personal efficacy, knowledge, satisfaction, temporal experience, and freedom. Each of these limitations covers something essential about the self. We fail to tap into divine omnipotence and omniscience. We desire particular objects because we lack the fullness of the absolute. We experience past, present, and future in place of eternity. Our consciousness becomes subject to the constraints of space and causation. The everyday experience of the limitations of space and time reinforces the separateness of beings, but the enlightened person may come to understand and overcome these forces.

The effects of these obscuring energies carry over from one life to the next through the work of the third *mala*. The karmic residue of thoughts and actions (*karmamala*) bind the individual to the cycle of rebirth and keep the individual alienated from the true self. As a result, human beings do the same things life after life and thus continually enter through the same door, the womb (K 77). Lalleśwarī distinguishes between the actions (*karmas*) that are performed with and without attachment (K 101). Actions done with attachment to a particular outcome, whether good or bad, leave impressions on the transmigrating soul. These traces bear fruit in future lives. Everyday unenlightened activity strands beings in the karmic tide of rebirth. Such efforts are futile for reaching the shore of Śiva consciousness.

> O [hu]man, wherefore are you trying to twist a rope of sand?
> You cannot tow your boat with it.
> Whatever God has written in your line of fate
> no one is competent to obliterate that.
>
> (K 15)

Fortunately, another type of action is possible: one can "dedicate everything to the Lord [*svatmas*, one's own Self (O 80)] without attachment" (K 49) to avoid creating further karma that binds the self to the cycle of birth and death.

The three impurities inhere in the body and material world only to the extent that a person identifies with them. Lalleśwarī says, "Do away with karmas two and causes three, and / you will gain insight into the inner world" (K 101). Individual selves burn off the *malas* until they realize their unity with the Self. Beings may have one, two, or all three of the impurities in various degrees. Supremely liberated beings operate with only a trace of *āṇavamala* (sense of individuality): they retain a body as an instrument of grace as they teach others, and they merge with Śiva when their work is done.[23]

DESIRE

The three impurities account for why human beings identify so strongly with the experience of duality. Lalleśwarī excels at making these metaphysical ideas concrete. Human beings experience the limitations of individual and worldly diversity in a multitude of mundane ways. The fact of difference bombards embodied perceivers with such intensity that we notice little else. The habits and dispositions with which we meet the world often impede spiritual progress by creating division in the mind. Lalleśwarī skillfully meets her audience's existential situation with insights from the realm of human emotion and perception. "Slay your mortal foes—lust, greed and anger," she writes, "or they will shoot you dead with their darts" (K 37). As consequences of the *mala*s that bind us to a sense of separateness, such toxic passions block the quest for unity.

Although one might multiply the list of emotions and habits that impede consciousness of ultimate reality, it is more helpful to view anger, hatred, greed, and lust as symptoms of the larger problem of attachment or misplaced desire. Awareness of desire may then become a means to achieve that consciousness. Desire restlessly quests for new and better satiations. Inner tranquility requires the severance of attachment to particular outcomes. As Lalleśwarī puts it,

> The mind will not be satisfied even if a kingdom is gained,
> Nor can it have peace if you give it away.
> The [one] free from desires will not die.
>
> (K 48)

Lalleśwarī repeats an age-old theme of Indian thought: one must not crave the fruits of one's actions.[24] The most spiritual pursuits can feed the endless round of craving when practitioners long for fewer distractions and better and quicker results. Whether a person rules a city or withdraws from society for contemplation, only with "mind free from attachment" can one "win the pleasure of the Lord" (K 109–10).

Not every desire is detrimental to spiritual progress. Sanskrit traditions praise persons who desire liberating knowledge (known as *jijñāsa*s or *mumukṣu*s). Lalleśwarī models this salutary yearning as she sings of her heart's desire for God. Her favorite metaphor for this desire is a kind of homesickness:

> With a rope of untwisted yarn
>   am I towing my boat on the ocean.
> Would that God heard my prayer and
>   ferry me across safely.

> Like water in unbaked plates of clay
>   my efforts are going to waste.
> How I wish I would reach home!
>
> *(K 1)*

Lalleśwarī imagines herself stranded on a lake. As in a bad dream, the rope for towing her vessel keeps unraveling. Her efforts drip away. A vast expanse separates her from her destination, and nothing she does can convey her there.

Longing pours from Lalleśwarī's many lamentations over her slow progress. As she meditates, studies, and prays, her anticipation mounts:

> I, Lalla, set out in search of Him;
> Singing His praises I strained my tongue a hundred times.
> But when I set my eyes on Him I found His gate bolted.
> This whetted my yearning all the more.
> I paused there itself and remained on constant vigil.
>
> *(K 74)*

Metaphors of erotic love aptly give voice to her need: "Maddened with love" (K 97), she sets out on the quest for liberation; and her passion "roasts" her heart until she becomes calm (K 75).

The intense desire for liberation burns off all urges for penultimate ends. Desire, therefore, is not an impediment in itself. The craving that binds the human person is overcome by the yearning that leads to liberation. In Lalleśwarī's words, "He who slays the three highway robbers, greed, lust and pride / ... seeks out the Lord spontaneously / rejecting all else as mere ashes" (K 36). Burning off the desire of attachment is the first all-important step toward the purgation of the impurities of individuality, delusion, and karma; and the cessation of craving frees the heart for its true love.

After one shifts the objects of desire, one may see in desire a model of the connection between the subject and its object. The moments in a single urge exemplify the dynamic nature of Śiva. First, a feeling of desire wells up in the subject. This initial state of intent mimics the unity of consciousness. The duality latent in the first instant then becomes manifest as a conscious desire for a specific external object arises. This moment mirrors Śiva's creation of objects for himself. By following the movement of desire, and by trying to grasp the moment of transition between unity and duality, one can glimpse Śiva, whose will to perceive impels him to expand into many centers of consciousness. The divine will to perceive resonates in the common human desire to experience the world and the more elevated wish to perceive Śiva in it. At the microcosmic level, human desire thus imitates Śiva's act of willing the material universe into being.[25]

BACK TO NATURE

Lalleśwarī marvels at the difficulty we have in turning away from the ordinary objects that attract our longing, toward our true identity. We are presented with "jars brimming over with wine, / but none cares to drink" (K 99). We hardly realize we are missing something. She laments,

> Though a royal swan you have become speechless.
> Someone, it seems, has carried away something of thine.
> When the mill came to a halt the grain channel was choked.
> Away went the miller with the grain.
>
> (K 106)

Our true nature cannot speak because the flow of consciousness is blocked. The channel leading the grain of our thoughts to the mill of self-consciousness gets stopped up with obstacles of many kinds. We thirst, forgetting that we are filled to the brim with divinity. Indeed, these metaphors, as with Lalleśwarī's general sense of homesickness, convey the human predicament of having lost something familiar and dear. We are missing our very own Self.

The Self that permeates all selves is none other than Śiva. As Lalleśwarī teaches, "Like a fine web is Śiva spread out. / He is there in all mortal frames" (K 82). Because Śiva *is* the power of consciousness, he is the basis of the perception of all beings: sentient creatures perceive with the same awareness that is Śiva. Self and self share the same attributes and activities. The microcosm of human activity replicates Śiva's five cosmic activities of creation, persistence, withdrawal, concealment, and grace: Śiva contracts his all-encompassing consciousness to enter into finite beings when he *creates* and *maintains* the world; he absorbs these external objects when he *withdraws* consciousness to focus inward; he *conceals* the unity of consciousness to make things appear as different from him; and subjects realize them as identical due to his *grace*. Kashmir Śaiva scripture states that Śiva continues to do these five activities in the empirical self as the individual perceives, enjoys, or ceases to perceive objects in the world. One's view of external objects can then either conceal one's identity or lead to a state of grace. Because it is Śiva's nature to engage in these activities eternally, Self never exists without selves who partake in them.

The impoverished condition of the stranded, homesick soul may be common; but according to Lalleśwarī, it is not natural. Time and again, she returns to the term *sahaj*, which means natural or something in its natural state.[26] The term denotes both the nature of the human being and the means for realizing it. *Sahaj* resides at the very core of her message: "to contemplate *sahaj* is the teaching" (my trans.; cf. K 59). As Lalleśwarī describes the most natural life,

> *Sahaj* does not call for restraint of the mind and senses.
> By devotion will you gain the portals of liberation.
> You may be merged as salt in water,
> still it is hard to attain *sahaj*-contemplation.
>
> (K 76, *modified*)

There is nothing more natural than union with the highest reality, despite a multitude of obstacles on both individual and cosmic levels. From among its various meanings, *sahaj* in the first line refers to the practices that are most true to one's nature. In contrast with more difficult ascetic approaches, we should cultivate simple means; nothing should be forced or false. In the last line, *sahaj* is the object of meditation: translators render it "the Self" or even "God."[27] This ambiguity echoes central Kashmir Śaiva concepts such as *sva-rupa*, in which the divine Self is "one's own form" and human nature is none other than the Self.[28]

SELF RETURNS TO SELF

Lalleśwarī favors an image from nature, water, to depict the separation and the return to the Self. In the ocean of life (*saṁsāra*), which flows from the Self, the self might feel as if it is stranded or drowning. It longs to cross to the other shore to unite with God. Not only does Śiva bring the self across to the other shore, but Śiva-consciousness enables it to see the divine pervading all reality (cf. K 29, 82). The self becomes merged, melted, dissolved, or absorbed into the Self. In contrast to those "stuck in the quagmire of ignorance" or pummeled by "the cascade let loose by the sea of delusion" (K 13), the adept becomes "merged as salt in water" (K 76).

Lalleśwarī's fluid way of thinking puts a unique stamp on a traditional Kashmir Śaiva teaching. For Śaivas, one of the most natural ways to witness the interplay of unity and duality with Śiva is to observe the states of waking, dreaming, and deep sleep. While waking, the senses and mind operate in the realm of subject and object. In dreams and mental meditation, thought constructs arise because of the impressions such objects make on the mind when awake. In both waking and dreaming, our awareness of external objects obscures the essential unity of consciousness. Deep sleep, in which all objects fade, approximates pure consciousness. The practitioner works to bring the unity that is unconscious in deep sleep into conscious awareness. One then enters the "fourth state" (*turīya*), in which one retains awareness of the nature of the Self even while acting in the world of diversity.[29] The practitioner's goal is to make this awareness constant.

Lalleśwarī combines this popular analogy with images of water and fluidity:

> The cold transformed water into ice and snow,
> giving rise to the conception of the three.
> When the sun of consciousness shines bright
> all three become one, and the world of the living
> and the lifeless are seen as Śiva Himself.
> *(K 83)*

The Self appears in the form of selves just as water condenses into states of ice or snow. The three states of everyday experience—waking, sleeping, and deep sleep—are, in the end, all modifications of the Self. In the fourth state, "When the sun of consciousness shines bright [and] / all three become one" (K 83), one sees this clearly. As Śiva moves fluidly between manifestation and dissolution, so, too, Lalleśwarī experiences different states of consciousness as one, permeated with Śiva.

Bodies of water figure prominently in Lalleśwarī's metaphorical depictions of union. She longs to cross to the other shore; instead, she gets "immersed . . . in the lake of nectar" (K 130). According to Gavin Flood, the image of immersion or absorption (*samāveśa*) into an ocean or lake has roots in early Śaiva possession cults; but in the metaphysics of the Trika school, this term denotes "immersion in the . . . ocean of consciousness, the immersion of the individual into the universal, or the realization of the identity between individual and universal consciousness."[30] Individual selves are waves or foam on the ocean of the Self. Thought constructs arise like waves on a lake, leading to a disturbance of one's sense of unity with pure consciousness. With practice, however, one sinks down into the source of these thoughts so that daily activities no longer disturb awareness.

Lalleśwarī recapitulates this dissolution or immersion in a series of verses with a single refrain: nothing mixes with nothing, or "the void gets merged into the void" (K 89–91). Each quatrain begins with an aspect of empirical reality and then dissolves it into an awareness beyond subject and object. For example, in K 89 she progresses from physical observances, to verbal mantras, to mental activity, to the void beyond the mind:

> [Tantric] rites drop, mantra remains;
> mantra drops, only the mind is left.
> The mind drops, nothing remains;
> the void gets merged into the void.
> *(K 89)*

Because the void that immerses, dissolves, and melts the self in the Self is beyond rational apprehension, the deity that abides in the void cannot be described (*na kenh*; O 16; K 24). In a mantric formulation, Lalleśwarī intones, "Something, or not; something or not; something or not; what is it?" (my trans.; cf. K 7). Union takes place in the emptiness beyond conscious experience. In the "wilderness of the void," one loses "both reason and sense" (K 103). From this perspective, where subject and object merge, Lalleśwarī says, "He was everything and I nothing" (K 100). The void pervades all.

THE PERSISTENCE OF DUALITY

Despite Lalleśwarī's apophatic statements about the void beyond subject and object, her understanding of duality differs from nondual traditions in which duality between *ātman* and *brahman* is only provisionally real. If the Advaita Vedānta school approaches the absolute through negation, the "Śaiva method is one of an ever widening inclusion of phenomena mistakenly thought to be outside the absolute."[31] Instead of "not this, not this" (*neti, neti*), Lalleśwarī elsewhere piles on more referents: "he or he or he" (*su va su va su va suh*; O 20; K 73). The many, with all their particularity, display the nature of divine consciousness.

Some collections of Lalleśwarī's work nevertheless contain sayings (*vaakhs*) that appear to teach the denial or annihilation of the individual self. Jaishree Kak Odin cites several verses that first appear in the collections of Anand Koul and the magazine *Koshur Samachar*, which seem to reject any immanent experience of divinity in favor of transcendence of name and form:

> Recite *So'ham* with every breath[.]
> Renounce the ego and mediate on the Self[.]
> She who renounces the ego finds the Self[.]
> Negation of the ego or "I" is the teaching.
> (O 133)

The "negation of the ego" in this verse finds echo in the notion of losing one's sense of I, me, and mine:

> I, Lalla, suffered the fire of love[.]
> Before death I died without a trace[.]
> Born without color or creed, yet what colors didn't I take[?]
> "I-ness" left me[.]
> What else could I do?
> (O 28)

Odin charges that Lalleśwarī's view of union negates her embodied particularity in an "identity model of reality" that too closely resembles ontologies of "the One" that close off difference.³² Lalleśwarī wants to "die without a trace," to be free of the tint she has acquired from being in the world. These verses set up self-negation as a prerequisite for merger with the absolute reality.

Does Lalleśwarī, then, come down on the side of a transcendent monism after all? The simplest way to refute this charge would be to dismiss such verses as inauthentic. Though several transmitters of Lalleśwarī's *vaakh*s attribute them to her, J. L. Kaul, who has come closest to assembling a critical edition of Lalleśwarī's work, does not. I argue, however, that we must situate this loss of "I" in relation to the cosmic impurity, *āṇavamala*, which creates a false sense of individuality. In this context, Lalleśwarī can distinguish "the true self from the false self" (K 82). The "I" that takes leave of Lalleśwarī is not her existence as an individual center of consciousness, but the ego or false sense of self that constrains, deludes, and blinds her from seeing her true nature. It is the latter self "who will die and who will be slain" (K 54–55) with the "realization of the self as consciousness" (K 117).³³

Depending on one's progress, one may experience various degrees of unity-in-difference. The emptiness of the void is one of these degrees. In the early stages of her practice, Lalleśwarī feels a great deal of difference from the Lord: "This is the difference between you and [me]: / that you are the master of the six / while I am robbed by the six" (K 128). Here she refers to the human failure to realize that we possess the six divine attributes of "omniscience, contentment, knowledge of the past from eternity, absolute self-sufficiency, irreducible potency, and omnipotence" and the propensity to be "misled by another six: . . . sexual desire, wrath, desire, arrogance, delusion, and jealousy."³⁴ Though God and soul resemble each other in their most essential attributes, they differ to the extent to which they can control these attributes.

Discipline and long practice gradually bring the faculties—mind, body, breath—under control. Contrary to the patterns often imposed upon "Eastern" thought, Lalleśwarī does not arrive at the void in order to abandon the physical and mental vehicles that conveyed her there. Her descriptions of the inner state of union are inseparable from the yogic practices which lead to it:

> *By constant practice* the manifested universe
> gets merged in the universal self.
> The world of name and form gets merged in the
> vastness of the void as one homogeneous whole.
> When the void disappears there remains the ineffable
>   Supreme alone.
> This, O Brahmin, is the true doctrine.
>   (K 133, *emphasis added*)

Kashmir Śaiva texts recommend practices of attention to the emergence of thought, perception, emotion, or desire. One does not cease *having* thoughts or perceptions but rather meditates upon the moments of transition, which are called "voids."[35] These spaces between unity and duality are windows into the expansions and contractions of universal consciousness. Because such instants admit no awareness of subject and object, one may concentrate on them to witness the unity in the midst of plurality.

The void is not the final destination for Lalleśwarī. Nonduality has an epistemological function as the singular moment in the cycle of Śiva-consciousness in which all differences merge.[36] It is the space where, as Lalleśwarī testifies, there is "neither word nor thought, . . . neither you nor I, nothing to contemplate nor the process of contemplation" (K 134–35). Yet nonduality is not the only moment, or even the final moment. Transcendence and the union of the void merely precede a return to the diversity of the world. The temporary dissolution of the faculties reorients her toward the other modes of consciousness and orders her perspective so that she can relate to others as they truly are. Union and differentiation eternally oscillate as selves ebb and flow in relation with the divine.[37]

Lalleśwarī's sense of duality, therefore, does not completely disappear after experiencing the unity of consciousness. Earth, body, and the void are equally Śiva, but they do not lose their particular features as a result of this realization.

> I roamed the ten quarters, and
> sped through the wind and the void.
> The nine apertures of the body I closed, and
> found Śiva everywhere.
>
> *(K 125)*

After enlightenment, God continues to appear in many forms; the self continues to take on particular characteristics. Lalleśwarī observes, "Though one I am caught in the war of two. / The same formless [lit., colorless] one appeared in various forms [colors]" (K 123). Because the highest realization encompasses not unity alone, but unity in duality, there is actually no contradiction in this "war of two." Śaiva rhetoric ranks various levels of awareness: awareness of difference as inferior (*apara*), unity-in-difference as middling (*parāpara*), and complete union as the highest (*para*) state of consciousness. The emptiness of the void is the "highest" (*para*) only insofar as it is most difficult to realize. The true adept sees the validity of many ways of describing the one and the many, including difference, unity-in-difference, and nondifference.

A degree of difference between Śiva and *jīva* is necessary for there to be relation between them. Lalleśwarī's occasional use of erotic imagery makes this point particularly well. She plays upon the resonances among love (*lola*; cf. K 97), her name (*lal*), and that of the beloved (*lala*):

> Rising in the last watch of the moonlit night
> I made my wayward mind repeat His name.
> I bore the pangs of his love, woke my beloved
> saying, "Here is Lalla, Lalla, Lalla."
> My body got purified when my mind attained oneness with Him.
> (K 88)

Love, attraction, and paradoxically, even union require at least two. As close as she is to her Lord, she retains her name, resplendent in the light of her true nature: she explains that only when "the lamp of knowledge shone bright for me, and revealed to me my true identity" (K 98) she "became known as Lalla" (K 86).

In contrast to the personal erotic image, a nonpersonal metaphor of a grindstone and its axle reiterates the difference between Self and self. The axle turns the mill, and the mill grinds fine flour.

> The mill turns steadily once you propel the wheel.
> The pivot alone knows the secret of the mill.
> Once the mill moves[,] turning out fine flour
> Grist will find its own way to the mill yard.
> (K 56)

Here, according to Odin, the axle is the Self, which provides the force to move the stones (the empirical self). I would venture to suggest that the grain stands for human beings attracted to the divine center becoming refined toward clarity. This metaphor, in which "the uniqueness of each constituent part remains intact,"[38] elucidates the synergy inherent in liberating knowledge.

The interplay of Lalleśwarī's images, ranging from dissolution of the faculties to the solidity of stone, points to the subtle nature of Śiva-consciousness. Lalleśwarī abides in the quivering liminality between unity and duality, where she can experience the divine expansion and contraction in every moment. The *yoginī* balances between transcendence and immanence, embraces subject and object without melding them, and cultivates a liberated mode of consciousness that runs through the three states of consciousness like a thread through the flowers of a garland. This awareness is Lalleśwarī's highest achievement, for it unites all the stages on her path and all the metaphors for her experience.

Lalleśwarī's corpus stands at odds with the construction of the essentially unitive or monistic East, but she is not some rare contradiction to the customary view of Eastern mysticism as nondual. Rather, she echoes the metaphysics of Kashmir Śaivism—one of numerous Indian systems that define themselves *against* Advaita Vedānta. Lalleśwarī stands as a testament to the duality preserved in Śaivism and in the oral legacies of women's wisdom in India.

Dismantling the view of the East as monistic is only half of the task at hand, however, because it is usually paired with a view of the West as dualistic. Jayant Lele observes that both the scholarship that created "orientalist" stereotypes and the scholarship that has criticized these stereotypes tend to obscure the heterogeneity of the West by constructing "an all-inclusive 'occidentalism.' . . . The main consequence of this strategy is that the internal dynamics of the western intellectual tradition . . . is flattened out in a manner that is counterproductive to [Edward] Said's own attempt to explain why the West continued to see the Orient as its other."[39]

The essentially dualistic West must come under scrutiny in the same manner as the nondualist East. To this end, we turn to Mechthild of Magdeburg, who doubly complicates Western scholarship. She has been called a "mystic" because her theology troubles the characterization of Western thought as basically dualistic; yet she also challenges the idea that "mysticism" is somehow an exception to predominant Western patterns. Her idioms of desire and fluidity recall Lalleśwarī's, but within differing structures, which will provide a basis for a comparison between the two theologians.

UNION IN DIFFERENTIATION IN MECHTHILD OF MAGDEBURG

Mysticism is well entrenched as an outlier in Western thought, especially when narrowly defined in terms of extraordinary and ineffable experiences of union with God. It is difficult to arrive at a precise definition of mysticism because of the broad spectrum of phenomena it has tended to encompass. It generally denotes a way of life oriented around a desire for and consciousness of divine presence. Mysticism has often been separated from the broader fabric of religious traditions and reduced to remarkable experiences such as visions, auditory experiences, and feelings of radical transcendence or divine immanence; but according to Bernard McGinn's magisterial history of the Christian mystical tradition, the term should encompass "everything that leads up to and prepares for this encounter, as well as all that flows from or is supposed to flow from it for the life of the individual in the belief of the community," including disciplines, texts, and institutions.[40]

In its various permutations, mysticism has often had a disruptive role in Western thought. Because "mystical experiences" have the potential to empower otherwise marginalized individuals, church officials over the course of Christian history have worried about claims of direct contact with God and their potential to circumvent their authority. For example, authorities censured the antinomian tendencies of individuals like Marguerite Porete and Meister Eckhart, tendencies in which law and the virtues take a backseat to contemplation. The hyperbolic erotic language of Mechthild and other medieval women who claimed intimacy with God also distressed the sensibilities of some readers. More troubling than these problems, however, the mystical goal of union with God has the disturbing potential to erase the essential difference between God and creation held so dear in the Western monotheisms.

The monotheistic religions of the West—Judaism, Christianity, and Islam—contain strong injunctions against idolatry. The Torah depicts the creation of the material world by a transcendent Creator, who is not to be identified with any created thing. Christians point to Christ as the *only* human being who was also fully God. In Islam, the sin of *shirk* designates the association of Allah with anything that is not divine. On the surface, the line between divinity and humanity could not be clearer. Yet each of these traditions contains strong lineages of contemplation, such as Kabbalah and Sufism, that facilitate union with God. We shall explore one Christian example of what "union" means; but here it is sufficient to note that the stereotype of Western religion as dualistic, in the sense of positing divinity and humanity as mutually exclusive categories, cannot hold up under scrutiny.

THE FLOWING TRINITY

The first place the Christian tradition breaks down the idea of dualism between unitary categories is its assertion of the triune nature of God: God is not a monad, but a being in dynamic relation to God's own self. References to the Trinity are ubiquitous in Mechthild of Magdeburg's work. Unlike some of the work of Marguerite Porete and Meister Eckhart, Mechthild never suggests a unity so strong that it melts the distinction of the persons into a single deity beyond Trinity. She repeatedly invokes one God in three persons, as in this explanation of their union:

> The Three Persons sent forth beautifully the beams of light in unison, each of them illumined by the other while remaining utterly one. The Father was adorned in his Person with the robust character of omnipotence; the Son was equal to the Father in infinite wisdom; and the Holy Spirit was equal to them in full generosity. (FL 3.9)

The Trinity is three, but its actions are inseparable. Augustine of Hippo, too, draws upon images of light to explain how the three are one, but his famous analogy of the triune God as lover, beloved, and the love best anticipates what for Mechthild is God's deepest nature: love.

Like her contemporaries Hadewijch, Beatrice of Nazareth, and Marguerite Porete, Mechthild employs the ideal of courtly love (*minne*) in expressing her vision of God. In her dialogues and visionary narratives, Mechthild often speaks directly to Lady Love (*vro minne*), the personification of God's most salient attribute.[41] Love cannot be indexed to any one of the Trinitarian persons (who also appear as dramatic characters), for Love embodies the entire Trinitarian mode of relation. God tells her, "That I love you passionately comes from my nature, for I am love itself. That I love you often comes from my desire, for I desire to be loved passionately" (*FL* 1.24). *Minne* can refer to God, to the personification of an attribute, and more inclusively, to "the active force by which we participate in and return to God."[42]

Mechthild encapsulates the dynamic movement of the love between the three Trinitarian persons in her unique term for their perichoretic interpenetration, the *dreierleie spilenden vluot*, or playful threefold flood (4.12). Margot Schmidt argues that *fliessende*, flowing, derives from the Pseudo-Dionysian tradition of desire (*eros*), procession, and return, but that *spilende* exceeds it:

> The word "spilende" adds a completely new dimension: it expresses something which divinely inspires bliss, something which is invigorating, whose joy, splendour and glory nourish the reciprocal life of the three Persons within the Godhead; that is to say, the Trinity itself is subject to its own law of *eros*.[43]

The term suggests overtures of life, joy, and play as characterizing the inner Trinitarian relations.

Mechthild's pervasive language of fluidity conveys the dynamic mutuality of the love between the three divine persons. The Father, the source of all, praises himself as "a flowing spring that no one can block" (*FL* 5.26). The Son eternally flows from the Father (5.6) and then out of the Trinity in the incarnation (1.22). The Holy Spirit, "an abundant outpouring of the Father and Son" (6.32), impels the Trinity to overflow in love and create the soul (6.8). Indeed, Mechthild tells us, "God could no longer contain himself" (1.22). God is compelled by God's own nature; and in all of its activities, the Trinity flows.

Mechthild crafts dialogues to imagine the unique, though inseparable, roles each member of the Trinity plays in creation. Before there was anything other than God, the Spirit "played for the Father, plucking the Holy Trinity" (3.9), sounding the first notes of the desire to create. The courtly musical metaphor suggests the beginnings of a vibration that would soon resonate with the created cosmos. At a key moment in this first divine council,

> the Father said: "Son, a powerful desire stirs in my divine breast as well, and I swell in love alone. We shall become fruitful so that we shall be loved in return. . . . I shall make a bride for myself who shall greet me with her mouth and wound me with her beauty." (3.9)

Creation ensues as divine love reaches its bursting point. The soul becomes God's bride, the "goddess of all creatures" (3.9). God's nature as love and the divine desire to be loved in return compels creation.

The Trinitarian relations exemplify a key principle for Mechthild: love opens persons to intimate participation in others, but this unity does not obliterate distinctions between them. The threefold flood of love does not wash away divine personhood; in fact, it enables the three persons to act in their characteristic triune way. Mutuality, equality, and generativity mark these relations; and in the overflow of love, others are invited to play in the tide.

THE FLOWING SOUL

As with Trinitarian love, the relationship between God and the soul that bears the Trinitarian image envelops both union and difference. The soul's creation out of love empowers human beings for full, agentive personhood; but although human agency is the precondition for genuine love, it also creates the possibility of estrangement. Salvation history issues forth from this dynamic.

Although the soul turns away from God and thus radically alters its original bridal relationship to divinity, God "kept his noble loving nature intact . . . [and] never gave up" on humanity (*FL* 4.14). A certain powerlessness forces God to overflow in acts of redemption: "He cannot withhold himself" (4.14).[44] Mechthild imagines that the spotless soul of Mary is created to take the place of the human soul in the cosmos, at least temporarily, so "he might have something to love; for his darling bride, the noble soul, was dead" (1.22).[45] Love impels God to restore humanity to its original state when, in a second divine council, the Son intercedes on the soul's behalf and offers to take flesh in order to heal her wounds.[46] When the Spirit concurs, the "Father then bowed to the wills of them both with great love" (3.9). Although there is no real conflict between divine justice and mercy for Mechthild (cf. 6.16

and 6.31), the dramatic device of the divine councils highlights the relational nature of salvation, which, like creation, pours from the divine nature. God is unable *not* to give love.

This powerlessness results in a dynamic of *eros*, procession, and return between God and the soul. The soul becomes "as godlike as one can be" (7.1) within creaturely limits. In this process of return, three instrumental causes, "Rising desire and sinking humility and flowing love . . . bring the soul up to heaven before God" (7.34). The soul ardently wings its way toward God through "rising desire":

> When you [God] pass through the soul, . . . and she then rises up and begins to fly with the wings of a dove, which are all the virtues, and she then begins to desire with the longing of the eagle, she follows the heat up to heaven, for she finds everything transitory to be cold and tasteless. (5.31; also see 5.4)

The soul then sinks again, not because it has sated its eternal desire but because humility is essential to Christian formation. Paradoxically, "sinking humility" moves souls *closer* to God (7.34), who as Redeemer "inclined himself" to earth (5.23). The sojourning soul climbs and plummets, drawing ever nearer to the heart of God. The third ingredient, "flowing love," unites this divinizing spiral as it purifies, sanctifies, and perfects the loving soul. The eddy of desire sweeps one into "a full exchange with God" (4.15), who promises, "Give me everything that is yours, and I shall give you everything that is mine" (7.55). A person becomes as divine as humanly possible without obliterating the distinction between the Trinity and the creation.[47]

The ebb and flow of creation and restoration permeate the whole of Mechthild's writing. The soul is always in motion within the

> . . . playful flood of love
> That flows mysteriously from God into the soul
> And through his power flows back again according to her ability.
> (7.45)

Mechthild's dialectic of union and separation thus seeps through the binaries attributed to her spiritual tradition.

THE DUALITY OF DESIRE

The soul may experience this fluid itinerary because it bears the image of God within as love (*minne*). The unlimited mutuality of desire between God and the soul is their deepest nature. The soul's native virtues are noble longing and boundless desire, and God's passion is insatiable as well: "He is as lovesick for her as he always was; for he neither increases nor decreases" (*FL* 1.4). Witness this exchange:

> The person said: "Dear Lord, I cannot control my longing; I would so dearly like to be with you."
> Our Lord said: "I longed for you before the beginning of the world. I long for you and you long for me. Where two burning desires meet, there love is perfect." (7.16)

The burning desire between God and the human being propels them toward one another in this life and anticipates everlasting union in the next.[48]

Nevertheless, between fleeting moments of presence, the bride-soul experiences extended periods of longing in absence. Alongside the commentarial tradition on the Song of Songs, Mechthild's courtly notion of *minne* also evokes a situation in which a lover (usually male) devotes himself to the service of a lady, often from afar, so that "the fruition of love comes to reside in the paradoxical nonfruition of continual yearning for the Beloved."[49] Like the hero of courtly literature, the soul labors in intense longing and the absence of full union. As she becomes impatient with ordinary modes of devotion, she insists,

> That is child's love. . . . I am a full-grown Bride. I want to go to my Lover.
> . . . .
> A fish in water does not drown.
> A bird in the air does not plummet.
> Gold in fire does not perish.
> Rather, it gets its purity and its radiant color there.
> God has created all creatures to live according to their nature.
> How, then, am I to resist my nature?
> I must go from all things to God,
> Who is my Father by nature,
> My Brother by his humanity,
> My Bridegroom by love.
>
> (1.44)

The soul's very nature as divine love creates the paradoxical dance of courtly longing. The relation of subject and object, lover and beloved, is always a relation of at least two: the soul encounters duality at the same time as it longs for union.

The separation between God and the soul intensifies when love turns in on the self. The capacity to love and desire is related to all of the permutations of the will (*wille*)—free will, goodwill, self-will, and God's will. The soul is endowed with free will at creation and maintains this dignity even now;

but one's future destiny depends upon its good use. When one gives self-will over to God, one "becomes one God with God in such a way that whatever he wills she wills as well, and they can be united in complete union no other way" (6.1).[50] Mechthild associates the will with the decision-making faculties, which can impede or yield to divine desire. She writes,

> The great outflow of divine love that never ceases flows on and on unceasingly and effortlessly in such a sweet course unfailingly that our tiny vessel becomes full and brims over. If we do not block it with self-will, our small vessel is always overflowing with God's favor. (7.55)

The notions of free will and self-will allow Mechthild to grasp why people do not automatically incline toward God as the soul was created to do. We would naturally flow back to God if not for the primary blockage to this flow, the accretion of a will turned in on the self. The will must be lured back to God so it will not only *assent* but *longingly ascend* after the divine.

Material creation furnishes another class of objects for the soul's love. Divinity cannot help but become embroiled in materiality. Because the soul bears God's image, we are drawn toward creation; yet the soul "gain[s] much praise from God" when she "[turns] the eye of her desire from all things" (5.4). Mechthild calls for practical discernment toward the cravings that arise from moment to moment. Some, including the most basic of physical desires such as hunger, "occur without sin for the reason that an evil will does not cause them" (3.18). Natural needs can become unhealthy attachments. Other objects of desire seriously threaten the soul's commitment to God.[51] Mechthild therefore supplies the dictum that "the more one satisfies oneself with earthly things here, the less heavenly bliss shall be left over for us there" (3.1). A proportional relationship inheres between the body's desires and the spiritual benefit one receives from treating them with moderation.

THE DUALITY OF SEPARATION

God-soul duality is painfully evident in the perception of God's absence. Mechthild often describes herself as *ellende*—lonely, abandoned, banished, and forsaken, a concept that covers a broad range of human experience.[52] Her text explores these nuances. For her, life in this world is a veritable exile (*ellende*) from God (*FL* 6.37; 7.48). Such loneliness in relation to the world is a positive means of identifying with Christ; but in relation to God, it marks the suffering of the soul during periods of divine silence.

Mechthild longs to be a stranger to the world and belong to God alone, like Jesus, who was born in exile (*ellenden geburt*) and suffered lonely distress (*ellenden not*; 7.18). The motif of entering a desert or a strange and foreign land functions positively as "an ascetical state of the soul conducive to receiving God."[53] Mechthild writes,

> You should love nothingness.
> You should flee somethingness.
> You should stand alone
> And should go to no one.
> . . . .
> Then you are living in the true desert.
> *(1.35)*

In even stronger language, she says,

> . . . I would rather be yet further removed—
> To the lowest place—
> Cast off like a raging dog
> And no one's friend,
> Unknown, in banishment,
> With poor people in a foreign land.
> *(6.19)*

Although Mechthild takes a radical step and leaves home at an early age for a city where no one knows her, this place of exile from the world primarily exists *within* oneself. In the solitude of one's own heart, one may whisper with God and enjoy "divine sweetness" unimpeded by distractions (6.2; cf. 2.23; 7.53). This ascetic process anticipates the preliminary "dark night of the senses" in St. John of the Cross, for it clears the way of obstacles to the flow of divine love.

The palpable absence of the Beloved, comparable to St. John of the Cross's "dark night of the soul," can occur at any time in the Christian life, especially after the soul has overcome lesser obstacles. Mechthild's poetry evokes the agony of anticipation as she waits for her Lover, accuses God of abandonment, and frankly acknowledges her own cooled ardor. Eventually she submits to God's whim:

> Love, your leaving and coming
> Are equally welcome to the well-ordered soul.
> *(5.30)*

Mechthild comes to rejoice in the experience of absence and even to seek it. She relates how after a "consolation" that goes on for eight years, her soul sinks to unprecedented depths. Considering herself unworthy of the divine favors, she chooses to descend to the place of the damned. God pursues her there, but she wishes to sink away from divine intimacy and keep nothing but unwavering memory to guard against unbelief. At last she reaches "constant estrangement from God" (4.12), which she welcomes with joy. But God never really abandons her. He tells her:

> I cannot be without you.
> No matter how far we are apart,
> We can still never be really separated.
> (2.25)

Paradoxically, the soul knows "full well that God would console her even in great estrangement," saying, "Now God is strangely with me, for now his estrangement from me is more welcome to me than he is himself" (4.12). Mechthild delights in knowing God in a new way, as simultaneously present and absent. She concludes:

> Ah, blessed Estrangement from God, how bound I am to you in love! You strengthen my will in pain and make pleasant for me the difficult long wait in this miserable body. By whatever means I make myself more your companion, the more intensely and wondrously God falls over me. O Lord, in the depths of pure humility I cannot sink away from you.
>
> But the deeper I sink,
> The sweeter I drink.
> (4.12)

Mechthild's paradoxical formula indicates that estrangement is not the final word in the Christian life. Given her frequent contemplations on the meaning of spiritual loneliness, we must ask: Is the duality of lonely alienation the final word for her?

SUFFERING AND STAGES OF THE CHRISTIAN LIFE

Some medieval Christian writers view the suffering of separation from God as the pinnacle of the spiritual life. Mechthild's predecessors in the erotic-mystical life, Richard of St. Victor and William of St. Thierry, would have viewed her frequent meditations on suffering and the cooling of her ardor as the final stage in her spiritual development. Richard of St. Victor's "Four Degrees of Passionate Charity" follow the experience of the bride in the Song of Songs. Wounded, the soul burns with desire. Bound, it can think of nothing but God. Sick with love, it is melted or liquefied in God. Fainting, it humbly flows where God directs it and suffers for Christ's sake.[54] In William of St. Thierry's four "ages" of love, the soul begins to taste the sweetness of divine illumination in its youth, feels tortured when it is removed, loses its vigor, and by old age patiently waits to go to God at death.[55] Both theologians culminate their progression with some degree of suffering.

Mechthild may have been aware of such schemes. Images from the Song of Songs that appear in Richard's work (wounding, bound love, etc.) are prominent in her book as well. She echoes William's "fourth age" when she describes her old age as "unproductive in resplendent deeds and cold as to graces" and "powerless . . . since it does not have youth with which to sustain fiery love of God" (*FL* 7.3). God affirms that "proper old age is joyfully patient and trusts in God alone" and offers a Trinitarian schema for this development:

> Your childhood was a playmate of my Holy Spirit.
> Your youth was a Bride of my humanity.
> Your old age is now a housewife of my Godhead.
> (7.3)

Several scholars today superimpose such a stagewise structure on the whole of Mechthild's thought. Barbara Newman reads Mechthild in line with Richard's theory of love and compares Mechthild's "stages" with those of Hadewijch and Marguerite Porete:

> For the earlier beguines, the bridal union takes place near the outset of the mystical life, but only as a foretaste of consummation to come. Through the sweetness of this union, God or Minne seduces the soul, luring her into the wholehearted commitment that will prove bitter and painful later on. Minne (for Hadewijch) or the Bridegroom (for Mechthild) then withdraws, leaving the *minnende Sele* to prove her loyalty through a long period of suffering as she 'lives Christ's humanity.' First comes the sweet, then the bitter.[56]

In this tradition of interpretation, sinking humility in imitation of Christ would be the final stage in Mechthild's spiritual development. As the ultimate renunciation of spiritual concupiscence, she would no longer hope for the soaring bliss of divine intimacy but humbly resign herself to bearing her cross through the final years of her earthly life of exile.

I suggest, however, that Mechthild does not share the Victorine tradition's investment in stages, which artificially carve up the fluid nature of progress in the Christian life.[57] Whereas Richard and William in passing mention that the stages are more or less concurrent with one another,[58] the flowing patterns of Mechthild's thought draw out this insight, which is masked by the earlier thinkers' structuring instincts. For Mechthild, suffering—whether in Christlike humility as in Richard or in the patience of weakened longing as in William—is not the last stage, or even a distinct stage in and of itself. Her path includes the agony of separation and the ecstasy of union, but she claims ultimacy for neither type of experience. Suffering from many sources—one's own sin, persecution by others, divine absence—recurs from the beginning to the end of the Christian life; and both suffering and consolation are necessary in the flowing (sinking, rising) nature of love.

THE DUALITY OF UNION

The duality inherent in longing and divine absence does not make Mechthild's theology "dualistic," nor does her concept of union imply monistic nondistinction. If duality is painfully evident in estrangement, it is blissfully so in union, for in order to love there must be an other, someone to love. Whereas some in the thirteenth century (such as Porete or Eckhart) would expand the idea of a union of wills to an ontological union without distinction in the ground of the soul, Mechthild stops short of this move. Amy Hollywood reads Mechthild as standing in a progression:

> While Mechthild does not go so far as to call for the annihilation of the will and the centrality of apophasis, her . . . understanding of mystical union, although expressed in a variety of more traditional formulas, *suggests* the idea of a union without distinction grounded in the preexistence of the soul within the divine.[59]

There is no final annihilation of the soul, no total dissolution into God; each retains its integrity so that one may mingle with another.

To be sure, many of the beguine's most beautiful passages on union seem to indicate loss of self. When God and soul "are united as water and wine, she turns to nothing and is transported out of herself" (*FL* 1.4). At such moments, she is unsure where she ends and God begins:

> . . . I was so lost in wonder
> That I could not find the boundaries of things.
> *(6.19)*

God affirms the completeness of their union, calling her "a loss of myself" (1.20) and telling her,

> When you love, we two become one being.
> And when we two are one being,
> Then we can never be parted.
> *(2.6)*

God avers,

> I am in you
> And you are in me.
> We could not be closer,
> For we two have flowed into one
> And have been poured into one mold.
> *(3.5)*

Mechthild depicts union in terms of melting or dissolving, becoming nothing, and a total exchange of one's being for God's.[60] She lays out how a person becomes "one whole person with the Holy Trinity": "a divine God with the heavenly Father" through detached humility, "a human God with Christ" through loving labor, and "God the spirit with the Holy Spirit" through Christian counsel (6.1). Divinization is not too strong a word for this process.

Two factors discourage an interpretation of union with God as the obliteration of distinction. The first is the poetic nature of the writing. Frank Tobin cautions, "God speaks in lyrical phrases and as a lover—not as a theologian—in saying he and the soul shall become one."[61] Bernard McGinn agrees that although sometimes "her expressions of merging in love are so strongly put that they might suggest total identity . . . [or] indistinct oneness with God of a permanent nature, . . . it would be a mistake to press these too far."[62] These caveats are well placed, but as Lakoff and Johnson suggest, metaphors are not arbitrarily applied: they structure the world in which Mechthild lives.[63] The presence of hyperbole is therefore not sufficient cause to dismiss the implications of her imagery.

The second and more significant reason to insist on union-with-distinction is the preponderance of *other* images in Mechthild's work, images suggesting that a person retains her integrity even in the most intimate union with God.

Mechthild's liturgical context provides one set of images for union: in the Eucharist, the human being meets God's own humanity:

> Mighty God received me.
> His pure humanity united itself to me.
> His Holy Spirit consoled me.
> *(3.15)*

Mechthild explains the "blessed union" of receiving the Eucharist in a Trinitarian manner: "Whenever we receive God's Body, the Godhead unites itself to our innocent soul and God's humanity mixes itself with our hideous body, and thus does the Holy Spirit make his dwelling in our faith" (4.8). Even as sacramental eating draws the human person into union with God, it is a "union" with three divine persons.[64] The physicality of the sacrament also highlights distinctions reinforced by the body.

Metaphors of airiness, weightlessness, and suspension further suggest a state of permeability by the divine that does not obliterate distinction. The verb most often used for this state is *sweben*, "denoting floating, hovering, motion without a goal, or motion for its own sake."[65] God wants to "lie weightlessly [*sweben*] in your soul" (3.2) and allows the soul to do the same: "Lord, ... if you were to flow, then she could swim [*sweben*]" (3.1). The matrix of the divine breath (*atem*), a quasi-corporeal synonym for spirit, envelops and transports the soul, invisible but nevertheless real: "Lord heavenly Father, between you and me there goes unceasingly an imperceptible breath, in which I come to know and see many marvels" (2.24).[66] God also suffuses the soul as the sun radiates in the air (7.55). These images suggest an alternate plane of experience, or a transposed physical condition, as the nexus for mysterious union that nevertheless leaves the self intact.

Erotic tropes illuminate union-with-distinction from yet another angle. McGinn comments that in contrast to the chaste kisses and embraces of Bernard of Clairvaux and William of St. Thierry's metaphorical readings of Song of Songs, Mechthild "often suggests, if indirectly, sexual intercourse itself as the most appropriate symbol."[67] In contrast to these theologians and some of her later editors, Mechthild does not eschew carnal images of desire. She pushes the eroticism of the God-soul relationship to extremes in order to explore all of its dynamics. Her desiring soul, the bride of the Trinity, leaves behind earthly things and "goes to the fairest of lovers in the secret chamber of the invisible Godhead. There she finds the bed and the abode of love prepared." The lovers speak:

> "Stay, Lady Soul."
> "What do you bid me, Lord?"
> "Take off your clothes."
> "Lord, what will happen to me then?"
> "Lady Soul, you are so utterly formed to my nature
> That not the slightest thing can be between you and me."
> . . . .
> "Lord now I am a naked soul."
> . . . .
> Then a blessed stillness
> That both desire comes over to them.
> He surrenders himself to her,
> And she surrenders herself to him.
> What happens to her then—she knows—
> And that is fine with me.
>
> *(1.44)*

Although the analogy between sexual and spiritual ecstasy, drawn from themes in the Song of Songs, is common in Mechthild's context, she elaborates creatively upon the soul's ineffable pillow talk with God. Her evocation of the erotic recalls the fact that human beings have bodies, and bodies ensure that no matter how intimate one is with human or divine others, we retain our physical integrity. God, the incarnate Christ, and human persons are eternally distinct, for bodies endure even in the afterlife.

Images of nakedness and clothing further highlight the intimacy-with-differentiation between God and soul. In the passage above, God requests the soul to disrobe; elsewhere God confesses, "I cannot be completely intimate with her unless she is willing to lay herself in utter repose and nakedness in my divine arms, so that I can take delight in her" (5.25). Clothing, too, symbolizes intimacy:

> You clothe yourself with my soul
> And you are her most intimate garment.
> (2.5)

The reversal from nakedness to clothing also plays out in the many ways in which God "adorns" the soul with virtues and eternal rewards:

> She is stripped of all things
> When God clothes her with the silk of fair love.
> She is delightfully crowned with manifold faithfulness.
> (3.10)[68]

No matter how completely they flow into one another in love, lovers remain two. Skin holds each separately together; each is like the garment resting against the other's flesh.

Divine and human persons mysteriously participate in the other's being. Lovers unite, and yet they are not numerically one. Mechthild writes of a "special intimacy with separation" (2.3) and states,

> When two lovers meet secretly,
> They must often part from one another inseparably.
> (1.44)

As I will discuss in a future chapter, much of the experience of absence and separation can be attributed to the limitations of the embodied human condition. Union is fleeting in this life, but Mechthild's erotic images indicate that God and soul remain two even as they become one in the afterlife.

SUMMARY

One of Mechthild's central concerns is to understand the mystery of the human soul: "What are you made of, Soul, that you ascend so high above all creatures, mingle with the holy Trinity, and yet remain whole in yourself?" (*FL* 1.22). She neither resolves the paradox in the direction of monism nor resorts to dualism but revels in the phenomenon of union-with-differentiation. On the one hand, the love between God and the soul ensures difference. I have read Mechthild against the stereotype of "mysticism" as a monistic transgression of the Creator-creature distinction. On the other hand, this difference is hardly a hierarchical metaphysical "dualism" since the fluid nature of love draws divinity out of itself and elevates the soul to God.

The metaphysics of union for Mechthild relies on a shared "nature" that is love. Unlike the Latin *natura*, Mechthild's *nature* (Middle High German) does not necessarily denote corporeality, for angels and God as well as human beings possess a "nature." She does not claim, as it would sound to modern ears, that human beings are made out of the same "stuff" as divinity. Some medieval theologians like Bernard of Clairvaux similarly make the important distinction "that that merging of God and the soul is a union of charity and will, not a merging of substance."[69] Grace Jantzen helpfully conveys the sense of such statements:

> It is anachronistic to read [Bernard of Clairvaux] in the post-Cartesian or post-Deist sense, as though there is physical stuff and mental stuff, or world stuff and God stuff, and Bernard is denying that these are the same. Without pretending that medieval writers were monolithic, it is a fair generalization to point out that they held to a much stronger sense of God as the continuing source and support of all things. . . . The modern interpretation of creation *ex nihilo* which sees the distinction between God and the world in terms of difference of stuff would be foreign to them. The stuff of the world flows out from God and is sustained in being by God's Being; it is not something independent of God in either origin or continuation.[70]

As a creature that flows from God, the soul for Mechthild is an independent locus of will. But because the all-pervasive divine and human nature is love, their mutual attraction unites them.

Critiques of Western Christian dualism and Christian denigrations of mystical monism both fit ill beside Mechthild's work. This juxtaposition helps us to see our contemporary constructs more clearly. A further juxtaposition with Lalleśwarī on the relation of self and divinity suggests that East and West are not so far apart after all.

COMPARISON

When the theological systems of Lalleśwarī and Mechthild emerge from the swamp of cultural essentialism in which they have been mired, they belie common generalizations about the metaphysics of their traditions. The above readings demonstrate the unhelpfulness and unrepresentative nature of the stereotypes. Our "Eastern" interlocutor maintains distinctions between self and Self, distinctions masked by the hegemonic colonial emphasis on Advaita nondualism. Our "Western" envoy exemplifies a much more dynamic interplay between God and the soul than the persistent stereotype of Western dualism usually allows. Attention to these women's theological imagery contributes to postcolonial interventions, for when we read Mechthild and Lalleśwarī together, they begin to break down the purported metaphysical barriers between East and West.

For example, both women employ images of water (solubility, mobility) to express union-in-differentiation that is neither monism nor dualism. This similarity of fluid imagery leaks out of such conceptual containers. Water and air share the same properties in India and Europe, and these elemental metaphors provide an experiential basis for reconceptualizing relations with divinity. Our interlocutors share an ontological structure of the self's origin and end in God. Both conceive of a process in which God overflows to give rise to beings that participate in divine attributes but are numerically distinct from God. Both theologians posit that God and the self share the same nature; yet as we investigate this nature, important differences begin to emerge.

Lalleśwarī's correlation between divine nature and human nature is more straightforward than that of Mechthild. Lalleśwarī's concept of *sahaj* evokes a single process of subjectivity that is identical on cosmic and individual levels. God and humanity share in common their deepest nature (*svasvabhāva*), the process of subject-object differentiation. For Mechthild, humanity processes from and returns to divinity; but this process is not its essence. She complexifies the degree to which humanity resembles the divine with her use of the term *nature*. God has a Trinitarian nature, human beings have a double (spiritual-embodied) nature, and angels have a single (spiritual) nature (4.14). Humanity shares its dual nature with the second person of the Trinity. Human nature resides in Christ, but God's nature as Trinity exceeds it.

Attention to the central mechanisms operative in the ebb and flow of the soul offers a more in-depth comparison than allowed by generalized categories of dualism and monism. Each theologian teaches union-in-differentiation, but the texture of each system depends on the means of union, which is love in Mechthild and consciousness in Lalleśwarī. Mechthild and Lalleśwarī negotiate duality differently, and these departures are rooted in the differing role of desire in how they come to know God.

DESIRING KNOWLEDGE

For Mechthild and her Christian predecessors in "mystical" theology, knowledge and love are eternal partners. Love fuels the spiritual search for knowledge of God and God's relation to all things. The soul, the aspect of the human being that is capable of both transcendence and immanence, knows and loves corporeal things but can never be satisfied by them. It longingly soars above all creatures to its divine source, climbing "the lofty mountain of powerful love and beautiful knowledge" in quest of God (*FL* 5.4).

Yearning similarly echoes in Lalleśwarī's cry, "Would that God heard my prayer and ferry me across safely.... How I wish I could reach home!" (K 1). Indian philosophical traditions tend to eschew attachment, with one important exception: the desire for liberating knowledge. Lalleśwarī's central aim is less a love relationship than the knowledge of her nature as consciousness. She invokes the trope of the distraught lover only rarely. For her, the movement of desire can reveal liberating knowledge. *Vijñānabhairava Tantra* 98 says, "When a desire or knowledge (or activity) appears, the aspirant should, with the mind withdrawn from all objects (of desire, knowledge, etc.) fix his mind on it (desire, knowledge, etc.) as the very Self, then he will have the realization of the essential Reality."[71] Kashmir Śaiva metaphysics teach that in the end, the subject and object of desire are identical; practices of attention to the movement of desire precipitate this realization. Lalleśwarī's search ends not when she finds someone to love, but when she knows her true Self.

This difference in desire has ontological foundations: love flows from Trinity, but consciousness flows from Śiva. Trinitarian love overflows to create nondivine beings that will participate in its flow, and desire prompts this erotic overflow of being. Śiva and Śakti, however, are first of all the nonpersonal dynamic of consciousness. Individual selves are objects of consciousness to Śiva as well as centers of consciousness that can recognize him. Despite this difference, the primary attribute of each deity attends the other. Kashmir Śaivas write of Śiva's will and Christians of the knowledge of God. Both poets invoke love *and* knowledge in their texts, but with reversed emphasis. Lalleśwarī uses the language of love in service of a particular kind of knowledge. Mechthild teaches that knowledge accompanies love; but, she insists, those who do not love cannot know God (cf. *FL* 2.23).

The divergence in primary metaphors for the God-self relation means that these theologians somewhat differently conceive of difference itself.

Lalleśwarī articulates duality between Śiva and herself in terms of subject and object. The self's narrative parallels the emanation of the cosmos from Śiva: as object, she originates in the consciousness of the divine subject. Lalleśwarī initially experiences her return in terms of a journey in which she has lost her way (K 5); but however circuitous the quest, there is actually nowhere to go. The Self resides within the self. External sojourn ceases when she stops fearing the ocean of *saṁsāra* and begins to see it as the all-pervasive flow that unites subject and object. The inmost nature of human beings as subjects is identical to that of absolute consciousness. When Lalleśwarī knows the divine subject as her own Self, she "experience[s] the bliss of consciousness and the light of knowledge" (K 118).

Lalleśwarī experiences difference as a problem to which the solution is intuition of the ontological identity of all consciousness. She analyzes duality in abstract terms of a perceiving subjectivity and its objects. Mechthild's imagery is more personal: her narrative of procession and return is a romance.

For Mechthild, difference is born of divine desire for an other. Personal images and dialogic forms depict the tenderness and risk accompanying God's urge to create. The Son requests, "Let us make man in my image. Even though I foresee great tragedy, I shall still love man forever." The Father replies, "I shall make a bride for myself who shall greet me with her mouth and wound me with her beauty. *Only then does love really begin*" (3.9, emphasis added). Divine love requires the risk that the beloved will wound the lover as well as return love. The soul does, indeed, wound herself and her lover, who then woos her back into intimacy. While Lalleśwarī finds knowledge of the Self, Mechthild returns to the arms of her Bridegroom. Śiva *knows* the other as other; the Trinity *loves* the other as other.

The juxtaposition of the analytical and the erotic highlights how each thinker might fund a theology of difference: in their narratives of procession and return, Lalleśwarī teaches us the facticity of difference, and Mechthild invites us to love it. From a liberated point of view, diversity is not a threat but something to be celebrated from the wellspring of the divine source. Both of our interlocutors trouble the stereotypes of their respective traditions, with an unsettling effect that reverberates through all the other relations in their theology. The next chapter considers the implications for the God-world relation that follow when monism and dualism cease to be hegemonic categories.

3

Coming "Down" to Earth?

"Can't this beautiful world and all the good it contains console you?"
"No, I see the snake of deceit and how treacherous cunning slithers into all the pleasures of this world. I also see the hook of lust in the carcass of base sweetness with which she catches many."
Mechthild of Magdeburg (FL 4.12)

Gently and gently shall I weep for you, O Mind.
You have been caught under the spell of delusion.
Even the shadow of worldly possessions will not stand by you.
Alas, you have lost your own identity!
Lalleśwarī of Kashmir (K 2)

The links between human industry and global warming, the extinction of species, and the pollution of earth, air, and water have never been clearer. The pros and cons of various solutions provide fodder for vigorous contemporary debate; but more basically, we are invited to reconsider the foundations of our way of life—our views of nature, of humanity, and of their respective purposes. Will we recycle and drive less because it is good for the earth, because it will help *us* to survive, or because it will save us money? Do we belong to an essentially different order than the natural environment? Is the earth merely some inert "stuff" for us to use and mold and conquer, or does it have some intrinsic worth? Are human beings, though embodied within this immanent matrix, really destined to rise above it all—whether because of some likeness to a transcendent deity, or because of our rational nature? If God is a part of this picture, are humans closer to the divine than the plants, animals, mountains, and streams? These questions drive at the heart of the worldviews that fuel our interactions with our environment.

Dualism has practical ramifications. In the last chapter, we discovered some of the imperial implications of stereotypes of the East and the West. A supposed philosophical divide between the *identity* of the one and the many in the East and a strong Creator-creation *distinction* in the West has been central to the supposed differences between the two. In this chapter, we explore how this dualism branches out into dichotomous ways of treating the natural environment. The epigraph from Mechthild of Magdeburg represents a tendency in her Christian tradition to associate the world with sin and temptation, with all that must be transcended in order to escape to the heavenly realm of an otherworldly salvation. The quotation from Lalleśwarī of Kashmir reflects a penchant within monistic philosophies to dismiss the empirical world as illusory, as an obstacle to seeing reality as it "truly" is, without distinctions of name and form. Each tradition ends up with a latent dualism between immanent nature and a better, transcendent reality so that "coming down to earth" truly is a descent from a superior plane.

Theologians interested in honoring the natural environment have cited such otherworldly impulses as a source of indifference to the natural environment: if this world is not our true home, or if it is merely an illusion veiling our true identity, then why should we preserve it? Rhetoric about the world's "cunning," "lust," and "delusion" in the epigraphs is of dubious use in a this-worldly theology. Many ecological thinkers challenge the radical separation between the divine realm and creation that this language implies.[1] Despite initial impressions to the contrary, Mechthild and Lalleśwarī have much to offer for valuing material creation in relation to divinity. Their visions of the world can provide practical insight for relating to the earth as now, more than ever, we need to revise our ecological sensibilities.

DUALISM AND ECOLOGY

In the West, dualistic views of nature are related to notions of the human being as something other than the material world: we are reasonable, spiritual, connected to divinity; "nature" is not. A rift within human existence results from this radical separation between divine and earthly realms: we must live here but find our true identities elsewhere. This essential separation from nature sets up a hierarchy of value. Human beings are the center of the universe. The natural world, which lacks mind and soul, may be used, subdued, or neglected to whatever degree is convenient for the human species.

How did we come to hold such views? Some critics locate this dualistic logic of domination in the advent of modernity with Descartes' cleavage of the "thinking substance" from the "extended substance" of the body and material reality. Others identify a deeper foundation in Platonic and Christian thought, where "the meaning of death is that the meaning of human life is elsewhere, not to be found in the earth or in human life as part of nature, but in a separate realm accessible only to humans, . . . the world of the Forms and the world of heaven."[2] These narratives, though useful for explaining how we have come to the current ecological crises, tend to neglect countervailing impulses in the Western tradition. For example, the early synthesis of Hebrew and Greek themes within Christianity did not fully resolve certain tensions surrounding the status of the material world. The Hebrew Bible conceives of the human being as a psychosomatic unity, but its creation narrative can be read as setting up an ontological "cleavage between the being of God and that of created beings."[3] The Neoplatonic Greek thought that so heavily influenced Christian orthodoxy envisions an "ontological continuum between God, the Logos of God, and the cosmos," which would seem to affirm greater continuity with nature;[4] but the soul in this system seeks to escape from the world and body as "lower levels" of existence and to return to God. The tensions in these themes can alert us to portions of our inheritance that deserve renewed scrutiny.

The untenability of a radical separation between heaven and earth in light of the current climate crisis has renewed interest in cosmology, the study of the origin and structure of the universe. Cosmologies are "cultural stories about the universe, the earth and the role of the human"—worldviews that include scientific, philosophical, and religious subplots.[5] A story depicting the universe as a watch set in motion long ago by a divine watchmaker who is otherwise unconnected to it will place different demands upon human beings than one in which every mountain and tree is inhabited by divinity.

In rethinking the impact of cosmology upon ethics, many Christian theologians have moved toward positions that affirm the presence of divinity in the world. For example, Sallie McFague offers the metaphor of the world as God's body and uses the term "monism" to express that "there is but one reality and it is God's; . . . all things have their origins in God and nothing exists outside God, though this does not mean that God is reduced to these things."[6] Grace Jantzen reclaims the term "pantheism" as a way of confronting contemporary revulsion for associating the material with the divine. She projects divinity as "mutuality, bodiliness, diversity, and materiality"[7] as the horizon toward which humanity should strive. Others such as Catherine Keller speak of panentheism, in which the all (*pan*) exists within (*en*) God (*theos*).[8] Each of these schemes imbues the natural world with the divine presence in hopes of inspiring reverence and care.

NONDUALISM AND ECOLOGY

Following the logic of these Christian rejections of dualism between God and the world, one might suppose that the "nondualistic" perspectives of the East embrace the material world more fully. Much of the recent attraction to Hindu, Buddhist, and Taoist thought stems from the perception of greater integration of spirit and nature in those systems.[9] It seems to follow that if cultures positing a great distinction between God and the world have a poor ecological track record, then those with more continuity would fare better. A series of major conferences on ecology and the world's religions at Harvard University yielded ambivalent conclusions on this question. Until quite recently, integrative or nondualist systems have not been mobilized for the preservation of the world's rivers, forests, and ecosystems. Many of these religions have in fact coexisted alongside frightening levels of environmental depredation.[10]

Hindu feminists and feminist scholars of Hinduism expose how cosmologies that purport to be nondualistic can nevertheless foster practical dualisms that devalue nature and women. According to Jaishree Kak Odin, in India, consciousness (rather than rationality, as in the West) is the standard that defines all else. Consciousness absorbs all relations—including the relation between God and the world, both of which are objects of a more basic divine awareness—but not before it breaks into hierarchical, gendered binaries. Several Indian philosophies posit that human beings must transcend matter (*prakṛti*) and its delusory qualities (*māyā*)—both envisioned as feminine—to reach spirit (*puruṣa*), the goal of liberation. For example, in traditions for which Śiva is the ultimate reality, the goddess Śakti—who emerges from Śiva as his active, creative, immanent other—is synonymous with the material world. The liberated transcend the world as they meditate on how Śiva reabsorbs Śakti, along with the body and the earth, into him once again.[11] Rita Sherma argues that for male practitioners, this meditation often goes hand in hand with ascetic dissociation from women and the body and efforts to control women and nature. Creation becomes a negative symbol associated with women, sexuality, social ties, and the external world, all of which are obstacles in a male-defined spiritual path.[12]

In view of this legacy, Hindu theologians now work to reconstruct the holistic implications of their traditions. Anantanand Rambachan is highly critical of the world-denying impulse in his Advaita (nondual) tradition. He insists that for the great teacher Śaṅkara, all that exists is "non-different" from *brahman*, which emits the world much as a spider spins out its web. Rambachan argues that the principle of *māyā* as a secondary creative principle and the source of illusion is an unnecessary later accretion that merely contributes to the erroneous idea that knowing the one devalues the many. For him, the world has value as the "celebrative expression" or "overflow of *brahman*'s undiminishing limitlessness."[13] Other scholars have worked to lift up feminine principles alongside the material world by focusing on nondualisms rooted in Tantric Śakta (goddess) systems;[14] popular worship of rivers as goddesses;[15] local festivals that celebrate menstruation as the flow connecting the goddess, earth, and women;[16] and grassroots reclamations of the feminine principle of nature (*prakṛti*) as the divine ground for creativity and the sanctity of all life.[17]

In the Christian and Hindu traditions, constructive theologians use terms such as monism, panentheism, pantheism, and nondualism to recast the difference of God and world in relational terms that give value to the earth. In eschewing dualism, they do not wish to swing to the other extreme and erase all qualitative distinction between Creator and creation. According to Val Plumwood, what is needed is a "recognition of a complex, interacting pattern of continuity *and* difference" that will resist oppressive hierarchies.[18] The voices of Lalleśwarī and Mechthild have not found their way into the larger cosmological narrative, but they offer yet another route to a more nuanced story about traditional cosmologies that may help us think continuity alongside difference. Read side by side, they open up ways to think of a world in which all things participate in God, without denying particularity or denigrating the material realm.[19]

THEOLOGY AND COSMOLOGY IN LALLEŚWARĪ OF KASHMIR

Lalleśwarī's tradition imagines the difference and continuity between the absolute and the cosmos in fluid terms: "The absolute is brimming over with phenomena. The streams of cosmic manifestation flow everywhere from it as does water from a tank full to overflowing."[20] Śiva and his Power (Śakti) manifest as the world of diversity while remaining one. Lalleśwarī describes her meditative insight into the unity of being:

> I saw Śiva and Śakti rolled in one.
> Overwhelmed with joy I got immersed there itself
>   in the lake of nectar.
> Now I shall die while alive; what can the world do unto me?
> (K 130)

Lalleśwarī's immersion in the bliss of the divine couple is possible because individual processes of cognition replicate the creative flow of awareness from unity to manifestation and back again.

Śiva as absolute consciousness, Śakti as cosmic manifestation, and the human being are all modifications of the divine; the liberated realize their unity. This expansive concept of divinity is not unique to Śaivism. Thus Vrinda Dalmiya explains:

> Gods and Goddesses in the Indian tradition are generally constituted in three layers. On one level (*ādhidaivika*), they are iconographically represented celestial beings whose intricate biographies are narrated in mythological tales. On the second level (*ādhyātmika*), they are vital principles of the lived-body of the devotee. Finally, on the third level (*ādhibhautika*), they are principles in the environment or cosmos.[21]

All three "layers" are present in Lalleśwarī's thought. As a personal deity, Lord Śiva continually performs the five cosmic activities of creation, persistence, destruction or withdrawal, concealment, and grace: "For ever Śiva creates and dissolves and creates again" (K 116). Creation is Śiva's perception: when he opens his eyes, he brings objects into being; and when he closes his eyes, he ceases to perceive external objects and they go out of existence. At the second and third levels, Śiva and Śakti are what they create. In the microcosm of the body, human beings recognize the Lord in the processes of breath and cognition. At the macrocosmic level of the universe, "the universe is eternally emitted and reabsorbed as it expands and contracts" from the pulse of the divine heart.[22]

Lalleśwarī's favorite metaphor for the union of Śiva (the one) and Śakti (the many) arises from her practice of meditation on the "unstruck sound," the syllable *Oṃ* (*Auṃ*), which unites all three levels of manifestation. According to Tantric texts, one accesses this mystical sound through chanting the syllable. Its culminating *ṃ* is the kernel of unity in all duality, for it represents the union of Śiva and Śakti. *Oṃ* resonates on several levels corresponding to the stages of the development of speech. It exists in potential form in the union of the divine with its energy; the audible sound is the corporeal voicing of the syllable. One hears the "unstruck sound" in the moment between this union and manifestation.[23] At an advanced stage of chanting, the yogi hears "the bell of truth ringing" (K 126) and merges into a union that has "the nature of ethereal sky, whose abode is the great void" (K 122). Through the practice, the yogi recapitulates the cosmic process of withdrawal, moving in sound through Śakti to Śiva.[24]

The Kashmir Śaiva accounts of the origin of the world illustrate a continuity between divinity and created diversity that troubles customary accounts of God-world dualism. Creation (*sṛṣṭi*) is Śiva's first cosmic act. Singh cautions that the "usual translation, 'creation,' is misleading because it implies that the creator acts upon an external material, and thus brings about the world process." He explains:

Sṛṣṭi is derived from the root *sṛj*, which means "to let go," "to pour forth," "to cast out." This implies that the world process is already implicitly contained in Śiva; he merely lets go or casts it out of himself. According to Śaivism, the world is not a creation, but an emanation; it is a theophany.[25]

Along these lines, Lalleśwarī expresses the matrix of creation as an infinitesimal lake in which all beings arise and submerge:

> To the lake too small even for a mustard seed
> all creatures come to drink water, and
> keep falling into it as soon as born—
> deer, jackals, rhinoceros[es], sea elephants and all.
> (K 113)

As a *yoginī* with memory of past lives, she recalls seeing this lake overflow in three cycles of creation and watching it dissolve again into the void (K 114). When divine consciousness manifests as subject and object in the cosmos, an increasing sense of difference emerges. Śakti, the very power of consciousness, is the first object in the process of differentiation, the first glimmer of duality in the absolute. Kotru identifies the miniature lake in the above verse with "the compact mass of Śakti ready to manifest as universe of name and form, . . . [which has] no dimensions yet is the source of all that exists in the universe."[26] The rest of creation follows in ordered succession.

We should pause to summarize this succession because it will help us understand the potency of Lalleśwarī's intervention in contemporary discourse on dualism between God and the world. One might visualize the cosmic stages (*tattva*s) as a chart that at the top begins with one thing, the pure consciousness of Śiva, and branches out into a multiplicity of created principles below it. The stages of Kashmir Śaiva cosmology evolve according to the increasing differentiation of a subject and its objects, as follows:[27] (1) The initial creative movement is the consciousness of pure "I" (*śiva tattva*). (2) The energy and intent to create (*śakti tattva*) emerges and, departing from pure "I-ness," consciousness now has a glimmer of "This." Subject begins to cognize object. (3) Next comes the awareness that "*I am* (this)." (4) Then follows the clear idea of the universe that is to be created: "*This* am I." (5) Next emerges an equal balance of "I" and "This." Consciousness remains "pure" (*śuddha*) because the true nature of things is not yet veiled to the knower. (6) A feeling of difference comes with the severance of "I" from "This" (*māyā tattva*). With *māyā*, the "impure" (*aśuddha*) creation begins.

Māyā is best translated as "artifice," the creation of the realm of duality. It consists of five aspects of limited individual experience, which mark the reduction of (7) divine omnipotence to the individual's limited powers; (8) divine omniscience to limited knowledge; (9) the fullness and satisfaction of the absolute to the desire for particular objects; (10) eternity to the experience of time as past, present, and future; and (11) freedom of consciousness to particular limitations of space and causation. (12) The individual subject (*puruṣa tattva*) emerges as a point of limited consciousness, followed by its object, (13) material nature (*prakṛti*). Matter differentiates into the remaining components of individual experience, beginning with the three *tattva*s or levels of mental operation: (14) intelligence (*buddhi*), which ascertains external and internal objects; (15) individual I-consciousness, or the ego (*ahaṃkāra*); and (16) mind (*manas*), which builds images and concepts in partnership with the senses. Next follow the *tattva*s of sensible experience, including (17–21) the five powers of sense perception—smelling, tasting, seeing, feeling by touch, and hearing; and (22–26) the five powers of action—speaking, handling, locomotion, excreting, and copulating. Finally, (27–31) the five primary elements of perception—sound, touch, form, taste, and smell; and (32–36) the five gross elements—ether, wind, fire, water, and earth—make up the sensible world.

For Lalleśwarī, God and world are not exactly two; they are simultaneously one and many, depending on one's vantage point vis-à-vis these thirty-six *tattva*s or levels of the cosmos. She refers to these levels in their traditional groupings:

> Alas! the five, the ten, and the eleventh
> scraped this pot and went away.
> Had they all come and pulled the rope together
> why should the eleven have lost the cow?
>
> (K 6)

The "five" are the gross elements at the bottom of this scheme. The "ten" are the five sense organs and the five organs of action, and the "eleven" are these organs plus the mind (*manas*).[28] Lalleśwarī notes here that the material world of sense and action distracts from the highest goal, but if one can train them to work together, they can harness the "cow," Śiva-consciousness, which is the one source of all.

A fundamental tension resides in the Kashmir Śaiva view of the world: is the multiplicity we observe real or illusory? The above scheme draws upon two Indian theories of causation, one in which effects are real transformations of their cause, like pots made out of clay (*satkaryavāda*), and another in which effects are the appearance of the single reality in various guises, like an actor who takes on various roles (*vivartavāda*). According to Gavin Flood, one can identify these two theories in Kashmir Śaiva literature through "emanation language" and "pervasion language": Śiva, as cause of the universe, either evolves (emanates) into the various levels described above, or he takes on (pervades) different forms in which his self is fully present but hidden to the untrained observer.[29] Lalleśwarī's references to the *tattvas* recall emanation language, for the cosmic hierarchy evokes the condensation, contraction, or emanation of consciousness into various degrees of objectivity. This scheme supports a gradual path to enlightenment through practices that follow the emanations back to their source. But when Lalleśwarī uses pervasion language, as when she says the universe is "permeated with" Śiva (K 83), she emphasizes the identity of the world with the absolute. From this perspective, because absolute consciousness is never truly altered, the practitioner may pass over all the different manifest forms to intuit their unity instantaneously.

Odin provides a fine translation of a verse that plays poetically upon the imagery of both theories:

> Cold changes water into ice or snow[.]
> Discernment shows the three states though
> different are not really different[.]
> When the sun of consciousness shines,
> The plurality is dissolved into oneness[;]
> Then the universe appears throughout
> permeated with [Ś]iva.
>
> *(O 39; cf. K 83)*

In the first line, Lalleśwarī depicts the modification of consciousness into plurality through the transformation of water into its liquid, solid, and gaseous states—an example of *satkaryavāda*, the theory in which effects preexist in and emanate from their material cause. However, in the second line the imagery shifts slightly to suggest *vivartavāda*, in which plurality is illusory: "The three states though different are not really different" (O 39). The three dissolve into water, their true form. The melting of these differences under the sun of consciousness reveals an ultimate oneness. Plurality is dissolved; the universe appears pervaded by Śiva.

The distinctions between the *tattvas* and the various theories of causation may seem unimportant, but the status of the world—as an illusion or as a real manifestation of consciousness—carries practical implications for its place in the quest for liberation. For example, the assignment of materiality to the "impure creation" would seem to imply a negative valuation of the world. Defenders of the tradition would point out that in Kashmir Śaivism "impurity" connotes neither defilement nor a state of materiality. Rather, "impurity is a state of seeming separation from consciousness," a misapprehension of the relation of God and world.[30] This interpretation might be the context for the following contrast between inner and outer purity:

> Some, though asleep, are yet awake,
> some, though awake, are yet sleeping.
> Some are impure even after ablutions, and
> some inactive despite householders' active life.
>
> *(K 111)*

"Pure" and "impure" refer to supreme and inferior knowledge. Impure awareness modifies absolute consciousness to support subject-object duality, but it does not fundamentally corrupt this consciousness.

Natalia Isayeva notes, however, that when Kashmir Śaivism and other Indian schools affirmed such a cosmic hierarchy, they "were clearly drifting away from . . . monism and tending towards potentially dualistic creeds and notions."[31] In practice, the hierarchical ordering of the cosmos is indeed value-laden, with the lower echelons specifically associated with materiality. Hence, Lalleśwarī describes worldly things as poisonous, binding, and not to be desired (K 118, 25)—an evaluation that accords with Kashmir Śaiva yogic rituals that "purify" the body from its taint of "the 'outer,' most coagulated world."[32]

Disaffection with the world is a tendency that runs throughout the tradition, but Odin finds Lalleśwarī's insights to be particularly limited. She criticizes Lalleśwarī for "creating a disenchantment with worldly things" and "stay[ing] locked out of any aesthetic experience of the world." In Odin's interpretation, Lalleśwarī's "most profound verses . . . reflect her desire to lose herself in mystical experience [rather] than to use it as the ground to lead to a more fulfilling material existence."[33] Given this apparent abandonment of materiality, we might judge that Lalleśwarī has nothing positive to add to our discussion of theology and the environment. We may test this assessment, however—here from the perspective of Lalleśwarī's epistemology, and in the next chapter from the perspective of her notion of *sahaj*, or what is "natural."

Lalleśwarī expresses her disenchantment with the world in a series of verses. The vicissitudes of karma and the cruelty of worldly power relations weary her:

> I saw a wise man starving to death,
> emaciated like a withered leaf falling in the winter wind.
> Also I saw a fool beating his cook
>   (who could not prepare food of his taste).
> Since then I, Lalla, am waiting for the day
>   when my lure of the world breaks up.
>
> *(K 9)*[34]

Lalleśwarī prays that the Lord will "cure me of the sickness of birth and death" (K 73; lit., "sickness of the world") and imagines her burden of worldly pleasure as a load of sweets that bends her body painfully in two (K 23). Desire and action bind a person to the cycle of life and death. Nonbinding enjoyment of the world is possible if one has the correct perspective, but two qualities make earthly reality particularly sticky: its impermanence and its ability to delude.

Even though the phenomena we perceive in the objective world are technically real, they are transitory and therefore less "real" than the eternal realm. Thus Lalleśwarī illustrates the ephemeral quality of the world:

> Now I saw a river flowing,
> Now neither a bridge nor a ferry.
> Now I saw a plant in full bloom,
> now neither a flower nor a thorn to be seen.
> *(K 10)*

> Now I saw a hearth ablaze,
> now neither fire nor smoke.
> Now I saw the mother of Pandavas[,]
> now was she a potter's aunt.
> *(K 11)*

Everything passes away, from the tree's seasonal blooms to the entire human world of bridges, ferries, and hearths. One's identity changes in an instant, from one life to another, like the woman who in one life has many princely sons and in the next is unfortunate. The main problem with worldly things, then, is that they do not last: not even a shadow of worldly affairs will remain (K 2). Lalleśwarī likens the failure to reconcile oneself to the impermanence of the world to dancing over a pit. "Everything amassed by you shall have to be left behind" (K 3; cf. K 12). From this perspective, we begin to understand why Lalleśwarī wishes to be done with worldly existence. Her world-weariness is her desire for the eternal.

Beyond life's ephemeral quality, Lalleśwarī is also concerned that its beauty and activity keep us "intoxicated" and "deluded" (K 14) rather than connecting us to their true source. Lalleśwarī chastises the mind: "You have been caught under the spell of delusion [lit., deluded by falling into *māyā*] . . . Alas, you have lost your own identity!" (K 2). This condition of human consciousness keeps us from reaching the "other shore" of Śiva consciousness. Instead, we choke and drown in the world-ocean:

> Why have you come under the cascade let loose
>   by the sea of delusion?
> Having dismantled the embankment
>   (which would have saved you)[,]
>   you have got stuck in the quagmire of ignorance.
> *(K 13)*

In medieval Kashmir, people crossed lakes by one of two ways: either on an earthen embankment built up as a bridge or in a ferry pulled by a rope. For Lalleśwarī, the embankment symbolizes knowledge: the way to cross the ocean of existence is to know its true nature. The ferry signifies effort, which ultimately goes to waste: the karmas one accrues in the lake of *saṃsāra* prove as effective for crossing it as "twisting ropes of sand" (K 15). There seems to be no way out of this "sea of delusion" (K 13) for we ourselves seem to have eroded the bridge-embankment of the knowledge of our true identity.

Kashmir Śaiva epistemology provides the key to interpreting the tension between Lalleśwarī's verses that rejoice in the all-pervasiveness of Śiva and those that reflect the transitory and comparatively unsatisfying nature of worldly experience. Lalleśwarī's acquaintance with the emanation cosmology of thirty-six *tattva*s enables her to discuss reality from various perspectives. *Tattva*s are psychological levels of awareness as well as cosmic levels of being: it is as if a person might climb up into any one of the levels of subject-object differentiation and view the world from each of these vantage points. Every level is a mode of Śiva's relation to Śakti corresponding to the various degrees of their union and differentiation. When one realizes the higher levels of consciousness, "I" predominates over "This." Lalleśwarī says:

> By constant practice the manifested universe
> gets merged in the universal self.
> The world of name and form gets merged in the
> vastness of the void as one homogeneous whole.
> This, O Brahmin, is the true doctrine.
>
> (K 133)

As she purifies her awareness, Lalleśwarī's sense of difference from the world recedes until, in the higher *tattva*s, only the void remains. Here, "Neither word nor thought is there, neither transcendent nor non transcendent.... Even Śiva and Śakti remain not there" (K 134). The highest level transcends even transcendence. "What remains is the truth to know" (K 134), for beyond awareness of the void lies the nameless consciousness of Śiva. Having intuited this void, one retains awareness of it even as one interacts with the realm of name and form.

No matter how liberated, persons continue to experience the "lower" *tattva*s. Some of Lalleśwarī's verses speak from the perspective of one enmeshed in the *māyīya*, or phenomenal realm, as when Lalleśwarī says: "Food and raiment do not pacify a restless mind" (K 30). But from her perch among the higher *tattva*s, Lalleśwarī sings of everything as an aspect of the all-pervading absolute. Though the universe is the contraction of Śiva's consciousness, it is also the Lord's own body:[35]

> What should we offer you in worship[?]
> you are the sky, you are the earth;
> you are the air, the day and the night,
> You are the sacrificial grain, the sandal paste,
> you the flowers, the water and all that exists.
>
> *(K 70)*

The poetess illustrates Śiva's all-pervasive nature with a number of analogies: he is like a fine net spread over everything (K 82), the sun that warms every place (K 79), the air that enters every home (K 79), the stone that is the substance of both temple and millstone (K 66, 78), and the water that cold transforms into ice and snow (K 83). He is the force or breath that animates every frame (K 82, 131).

In such passages, Lalleśwarī exults in the common, everyday world of stone, earth, sun, and rain. Consciousness emanates and suffuses every created thing. Śiva pervades all, but it is difficult to see him because of all the diversity that we perceive so clearly. For Lalleśwarī, the religious urge to transcend the mundane, whether through permanent renunciation or through antinomian behavior, is one of the ways *māyā* veils the unity of reality. She therefore admonishes those who renounce home to look for God at places of pilgrimage, for they are misled by grass that looks greener from afar. She also eschews heteroprax Tantric rites, such as the ritual consumption of taboo substances like wine and meat. Although these practices accord with the idea that Śiva is so pervasive that "there is no reality which is impure,"[36] Lalleśwarī refuses to roam so far from ordinary life. One will glimpse God inside the self if only one can stay in one place long enough to see it (K 107, 108).

Lalleśwarī insists that the Lord is in no way sullied or diminished by having the world as his body. He is both omnipresent and stainless (K 109). A charming *vaakh* attributed to her in some collections conveys how seeing the world in this light enables her to embrace the world and her embodied state:

> In the midst of being lost, I lost the sense of being lost[.]
> After being lost I found myself in this worldly ocean[.]
> Laughing and playing, I attained the all-pervading Self[.]
> This philosophy became a part of me.
>
> *(O 29)*[37]

This attitude of play frees her to act for the benefit of the world. As the Kashmir Śaiva teacher Abhinavagupta puts it, "People, occupied as they are with their own affairs, normally do nothing for others. The activity of those in whom every stain of phenomenal existence has been destroyed . . . is intended only for the benefit of the world."[38] With a proper understanding of things, one may embrace the world; one may swim in the worldly ocean without fear of being lost at sea.

For Lalleśwarī, then, there are multiple levels from which one can view the world. From the lower *tattva*s, where duality predominates, a beginner's longing for union with divinity may lead to expressions of frustration with the body or the material world. The liberated individual, however, moves between the *tattva*s while retaining the all-pervasive consciousness. She no longer views the world as an obstacle to overcome but sees the divine nature in and through it. Whether immersed in the unity of consciousness, attending to the relation of subject and object, or partaking in daily activities in which plurality predominates, one can recognize all of these states as Śiva's nature.

THEOLOGY AND COSMOLOGY IN MECHTHILD OF MAGDEBURG

As with Lalleśwarī, Mechthild of Magdeburg's cosmology supports both continuity and difference. She is somewhat unique in her focus on the span of creation. One translator comments, "It is this cosmic dimension of many of her visions that distinguishes Mechthild from the women visionaries to follow, who confine themselves to reporting visionary experiences of a personal and private world."[39] Mechthild's relational cosmology is rooted in her conception of the triune God, whose nature is love (*FL* 7.48; 1 John 4:8). The divine flow of love spills out of its internal relations to embrace nondivine others so that the entire cosmos participates in the overflow of divine mutuality and generativity. The scope of her visions corresponds with her calling to instruct all of Christianity; her book, which flowed from God's mouth (2.26), becomes an instrument in returning creation to its source.[40]

Several of Mechthild's images demonstrate the continuity between God and creation. She elaborates an allegory of an eternally burning fire of divine love. Angels, saints, the blessed on earth, the bodies of the blessed, earthly things, God's comfort and judgment—"these things have come out of this fire and flow back into it" (*FL* 6.29). Water also evokes the connective flow of being. In heaven, the blessed enjoy uninterrupted participation in God as the "threefold stream flows out playfully from God, filling their minds and hearts so that they sing the truth effortlessly with joy" (3.1).

In addition to the elemental images of fire and water, Mechthild imagines that before creation, God was in the form of a sphere, in which "all things were enclosed within God" and "present" to God (6.31; cf. 3.9). Like many medieval thinkers, Mechthild differentiates between spheres within the cosmos, spatialized gradations arranged vertically from heaven to hell. For example,

De proprietatibus rerum, an encyclopedia written in Magdeburg during Mechthild's lifetime, enumerates seven spheres of heaven and their subdivisions.[41] Mechthild encases this whole within another, ultimate sphere, which is God. She writes that this sphere remained whole when God began to create, and it will remain whole for eternity. God is "in all places and in all things" (2.25), and all things remain within God. She goes beyond many of her predecessors by including even the depths of hell as "the lowest part of the sphere, . . . a bottomless foundation beneath all abysses" (6.31). It is inconceivable to Mechthild that anything should exist outside of God, including the places where evil is punished and virtue rewarded.

The participation of creation in the very being of God does not rule out the difference of created beings. God is not only "the life of all that lives" but also "the ordering of all that is" (3.2). Each creature manifests within the divine sphere with a unique nature and task: "human beings in order to love God, to enjoy and know him, and to remain obedient; birds and animals to live according to their nature; inanimate creatures to remain firmly placed in their being" (6.31). *De proprietatibus rerum* exemplifies a common medieval organizational scheme. Based on the degree to which each class of beings participates in the divine attributes of being, intelligence, and so forth, the hierarchy descends through the angels, the reasonable soul, the human being, and the animal, vegetable, and mineral kingdoms. In this tradition, human beings take their place between the intellectual being of the angels and the physical nature of beasts.

Many passages in Mechthild's book also rank beings progressively. In reverse (ascending) order, she lists "fiends of hell, . . . those in purgatory, . . . sinners on earth, . . . good people on earth, . . . the chosen pure, . . . holy angels, . . . saints" in heaven (7.52). When she alters the common scheme by reversing the last two positions, with human beings ranking above the angels, she testifies to the importance of the material realm. For her, the incarnation alters the ontological hierarchy so that "divine nature now includes bone and flesh, body and soul" (4.14). Humans actually resemble God to a greater degree than angels because human beings have bodies.[42] The fallen angels, who did not have bodies but "only a single nature, . . . could not return" from their fall (4.14).[43] Only embodied beings can be restored to God through the incarnation, participate in the Eucharist, and imitate the humanity of Christ through the virtues.

Mechthild makes the unique placement of human beings the base for navigating the entire created order. The structure of the universe within God is something like an hourglass through which individual souls move like grains of sand. Heaven is at the top and hell at the bottom. Mechthild describes heaven from the top down.[44] Above everything "is nothing but God, God,

God" (3.1). Then comes God's throne, in which one can see the reflection of the Trinity. Mary sits upon the throne as incomparable "goddess" (3.1; cf. 3.4).[45] Below, the realm of heaven consists of the nine choirs and the "desolation"—the upper levels of a breach created when Lucifer and other souls fell out of the choirs—sparkling above it.[46] Human souls are destined to fill this breach, which is currently empty. After the last day, John the Baptist will take Lucifer's place in the desolation and serve as a prince before the throne. Apostles and "pure spiritual virgins" dwell near the throne, above the seraphim and in the empty places among them (3.1). Below the seraphim stand virgins whose thoughts may not have been quite as pure as their deeds (3.1). The cherubim are in the next choir; martyrs, preachers, and "spiritual lovers" (who are "not virgins") can enter into their ranks (3.1). The remaining Christians (widows, married people, the newly baptized, and children up to age six) take their places in and below the sixth choir. Finally, there is a comfortable place for unbaptized children under five, who receive honor but no reward. Though fixed in place, the choirs are permeable due to the mobility and individuality of souls, whose rank and rewards are commensurate with their individual lives.

Hell, the lower half of the hourglass, is an inverted image of the heavenly hierarchy. It, too, has an ordered structure, which "is so perverted that the highest are consigned to the lowest and basest place" (3.21). Lucifer therefore occupies the deepest abyss.[47] Hell's jagged foundation is built "from all kinds of stones of huge capital sins" carried there by familiar figures such as Adam, Cain, and Judas (3.21). In closest proximity to Lucifer dwell the baptized Christians who, despite knowing the gospel, did not repent of their sins and therefore suffer the most. In the middle are the Jews, who at least had the law; and at the top, where the torment is least severe, reside the heathens. All are ranked according to their works and, with a vividness rivaling Dante's *Inferno*, undergo graphic punishments to fit their various crimes. At the very top of hell (just below purgatory proper) is limbo, "the worst purgatory that a sinner can enter," reserved for sinful church officials and the patriarchs of the Hebrew Bible (3.21).

In the middle of the hourglass, purgatory is "so large that it begins at the mouth of hell and ends at heaven's gate" (6.8). This realm affords the most movement in eternity. No one can ease the pain of the souls in hell, and those in heaven rest blissfully content with their reward. But in purgatory, souls undergo penance for their sins, acquire lacking virtues, and eventually enter heaven. Others may help, as when one man through a vision tells Mechthild quite specifically the penance that will suffice for him: "a hundred *venias* [prostrations], twelve disciplines [penitential whippings], and many tears with a sorrowful heart from pure eyes every day for a year. And one should say masses" (3.17). The soul's cosmic itinerary is a communal affair that spans this life and the next, and Mechthild considers penance on behalf of departed souls a principal part of her work.

Mechthild's preoccupation with heaven, hell, and purgatory seems to confirm our suspicions of otherworldliness; yet for her, human activity in this life is not only meaningful in terms of its future reward. It also begins the process, which continues after death, of developing virtues that make human beings like God. Mechthild's prayers for those in purgatory evince a belief in the continuity of this world and the next. In her view, purgatory has a twofold temporal structure: suffering and afflictions in this world begin a process of purification that continues after death. Earthly souls make progress through penance, which passes at death into the disciplines of purgatory's demons and the torment of one's own internal accusations. "Thereafter," Mechthild explains, "through help and forbearance they pass beyond all distress" (6.8). Purified souls reside very near to heaven, where they lack only the direct vision of God and the reward that will come at the end of time. For "those souls who have no need of purgatory but have not yet come into God's kingdom" (7.57), "a twofold paradise" that similarly spans both lives serves as an alternative point of transition. This vast, complex structure undergirds the idea that the "other" world is continuous with earthly experience. Spatially, we might imagine with Mechthild that "this" world—bodies, history, church, and the sacraments—lies right in the middle of the hourglass. Earth is central in importance as well as in its location, for human beings there exert the most influence upon their eternal destinies and that of others.

In Mechthild's two purgatories and paradises, the present world is not only continuous with but also *overlaps* with the eternal hierarchy. Bliss and suffering are both present realities. The earth gives a foretaste of both destinies. It is, as it were, the microcosm in which all of the "places" exist concurrently:

> We are now present in heaven. Just as we are now on earth clothed with virtues and adorned and permeated with holy love of God, so are we now visible to all the blessed. . . . We are also present in purgatory as soon as we have earned it on earth. . . . The sinner's presence is also manifest in hell. . . . Thus does our presence go in and out of heaven, purgatory, and wretched hell according to where our own free will seeks to align itself. (4.25)

This "interpenetration of the temporal with the eternal" infuses worldly experience with ultimate significance.[48] Heaven is present on earth; purgatory is an aspect of this life; and hell is the wretchedness we choose for ourselves.

The universe is also permeable through the mystical itinerary in which, like Augustine's vision at Ostia or the Pseudo-Dionysian ascent, the soul "turns the eye of her desire from all things in order to be able to gain much praise for God" (5.4). The soul perceives all the degrees of difference between creatures and Creator and thus lovingly attends to all levels of being. In Mechthild's description, the soul's motion resembles the natural course of the rising and setting sun. It ascends to the Trinity in the heat of her desire. After she "has been permeated by the radiant heat of long love and has thus become faint in the embrace of the Holy Trinity" (5.4), she descends again. The ecstatic human soul returns to its senses. The soul is thus always in motion, soaring and sinking, while the body remains, anchoring it to the earth.

Mechthild's yearning for the source of God's good creation makes her susceptible to the charge of otherworldliness. Her eagerness to leave behind the things of this world can give the impression that they are of little value. She prefers the ecstasy of union to the struggles and limitations of everyday life and complains when God commands her soul to "go down" (1.2). She rejects all consolations: "Oh, get up and depart from me, all you creatures! You cause me pain and you are not able to console me"; and as she moves among "this beautiful world and all the good it contains," she observes that "nothing tastes good to me but God alone" (4.12). Such dialogues certainly do convey ambivalence toward created goods.

This ambivalence is rooted in a theological tradition in which the pedagogy of a gradual, ladderlike approach to God through the scale of natural forms was often seen as a concession to human weakness. As she grows old, Mechthild complains that she longs for earlier days when she could seemingly fly directly to God, without the support of worldly things: "Oh, what a wretched person I am! I complain to God in heaven that I am worse than I was thirty years ago. For the creatures that then helped me bear my misery did not have to be so noble to help this poor body thrive" (6.4). In the midst of her human desires, she learns to practice discernment, to "constantly station two guards between my soul and all earthly things, so that she may find just that amount of pleasure in my flesh that my meager needs require, . . . so that these earthly things do not lead me astray into a greedy desire to possess much or to linger in pleasure" (6.4). Mechthild, like other Christian ascetics before and after her, would prefer not to need or want anything other than the pure, unmediated presence of God, for earthly supports can distract from the ultimate goal.

The wisdom of this tradition, though it would seem to want to transform human beings into angels without the support of the physical, is its fundamental reorientation of all things in relation to God. There is nothing intrinsically evil in the created realm. Mechthild and others fear the *disorder* of their loves. She warns, "Be careful! No, this is not your Beloved. . . . Don't let the rich delights of earthly things push you away from him" (6.5). The internal dialogues above express Mechthild's growing pains. People have a great capacity for self-delusion, to convince themselves they need more than they do in order to serve God. Instead, Mechthild detaches her grasp from the beautiful things of the world, learns to "love God and not myself . . . in the nobility of creatures" (6.5), and "arranges all things in such a way that they are used entirely according to God's will" (6.4). The world is not negated but ordered in relation to God. Proper use trains the soul, and moderation frees it of attachment and the cares that come with loss.

Continuity and difference ebb and flow in Mechthild's visions of the God-world relation. The flow of the cosmos from God crystallizes into order; it is a structured flow, not an undifferentiated chaos. The flood of love deposits on the shores every degree of living thing, graded according to their created nature and their degree of participation in the goodness of God. The pattern of overflow and return does not reduce world to God. All things, while distinct from God and one other, share their foundation and goal in the divine. Human beings find their place both in the eternal choirs of heaven and hell and in the lived experience of these realities as they penetrate earthly existence. As the most mobile of all creatures, they image both the spiritual and bodily natures of the incarnate God; and they image God all the more as they order their love of the earth according to its relation to divinity.

COMPARISON: AN ELEMENTAL COSMOLOGY

Having surveyed the cosmologies of both theologians, certain similarities immediately emerge. The cosmologies of both Mechthild and Lalleśwarī feature elemental images of water and fluidity that convey divine presence in the midst of differentiation in the world. Tactile experiences of water and air flowing over bodies, quenching thirst, plummeting from high cliffs, and traveling from fresh springs to the ocean orient the seeker to the divine in this-worldly terms. The charge of otherworldliness sits uneasily with the imagery of their texts. Both women agree that the empirical world is not all there is, but their desire for something more results in a deeper awareness of the divine presence *in* the world. The interplay of immanence and transcendence develops into layered cosmologies that express relative levels of perception of the divine—not levels of separation from God.

The central divine attributes of love and consciousness initiate the creation of external objects. The relationship between God and world is one of divine overflow, branching into ordered hierarchies of beings that humans navigate as both embodied and conscious/spiritual. For both authors, the world returns to its divine source, flowing back to the divine fire (6.29) or becoming reabsorbed in cosmic dissolution (K 113–114). Lalleśwarī can view the world from the various *tattva*s, seeing the continuum of God-world unity in its many degrees of difference. In her visions Mechthild rises to God in heaven, sinks back to earth, and earns an eternal place in the heavenly hierarchy. Both participate in traditions that express practical ambivalence about material and temporal reality through a preference for immediate access to the divine. But their best wisdom about the nature of creation enables them to see the divine in the all, to "laugh and play in this worldly ocean" (O 29), and "in the nobility of creatures . . . [to] love God" (*FL* 6.5).

Both women evoke the emanation of the world from the divine; but the complexity of their cosmologies, including the Mechthild's insistence on *ordering* beings in relation to God, can give the impression that the "lower" realms are of little worth. The position of material reality in the big picture might be taken as an excuse for its pollution, consumption, or neglect. Yet the elemental imagery flows throughout every level of the cosmos for these thinkers. The flow of divinity pervades all of reality, connecting heaven and earth. Emanation and pervasion serve as essential counterparts to one another in these accounts—emanation accounts for difference; pervasion accounts for the continuity that keeps creation in contact with its divine source.

This elemental connectivity means that the human desire to return to our divine source does not remove us from the world. The longing of Lalleśwarī and Mechthild draws them into true knowledge of God, world, and self. Yearning moves in both directions, as evidenced by the role of desire in their epistemologies. Desire fuels the spiritual quest, but the seeker quickly realizes that it often strays toward objects that, though attractive, fail to satisfy. Saturation with penultimate goods temporarily dampens one's taste for the wine of true love. Therefore Mechthild says,

> . . . My heart's delight
> . . . I have taken back from the world,
> Retained for myself
> And denied to all creatures.
> (*FL 1.42*)

Lalleśwarī tenderly mourns the tragedy of such infatuations:

> Gently and gently shall I weep for you, O Mind.
> You have been caught under the spell of delusion.
> Even the shadow of worldly possessions will not stand by you[.]
> Alas, you have lost your own identity!
> (*K 2*)

Earthly things slip through our grasping hands in proportion to our desperate hopes that they can satisfy our deepest longing. Both women advocate detachment from earthly objects and moderation in their use. Mechthild values ascetic practices because they discipline desire to love all things in relation to God. Lalleśwarī finds that clearing the heart of common craving sharpens her sights on the true goal: "He who slays the three highway robbers, greed, lust and pride . . . / seeks out the Lord spontaneously" (K 36). The cosmological hierarchies in the thought of both women must be viewed in relation to this fluid epistemology of desire: the hierarchies express ways of approaching Absolute Being through beings. Such schematization trains the seeker to value the material world as it truly is, no more and no less.

Desire's movement in the world, we have discovered, reveals the divine, though differently for each theologian. For the beguine, love (*minne*) is God's nature and ours. The fluidity with which the soul soars in the cosmos is due to the inexhaustible

> . . . playful flood of love
> That flows mysteriously from God into the soul
> And through his power flows back again according to her [the soul's] ability.
> (7.45)

This empowers the human being to know and enjoy all of creation. For Lalleśwarī, desire's movement reveals the dynamism of consciousness:

> Maddened with love I, Lalla, set out in search of Him.
> Day and night I strained myself,
> and, lo, I found the wise one in my own house[.]
> That was the most auspicious moment of my life.
> (K 97)

Desire is a subject-object relation that flows between the two. When Lalleśwarī's restless desire sends her out into the world, she comes to know it as the movement of Śiva's consciousness within. For both, the overflow of a fluid divinity creates a cosmological pattern of differentiation and return. The world appears as permeated with divinity as one perceives this flow.

The elemental imagery of water grounds heaven and earth, the void and the material world, in a sensory continuum. The human being need not become disembodied to perceive divinity. Rather, the world becomes the site for recognition of the divine.

DIFFERENCE-IN-IDENTITY

We may now situate Mechthild and Lalleśwarī's cosmologies amid contemporary ecotheological paradigms. The proposals I surveyed at the beginning of this chapter express the God-world relationship in integrative and holistic terms, yet none advocates a complete collapse of the God-world distinction. As the divine "horizon" in Jantzen's pantheism, God is immanent in the world and yet transcends complete identification with what presently exists. Keller's panentheism expresses created difference through the metaphor of the ocean of the depths of God that remains full even as it empties itself in drops and waves of differentiation.[49] Sherma, too, upholds the dynamic relation of Śiva and the world, even as she restores the markers of divinity and purity to the material realm. Each of these systems retains roots in difference that recognizes dualities between beings without capitulating to dualism.

Lalleśwarī and Mechthild resist dualism not only by revaluing the material realm, but also by fracturing the binary categories that we bring to their texts. Both relational visions find their source in a triadic conception of divinity. The Holy Trinity is a threefold flood of love (*FL* 4.12) that manifests as lover, beloved, and the love between them: Father, Son, and Spirit. Lalleśwarī's meditation on Śiva and Śakti recognizes a divine triad that includes humanity among the centers of dynamic consciousness that can be immersed in the bliss of union (K 130). The divine nature grounds union and guarantees internal difference that goes beyond binaries. It gives rise to creation with multiple levels of spheres.

Comparison of Lalleśwarī and Mechthild draws attention to the range of possibilities that exist between the poles of continuity and differentiation. David Lawrence highlights the dynamic interplay between these poles in both Śaivism and Christianity. Contrary to the East/West stereotypes,

> there is, paradoxically, a dualistic moment in the Śaiva notion that the multiplistic experience of the world and the individuals in it are *real*, as the emanation of Śiva. Much of the Śaiva devotional literature in fact has a dualistic, supplicatory quality. Likewise a moment of identity between God and the world is found in much of Christian theology, particularly when it makes use of features of Neoplatonic emanationism.... The understanding of identity in difference found in both traditions permits a degree of rapprochement.[50]

"Identity in difference" between God and world resonates in our two interlocutors, multiplying the options between dualism and monism for viewing the natural environment.

Significant differences remain between the two traditions, however, between "the divine self-recognition that constitutes all experience" in Kashmir Śaivism and the Christian "endeavor to limit the logic of *esse est percipi* [to be is to be perceived] to maintain the orthodox monotheistic position of the difference between God and the world along with the souls in it."[51] For

Christians, the world does not disappear when God "closes his eyes" as it does in the case of Śiva, for whom the world comes into being as an object of his perception. The Trinity creates genuinely nonidentical centers of consciousness so that they can enter into loving relation. We might imagine Mechthild and Lalleśwarī on either side of the fulcrum, the "in" of Lawrence's term "identity-in-difference." Reading them together finds them on opposite sides of the seesaw of continuity and difference: they balance into a middle space of ontological relation, but Mechthild typically sits on the side of *difference*-in-identity, with Lalleśwarī usually taking the seat of *identity*-in-difference. Lalleśwarī journeys through all the levels of manifestation (*tattvas*) but feels most at home above them in the void of pure consciousness, where one perceives *I am* (this). Mechthild visits her there but, retaining the Śaiva framework for a moment, does her real work on the border of the "pure" and "impure" creation, drawing on concepts requiring the ontological difference of *I* and *this*.

Can these complex and rather neglected views of the God-world relation be the source of positive attitudes toward the world today? One important contribution is their capacity to reframe our assumptions about particular religious traditions. Christian theology has been charged with too much separation between divine and earthly reality. In Plumwood's evaluation,

> the salvation awaiting them beyond and above the world of nature, a fate marked out for humans alone, confirms their difference and separation from the world of nature, and their destiny as one apart from that of other species. The real self is the soul; . . . it is not merely discontinuous from and outside nature, but is oppositional to it, and is in conflict with the basic conditions and fact of its physical existence.[52]

If we carry the assumption that Christians only want to escape material nature, Mechthild's longing to ascend to God seems to fall prey to this accusation; yet a closer reading has revealed more nuance and complexity. For the beguine, the "real self" is always the created, embodied self. It flows forth from God along with all of material creation. Material nature persists in the return of creatures to their divine source, for bodies are necessary to experience the eternal reward or perdition she anticipates in her visions. One need not deny the existence of a transcendent realm in order to pay attention to this world. Mechthild's heaven, purgatory, and hell do not await her "beyond and above the world of nature." These realities overlap and interpenetrate one another in the present life for those with the eyes to see it. Lalleśwarī's system features continuity even more strongly than Mechthild's: there is absolutely no conflict between physical existence and the identity of the liberated self, for everything in existence possesses the nature of Śiva's consciousness. Neither theologian advocates hyperseparation between divinity and creation, as ecological activists routinely allege of the Platonic and Cartesian models. The continuity they envision may provide the basis for developing the ecological consciousness of their respective traditions.

Neither theologian completely subsumes God and world into one another, which is a worry for some critics of systems that view the world as divine;[53] but we must also ask whether they preserve the value of diversity that would hold individual beings, species, and ecosystems as worthy of preservation and care. The charge of too much continuity would fall more heavily on Lalleśwarī than on Mechthild. Lalleśwarī's meditation and visions of cosmic reabsorption dissolve difference to an extent that Mechthild, with her belief in the triune God and the eternal choirs of heaven, could never brook. But even in Śaivism, creation and dissolution are eternal activities: oneness always flows back out into differentiation. Continuity and difference are an eternal dialectic in both visions.

Here I have proposed that a "complex, interacting pattern of continuity and difference" of the sort necessary for responsible ecology can be found through the retrieval of traditional cosmologies such as those of Mechthild and Lalleśwarī.[54] Many of the options today have lost this complex interplay. Traditions that emphasize difference between God and world can go too far, making the world the antithesis of the divine. Those that emphasize continuity run the risk of an economy of the same that values beings only insofar as they resemble the one true Being. Mechthild and Lalleśwarī, who mediate continuity and difference through their hierarchical epistemological schemes, can be read as instrumentalizing the world, discarding each rung of the ladder as they climb away from the earth up toward the divine realm. But as I have demonstrated, this reading is a distortion of their mature teachings about the universe as the celebrative overflow of the divine nature.

These dynamic cosmologies hold much capacity for an ecofriendly balance, even with the possibility of overemphasizing continuity on the one hand, or difference on the other. The limits and possibilities of these two systems illustrate the lack of an inherent correlation between cosmology and practice. Rosemary Radford Ruether cautions of "the difficulties of assuming a straightforward relationship between the worldviews of particular religions of the world and the treatment of nature."[55] Indeed, distortions in Eastern and Western worldviews have permitted and even encouraged the escalating harm of the natural environment since the industrial revolution. We therefore must not fail to retrieve positive intellectual and spiritual streams where we may. The fluidity of the divine relation to the world, as neither identical with nor radically separated from one another, is one such stream.

CHALLENGES AND GIFTS FOR AN ECOFRIENDLY THEOLOGY

We have seen that Lalleśwarī's and Mechthild's cosmologies, in which all beings flow from divinity, have great potential to answer the call of contemporary ecotheologians for worldviews that honor the natural environment in concrete ways. But juxtaposing them together with the proposals at the beginning of this chapter, two features push back at contemporary norms: the affirmation of hierarchy and the presence of ascetic tendencies. Each of these challenges may be gifts to the contemporary conversation.

First, the elaboration of hierarchies (of heavenly rank, created beings, or modes of consciousness) shows a level of attention to difference that monistic or pantheistic proposals often lack. In our affirmation of difference, we need to be prepared to describe what these differences are and find conceptual frameworks, however provisional, for thinking about them. Such frameworks can bring a greater range of difference into view. They can facilitate ethical decision making about beings in their complex relations to one another. The hierarchies we have examined are not static; in fact, the human being exhibits a remarkable mobility in the realm of created difference to see things from the perspective of heaven *and* earth. By stepping out of a reified place for humanity in relation to the rest of creation, theologians can better theorize toward mutual care and responsibility.

The ascetic strains in both thinkers may also be positive resources. For these women, inordinate attachment to created goods hinders the development of a mature perspective. Lalleśwarī sees how much misery results when people cling to material wealth as if it were essential to their identity. Only by letting go can we enjoy the ocean of this world without drowning. Mechthild knows how worldly goods can capture desire and prevent the full flourishing of the desire that loves all things in God. She pursues ascetic practices further than Lalleśwarī, who eschews its extremes. If we shift our comparative lens to include contemporary scholarship as well as medieval voices on this issue, the value of comparison emerges even more strongly.

Recent work on Hinduism and ecology suggests additional ecological possibilities in practices of asceticism. Harry Blair has constructed a fourfold typology of Hindu perspectives on ecology that shows increasing commitment to the natural environment: (1) mastery over nature; (2) sustainability through reciprocal relationships and stewardship; (3) a "romance" view of the world as a manifestation of ultimate reality; and (4) asceticism that renounces use. The fourth, the "renouncer" perspective, was rehabilitated by Mahatma Gandhi in his teachings of nonviolence and self-sustainability and is now the basis for a Gandhian ecological movement.[56]

In light of the fact that Mechthild and Lalleśwarī do not directly address the ecological issues that have now escalated to crisis levels, they may not fit clearly into any one of these models. We may think with them, however, to extrapolate their teachings. For instance, Mechthild writes of "using" all things for God's praise, an approach that could support either of the first two relations, of mastery or mutual sustainability. Her view of the cosmos as the effusion of divine love could also place her in the romance model. Lalleśwarī similarly has features of the romance view, with her teaching that the world is the externalization of Śiva's nature. In view of their potential to challenge contemporary assumptions, however, I focus here on their resonance with the renouncer model.

Many theologians eager to embrace the created realm as divine (along the lines of the romance model) condemn withdrawal from earthly things as otherworldly, antibody, and antinature. Yet ascetic teachings glimmer with new possibility next to the fourth and, in Blair's mind, most committed ecological position. Gandhi's followers have developed his principles of truth, nonviolence, self-purification, and simple, sustainable life in community into an ecological logic.[57] Vinay Lal argues that although Gandhi precedes the "environmentalist" movement, his sensibilities are deeply ecological. The Mahatma was a critic of the development model of modernity; and he advocated vegetarianism, natural cures, walking as a primary mode of transportation, and reuse of materials, including human waste.[58] Abstinence runs counter to the omnivorous impulse of the mastery model. Asceticism can be ecofriendly insofar as restraint with respect to natural resources counterbalances the tendency of contemporary society to enjoy the world through its consumption.[59]

Juxtaposed with this reassessment of ascetic restraint, Lalleśwarī's teachings ring true: "Only such clothes are helpful as ward off cold. / Such food alone is beneficial as can appease hunger" (K 33). Though she cautions against extreme physical deprivation, her ideal attends to basic needs as it counsels, "Be moderate and you will become even minded" (K 27). Compared to the standards of much of the so-called first world, her ideal is ascetic; but in the long term it may also be the only feasible alternative. Larry Shinn comments that it is hard "to imagine large numbers of Indians, let alone Americans, abandoning their lives of comfort—usually in cities or suburbs—for such self-disciplined, simple living," but it is even harder to imagine that current levels of consumption are sustainable: "Gandhi would call us to the simple life before we or our children are forced to adopt diminished lifestyles by necessity."[60] Renouncing unnecessary use may be the most important habit to develop if we are to have a sustainable future for the human and natural world.

Mechthild's more rigorous asceticism sharpens the critique of current habits of resource depletion. The penitential aspect of her discipline implies the need to rectify the effects of greed. As a first step in her vocation as a beguine, Mechthild abandons the finery of the court to join Christ's poor. Her radical gesture stands as a challenge to the affluent, then and now. As with her beloved mendicant preachers, the Dominicans, her calls to voluntary poverty sound a prophetic note to the affluent whose "needs" are excessive. She contrasts "two kinds of poor people": "The ones are cheerfully poor and are always in fear that they will receive too much of this poor earth. The others are involuntarily and quite unhappily poor, and they constantly run around in great anxiety that nothing on this poor earth will ever be theirs" (3.19). Contemporary readers might claim the wisdom of Mechthild's insight that the "involuntarily and . . . unhappily poor" will remain so insofar as their restless hearts are fettered with anxiety. No matter how much they accumulate, they will always run after more. Voluntary withdrawal from earthly things, and the heavy layer of dust these things leave upon the heart, clears the way for new methods of inhabiting the world.

As we reconsider the ecological virtues of asceticism, however, we must not expect our medieval ascetics to have all the answers. For example, in the same passage above, Mechthild teaches that the plight of the involuntarily poor is just: God "must win them by being very hard on them," since they would not return God's love if they lived in abundance (3.19). The implicit theodicy is unhelpful insofar as it suggests that impoverishment may be divine punishment. Some may also criticize the thirteenth-century Christian valorization of poverty as romantic and disconnected from the grinding reality of those lacking the luxury of choice. Furthermore, Lalleśwarī's simple teaching of moderation may be just a bit *too* simple: who is to say what one really needs? Where do we draw the line in our consumption as individuals and as a society? Even though these women were not responding to the perils of air pollution, rising sea levels, and perishing ecosystems, their teachings on moderation and their ascetic practices may suggest to us habits more conducive to respect and care for the earth. Their vision accompanies us as we embark upon the important critical ethical tasks that await us.[61]

CONCLUSION

The charge of otherworldliness in beguine and yogic spirituality proves to be misplaced. No other world provides an escape for Lalleśwarī; for Mechthild, the "other" world permeates every atom of worldly existence. Their interaction with material reality inspires longing for the divine—not the desire to evade ecological responsibility, but the hope of loving all things rightly in relation to their source. Retrieval of their relational systems for theology can ameliorate the oppositional cast that God-world duality has taken in the modern period, but we must also inhabit these traditional myths anew. The next chapter picks up the questions of materiality and asceticism to consider the role of the body in a theology of difference.

4

Body: Prison or Partner?

> Ah, dearest prison in which I have been bound, I thank you especially for being obedient to me. Though I was often unhappy because of you, you nevertheless came to my aid. On the last day all your troubles will be taken from you.
> *Mechthild of Magdeburg (FL 7.65)*

> O embodied one, should you be too much obsessed with your body, embellishing and adorning it and providing sweet dishes,
> of this body not even ashes will endure.
> *Lalleśwarī of Kashmir (K 31)*

Today,[1] we often hear that mind, body, and spirit are, at a fundamental level, inseparable. Contemporary physics tells us of the interchangeability of energy and matter. Holistic medicine assures us of the importance of a healthy spirit for a healthy body. Research on meditating monks shows the physiological correlates of religious experience, and other studies demonstrate positive effects of prayer on the ill. In a discussion of neurotransmitters, Christiane Northrup asks, "If the uterus, the ovaries, the white blood cells, and the heart all make the same chemicals as the brain makes when it thinks, *Where in the body is the mind?* The answer is, *The mind is located throughout the body.*"[2]

Although in a variety of fields the prevailing wisdom would integrate the sensory and mental faculties, persistent rhetorical patterns keep us under dualism's thrall. The Cartesian project of achieving certain knowledge through separation of mind from body has had lasting effects: "While adherence to such a *doctrine* has largely disappeared, utilization of the *critical rhetoric* stemming from it, even after determined efforts to expunge it, persists."[3] One form in which the critical rhetoric of dualism continues to hold sway today is in the way dualism's critics tend to see it everywhere. Below, we shall see examples where this anachronistic separation of the mind (or soul) from the body is read into Mechthild and Lalleśwarī's thought. We cannot break our dualistic lenses until we have good alternative models.

This book has wagered that if modern dualistic categories are the problem, premodern exemplars might offer other patterns as we move toward a postmodern way of viewing the world and the human person. As with our investigations of the relations between divinity and humanity (in chap. 2) and between divinity and the world (in chap. 3), a search for alternatives must not simply import premodern concepts unaltered. Our two-way conversation will question certain aspects of premodern worldviews, just as the premoderns will certainly have something to teach us today.

I have also wagered that a comparative approach will do more to break our dualistic spectacles than investigation of a single tradition alone. On the issue of Western mind-body (or soul-body) dualism, others have similarly turned to the East. Philosopher Luce Irigaray discovers in the theories and practices of yoga "that the body is itself a divine place"; and she learns from them "how to cultivate [one's] body, and to respect that of others, as divine temples."[4] In particular, Irigaray works with the image of breath as connecting or infusing the body with spirit. The retrieval of voices from a number of locations outside the modern West is well under way. Here, I bring together interests in both *Eastern* and *premodern Western* approaches to the body.

The question that will guide this comparison is whether the body is a prison or a partner in the human quest for ultimate liberation. In other words: does it inhibit or facilitate spiritual goals? Hindu and Christian traditions both harbor some ambivalence on this question. Practitioners of both traditions baffle many students of religion today with the intensity of forms of asceticism that restrict the comforts and pleasures of the body. I follow scholars such as medievalist Caroline Walker Bynum, who attempt to push past an initial repulsion from ascetic practices and come to view "efforts to discipline and manipulate the body . . . more as elaborate changes rung upon the *possibilities* provided by fleshliness than as flights from physicality."[5] If we remove our Cartesian lenses and try to understand what Christian and Hindu ascetics hope to accomplish through bodily discipline, we ourselves may be able to imagine new forms of partnership with the body.

On these issues, Mechthild and Lalleśwarī challenge us at every turn. These theologians demand careful reading if we are to see how their fluid patterns of thought break out of the dualisms habitually attributed to them and their traditions. We will investigate their pluralist anthropologies, which claim that human beings are not made of two things called mind (or soul) and body but are infinitely more complex. Where their narratives appear to reject the body, we will look more closely at the role of physical practices in their journeys. And where they part ways with one another on the importance of suffering in the spiritual life, we may wish to temper our postmodern celebration of the body through attention to its pain.

FROM DUALIST TO PLURAL ANTHROPOLOGIES: LALLEŚWARĪ OF KASHMIR

In the last chapter we discovered that Mechthild and Lalleśwarī dissolve the dualism between heaven and earth, or between divinity and the world, through complex cosmologies with a great deal of mobility between levels. Because in their systems the divine being overflows creatively by nature, we should not be surprised if divinity similarly flows forth into human beings whose capacities mirror the complexity of the cosmos. One of the primary benefits of their thought, then, is that they provide alternative templates of the human person that do not dualistically reduce humanity into bifurcated physical and mental/spiritual capacities.

Lalleśwarī's philosophical tradition cannot conceive of the body either as a singular thing or as something excluded from the realm of the spirit. For Kashmir Śaivas, "The perceptible is [God's] body."[6] The individual body is seen as a modification of the material levels of the cosmos described in the previous chapter. Recall that the intelligence, ego-sense, and mind are all evolutes within the *physical* world. They are part of the "subtle body" (*sūkṣma-śarīra*) that transmigrates between lives, which consists of the eight *tattva*s from intelligence (*buddhi*) down to the primary elements of perception (sound, etc.). The gross body (*sthūla-śarīra*) is the physical aspect, which does not transmigrate; it is made of the five gross elements. All of these diverse components, representing thirteen levels of divine emanation, make up the human body. By means of this participation in the *tattva*s and the consciousness that imbues all of them, the human world of experience may extend to the most subtle levels of cosmic manifestation, up through pure consciousness itself. While traversing these worlds, the yogi experiences them as one's own body, just as Śiva does.[7]

Consciousness flows with the breath in the gross and subtle bodies through a network of rivers or channels (*nāḍī*s). Contemporary practitioners of yoga will be familiar with the idea that these channels carry *prāṇa* (energy or breath) to energy centers (chakras) along the vertical axis of the body. Lalleśwarī calls these centers *mandal*s; referring to the twelve centers outlined in the *Vijñānabhairava Tantra*, she ascends simultaneously through the body and through the cosmos.[8] She envisions breath passing through the fiery navel region, the abode of the mystical sun, where one gains "insight into the inner world" (K 101). The breath stokes the inner fire as it moves in and out like a bellows and then proceeds to the heart center (K 98). The breath finally rises to the cool place in the head where the ultimate, *brahman*, resides. This is the abode of the moon, the source of "nectar" that flows downward through the *nāḍīs* (K 71, 96). The circulation of breath through these centers replicates the vibration of the universe: consciousness becomes more subtle as it rises toward the head before descending again.

This abbreviated map of Lalleśwarī's view of the body should suffice to illustrate that, for her, the body is no single thing, and it includes and exceeds the faculty called mind. She also expands her concept of the mind with two Kashmiri terms: *man* and *tsyeth*. The first corresponds with the *tattva* of *manas*, which evolves from the higher evolutes of intelligence and ego. It can be translated as "mind" or "heart," for it is the storehouse of beliefs and emotions and the faculty with which one pursues one's desires (cf. K 32). *Man* is not necessarily a cool, reasonable, or superior faculty. Lalleśwarī likens it to a dangerous ocean when allowed to boil over: "In fury the mind and the ocean are alike, constantly emitting fire of wrath" (K 41). The mind often resembles an unruly colt or a stupid donkey; but if reined in it can, in turn, control the inner breath channels and the other physical faculties (K 35, 43).

The second Kashmiri term, *tsyeth*, which can be rendered "mind" or "individual consciousness," shares many of the qualities of *man*. It must be tamed with the bridle of intelligence and knowledge so that the Self can pacify it.

> The steed of the mind roams over the skies
> traveling millions of miles within the twinkling of an eye.
> Yet the faculty of discrimination can control it
> with the bridle of consciousness after breaking
>   the two wings of *prāna* and *apāna* [sic].
>
> (K 52; cf. K 55)

Despite its unruliness, *tsyeth* is the individual correlate of universal consciousness. The word for "consciousness" (*tsetani*, O 89) in the fourth line above is closely related to the word for "mind" (*tsyeth*, O 89) in the first line—both share the same Sanskrit root (*cit*): human consciousness (*cit*) is the microcosm of the divine attribute of *caitanya*. Thus, although *tsyeth* partakes in the limitations of individuality, it is the consciousness within the human being that expands to share the awareness of Śiva himself, the "sun of consciousness" that melts and absorbs differences into itself (K 83). In its contracted form, individual consciousness is drowned by *māyā* (K 2), comes under the influence of others (K 15), and tends to stray (K 29, 52, 53, 55). But because it is a temporary appearance of *caitanya*, it can melt and dissolve back into divine consciousness through yogic discipline (K 33, 83, 89). Like the body, then, the mind, which is not a unitary and self-contained faculty, reflects the very nature of divinity.

FROM DUALIST TO PLURAL ANTHROPOLOGIES: MECHTHILD OF MAGDEBURG

Some readers of Mechthild have projected a dualistic anthropology onto her thought. Thus James Franklin writes, "Mechthild considered man [sic] to be a being composed of two completely antithetical essences, spirit and flesh."[9] He assumes a simplistic equation of the body with evil, eliding the crucial difference between the empirical body and the symbolic significance of the "flesh" in the Pauline Christian tradition. He also points to her dialogues between Body and Soul, which we shall discuss shortly, as evidence that the needs of the body directly oppose the needs of the soul, and that the body must be subjugated and punished.

A careful reading of Mechthild's body language corrects this misunderstanding. Like Lalleśwarī, Mechthild has a rather complex anthropology. She writes of the soul (*sele*), spirit (*geist*), senses (*sinne*, which include the mind), and body; and rather than positing a singular, unified concept of the body in stark opposition to the "spiritual" faculties, Mechthild employs at least three terms for the body—*fleisch*, *licham*, and *libe*. In her mature thought, these entities are capable of radical participation in spirit and integral to the flow of redemption.

Mechthild uses the term "flesh" (*fleisch* or *vleisch*) in at least two ways. First, the flesh is a Pauline-Augustinian metaphor that signifies a total way of life in contrast to the embodied life of the spirit. The spiritual way of life is turned toward God, the fleshly away from God; both involve the body.[10] Mechthild frequently contrasts *fleisch* with *geist* (spirit) as being fickle, weak, or sick, having perverted desires, and limiting the senses to physical realities. "The loving soul . . . mortifies her flesh" as she imitates the passion of Christ (*FL* 3.10). Second, mechthild uniquely incorporates the symbolic, scriptural meaning of the flesh into the story of redemption. At pivotal moments she attributes flesh to those who live the total life of the spirit: God, Mary, and Jesus. At the incarnation,

> the whole Holy Trinity . . . placed itself in the open heart of her [Mary's] most pure flesh, and united itself with all that it found in her, so that her flesh became its flesh in such a manner that a perfect child grew in her body and she became a true mother of his flesh. (5.23)

The incarnation renders a positive ontological effect in human beings. Because "divine nature now includes bone and flesh, . . . the soul alone with its flesh is mistress of the house in heaven" (4.14). As the human being grows in perfection, even *fleisch*, that orientation of the human being polemically most associated with sin and physicality, participates in the goodness of God, and "she begins to taste with delight his love on her flesh" (6.1).

In contrast to the theologically laden *fleisch*, *licham* (related to the modern German word for corpse, *Leichnam*) is decidedly more corporeal. When Mechthild visits her confessor's grave, she visits his *lichamen* (4.22). It is also the word used to refer to holy relics and the sacrament (*gottes licham*). The soul separates from *licham* at the moment of death, to be reunited with it at the last day. Although the souls in hell, limbo, and purgatory are imagined with bodies so they can do penance, they do not retrieve their corporeal selves until the last judgment.

Lip or *libe*, like the modern *Leib*, also signifies the body in its material sense. Thus it is nearly synonymous with *licham* in some passages referring to the empirical body in which soul nests: "*sele in disem armen libe, . . . sele in einem licham*" (5.1). Mechthild most often expresses the unity of body and soul with the pairing *lip und sele*, a holistic signifier that indicates the experience of the total person. It is the same word used for "eternal life," *ewigen lip* (1.22; 1.44; etc.), in which *lip und sele* reunite to receive their reward (5.25).

In Mechthild's vocabulary, then, *fleisch*, *licham*, and *lip* all correlate to physicality. *Fleisch* often retains a symbolic sense in opposition to spirit as a total way of life, but it can also indicate how the incarnation unites Christ's life to humanity. *Licham* is the empirical body, what is left behind at death. *Lip* is that which partners with the soul to constitute a living being. Although we can draw these general distinctions, the three overlap significantly. The flesh (outside being drawn into the Trinity) is in itself most troublesome in its association with sin, but it has the least to do with the empirical body; whereas *licham* and *lip* are afflicted with sickness, suffering, and death in this life but will live without pain in the next.

It would be difficult to distill a pure dualism out of the anthropologies of either theologian due to their pluralistic conceptions of the human person. Rather than soul and body or mind and body, the human person is an aggregate of numerous overlapping material and transmaterial faculties. To be sure, reading them in translation can mask the complexity of their views of the human being and make it easier to read dualistic assumptions into the text. Now that we recognize the plurality of their grammars of the body, we may consider the arc of their narratives.

NARRATIVES OF THE BODY: CONFLICT

Although both women have complex views of the human person that do not divide its faculties between purely mental/spiritual and purely physical activities, they may still be subject to critique if they fall into a *practical* dualism. Indeed, both have been accused of just that: Lalleśwarī of wanting to transcend the body in meditation, and Mechthild of wanting to escape in ecstasy and in death. These readings of Lalleśwarī's verses of longing and Mechthild's colorful dialogues do have some basis in the texts.

Lalleśwarī's emphasis on the conundrum of the unenlightened state in her own journey has caused some translators to read her as a vigorous ascetic with an antibody stance. Take, for example, some lines (K 129) that I translate as follows:

> O Lord, I understood neither self nor others.
> I always knew one body.
> You are me, I am you; I did not understand this meeting.
> Who are You, who am I? I have doubt.

Grierson and Barnett follow a variant manuscript and render the second line "Continually I have mortified this vile body" (GB 7). Kotru (129) has "always I took the body as myself," a translation that draws out the problem of identifying too narrowly with the body rather than with consciousness.[11] Both of these translations present the body as a problem to be overcome.

Other verses imply that Lalleśwarī eschews basic needs such as clothing and food. In a *vaakh* that addresses such concessions to the body, Grierson prefers a variant that states, "Recognize thy body as but food for forest crows" (GB 28; cf. K 33). He also interprets the guru's teaching to look inward (GB 94; K 97) as slighting the body: Lalleśwarī ought "to recognize the external world as naught but an illusion, and to restrict her thoughts to meditation on her inner Self" (Grierson and Barnett, 107). Odin rightly points out that this interpretation minimizes the Śaiva insistence on the reality of the world. Yet she too criticizes Lalleśwarī's "austere lifestyle and her approach to her bodily needs" and charges that for her the "body is only important as long as it serves as a means of transcendence."[12]

We have already seen that James Franklin attributes an anti-body dualism to Mechthild. This view disregards Mechthild's vision of the entire person, soul and body, united with the second person of the Trinity (*FL* 6.24), as well as her insistence on the goodness of the created body. She writes that Adam and Eve's "bodies were to be pure, for God created for them no shameful members" (3.9). The gendered body was created good; but the fall (which results not from sexual temptation, as is often adduced from the Eve story, but from eating) has consequences for sexuality: "When they had eaten the disgusting food that did not agree with their pure bodies, they became so filled with poison that they lost the purity of the angels and forgot their virginal chastity" (3.9).[13] Franklin's reading has warrant, however, insofar as the body loses its created goodness after the fall.

For Mechthild, the fall into sin means that the embodied soul now struggles to ascend to God. Two related limitations make corporeality an apparent obstacle to the spiritual quest. First, the unsuitability of the body's senses to share in the soul's ascent makes these flights painful for the body. During the soul's ecstasy, the body is first exhausted and then left behind:

> God's true greeting, coming from the heavenly flood out of the spring of the flowing Trinity, has such force that it takes away all the body's strength. . . . Then the soul leaves the body, taking all her power, wisdom, love, and longing. Just the tiniest bit of her life force remains with the body as in a sweet sleep. (1.2)

Bereft of its power, the body sleeps—peacefully, from the soul's perspective—as the soul plays with the Trinity "a game that the body does not know" (1.2). But the body feels tormented, saying to the returning soul,

> Where have you been?
> I can't take it anymore.
> *(1.5)*

Mechthild weighs these effects in an exchange between Lady Soul ("Mistress and Queen") and Lady Love:

> "Lady Love, you have brought me to such a pass that my body is racked by a strange weakness."
> "Mistress and Queen, in exchange I have given you much sublime knowledge."
> "Lady Love, you have devoured my flesh and blood."
> "Mistress and Queen, you have thereby been purified and drawn into God." (1.1)

The soul's knowledge and purification cost the body its comfort. The body's untrained powers are so unsuited to the work of contemplation and the exertion of rapture that Mechthild knows many religious people who avoid "divine inwardness" altogether in order to "spare the body" (6.13). But the exchange with Lady Love demonstrates that for Mechthild, the discomfort of the body is but a small price to pay for the bliss of love.

The second major impediment to the soul's full, lasting union with God is that the body's comparative weakness makes it difficult to sustain the full divine presence for long. Lady Soul becomes disconsolate when the "game" of love ends and she "must go down," awakening the body with a sigh (1.2). Already in the midst of ecstasy she begins to fault the body for God's decision to limit the intensity of their affair. She warns, "Lord, you have raised me up so high here that I shall not be able to praise you in any fitting degree when in my body. Rather, I shall suffer as an outcast and struggle against my body" (1.2). Upon returning from her tryst, the full extent of the soul's marital conflict with the body breaks out. The body now apprises her of its perspective: "Well, woman, just where have you been? You come back so love-struck, lovely, and vibrant, free, and witty. Your carrying on has cost me my appetite, sense of smell, color, and all my strength" (1.2). Accustomed to leading the way in experience, the body is left insensate in its "sleep" and feels, frankly, left out. The peevish soul snaps back, "Shut up, murderer! Quit your bellyaching.... That my enemy has been wounded—what do we care about that? It makes me glad" (1.2). The partnership between body and soul is clearly not always harmonious.

As a result of these perceived impediments to her spiritual goals, in the course of Mechthild's text, the soul's resentment toward the body modulates into various keys of irritation and resignation. She refers to the body as her enemy (4.2), a prison (3.10; 7.48), a "beast of burden, ... bridled with worthlessness" (1.46), a stinking "dead mongrel" (3.5), and "an old pensioner who can no longer serve at court" (3.1). Alongside readings of Lalleśwarī that style the body, at the very least, as an obstacle to realizing one's true identity, and at worst as food for carrion animals, does the charge of antibody dualism stick to these women after all? Is their deepest longing simply to escape the body's constraints and let the true self/soul ascend to a more transcendent realm?

I propose to read the above frustrations with the body as but one moment in the two women's processes of spiritual discernment. Many readers would certainly be able to identify with these frustrations; these teachers vividly acknowledge the reality of the body's limitations. But it would be a mistake to read this moment as the final act. What happens next in their narratives of the body is crucial: they begin to employ their bodies in practices that lead to liberation.

LALLEŚWARĪ'S PRACTICES

In order to move past her initial difficulties with the embodied condition, Lalleśwarī practices yoga. Specifically, her verses reflect the forms of meditation outlined in the Tantric texts of the Kashmir Śaiva tradition, in which a practitioner aims to recognize the body as a microcosm of the cosmic flow of Śiva's consciousness. These exercises will reframe the question of whether or not Lalleśwarī quests to escape her physical existence.

Lalleśwarī accords with the major schools of Kashmir Śaivism in teaching that the most effective religious disciplines participate in, are vitalized by, and reveal the flow of divine consciousness. The flow of the cosmos is replicated in the microcosm of the body. Lalleśwarī expresses the identity of the divine and human nature through her principle of *sahaj*, which means natural, naturally, or something in its natural state. J. L. Kaul defines the Sanskrit term *sahaj* as an adjective and a noun: "adj., inborn, natural, easy; n., true nature, the nature of the Self, the true reality; used by Lal Ded as an epithet of the Supreme Siva [sic], He who is the real and true."[14] This principle indicates that, in order to realize one's true nature, one should use natural means.

Kashmir Śaiva texts attest that practitioners achieve this realization in various ways. Some come to it instantaneously, an occurrence called "no means." Some experience the "divine means," in which divine grace grants direct apprehension of identity with Śiva; others follow the "empowered means" by attending to the subtle internal processes that replicate the vibration of consciousness. Still others employ the "individual means," which focuses on physical activities such as postures, breathing, worship, and the chanting of mantras. In all such practices, the aim is to catch hold of moments of transition, such as the initial moment of intent in any thought or action, where one can best perceive the subtle movement of consciousness.[15] Lalleśwarī focuses on the flow of the breath, a method that can easily be taught to others. Some in the tradition view direct apprehension of Śiva without physical practices as the superior path, but Lalleśwarī's meditation on the breath does not reflect any lack of competency on her part. It may instead signal a preference for an "emanation" scheme that retraces the path of manifestation through embodied experience, as opposed to a "pervasion" cosmology in which realization bypasses the body and is instantaneous.[16]

Lalleśwarī describes how breath becomes more subtle as it ascends, gradually dissolving everything it touches in imitation of the cosmic process of dissolution. The breath progresses through the navel to the head, the abode of the mystical moon, which drips nectar into the channels of the body (K 96):

> I reined in the steed of the mind blending thoroughly
> with the vital airs coursing through the ten nadis [sic].
> Because of that the nectar of the moon melted down,
> and the void got merged into the void.
>
> (K 91)[17]

Lalleśwarī says, "The nine apertures of the body I closed, and / found Śiva present everywhere" (K 125). Microcosm thus merges with macrocosm in the breath.

As complex as Lalleśwarī's esoteric breath imagery may seem, it revolves around one of the body's most natural impulses: as *Śiva Sūtra* 3/44 says, "The link with the vital breath is natural."[18] Lalleśwarī describes breath (*prāṇa*) as vital energy, the "life ... the Lord breathed ... into all skeletons" (K 131). The first divine out-breath initiates life even before the world emerges, and the in-breath reabsorbs its manifestation into the unity of the subject. Thus yogis also find in the exhalation, retention, and inhalation of breath a microcosm of Śiva's creation, persistence, and withdrawal of the world. Bordering inside and outside, immanent and transcendent, breath is the most simple, natural link to God, intricately infused into human nature—a criterion that many arduous physical and mental religious practices fail to meet.

What is the relation of the breath to the body? Each faculty, from the individual consciousness to the five senses and mind, reflects some level of cosmic manifestation and grants a glimpse into the divine nature. Without training, however, these abilities are leaky vessels. Lalleśwarī styles "the five senses" as a "lake that ceaselessly oozes away" (K 119, 120) and says that her efforts go to waste "like water in unbaked plates of clay" (K 1). In order to harness the divine flow in the body, seekers must neither suppress the workings of body and mind nor overly indulge them, but instead attend carefully to their homology with divine consciousness. By focusing on breath and body, Lalleśwarī focuses on the divine immanent in herself. Some tantras teach that only a deity can worship a deity: the human being must first assimilate herself to the god through its mantra or some other means. Lalleśwarī finds the mode of assimilation in the centers in the body through the breath:

> He who knows the regions of [the subtle body] as the abode of God,
> and also the *prāṇas* [sic] that move between them through the nasal passage;
> he who knows the unstruck sound [i.e., Oṁ],
> ....
> Having become Divine Himself, who else is there to worship?
>
> *(K 71)*

Practices of the breath thus keep the practitioner solidly in the body while connecting to its life source. When Lalleśwarī realizes that all—including her body—is divine, she has no need to transcend the physical.

In addition to permeating the body, the breath has an intimate link to the mind. Lalleśwarī advises, "Try to join your *prāṇa* [sic] with the mind" (K 66). Working with the breath restrains the mind (K 52, 91), and reining in the mind can help to control the breath (K 80). Kotru explains the relation of breath and mind, which

> permeate the whole body, and are inextricably related to each other. If one is controlled the other is controlled automatically. . . . The uneven movement of [the in-breath and out-breath] creates restlessness in the mind. Through the practice of yoga the rhythm of the breath is slowed down and it becomes even.[19]

Mind and breath mutually discipline one another. This emphasis on control and restraint of breath and mind reinforces the paradox of *sahaj*: although these processes belong equally to ourselves and the Self, in their distracted, diffused state we must harness them or seal them from leaks. Lest the flow run dry, one must control one's natural faculties without cutting them off from their source.

The middle space between inner and outer, Śiva and Śakti, one and many, resides *in the body*. It is palpable in the moment of transition between the breaths; but according to the great Kashmir Śaiva teachers Abhinavagupta and Kṣemarāja, even enjoyment of a good meal, music, or an aesthetic object can lead to bliss, as "consciousness is free on such occasions of thought constructs, given over as one is to the pleasant experience."[20] In this spirit, Lalleśwarī teaches,

> With a loving heart search within this very body.
> This body is known as the abode of the Supreme self.
> Greed and delusion dispelled, this very body
> will acquire grace and a halo of illumination.
>
> (K 32)

When Lalleśwarī massages life into the self's atrophied faculties with such practices, the restored natural (*sahaj*) functioning of the body becomes the boat in which she reaches Śiva-consciousness.

If one expects to find denigration of the body in Lalleśwarī's teachings, one can find it; but the framework of her embodied yogic practices reveals precisely the opposite effect. Lalleśwarī does not participate in the Indian ascetic trajectories that seek to transcend or deny the body. Several aspects of her work, then, caution against reading hyper-asceticism into her text.

First, as we have seen, the body is integral to realizing one's identity with Śiva. Lalleśwarī employs body and mind (*tana mana*) in her search for God (O 26, K 126). Her own struggles show little evidence of the more rarefied or instantaneous paths to enlightenment. The practices she prescribes—particularly her pairing of the mind and the breath—fall under the "individual" and "empowered" means, those that employ physical practices and mental concentration toward the realization of unity in duality. Other bodily practices such as the chanting of *Oṃ* also help to bridge the divide between unity and difference, the unmanifest and the manifest, and absorb the practitioner in the middle space between Śiva and Śakti.

Second, once Lalleśwarī knows her true nature, she finds that though she is indeed the psychophysical conglomerate, she is so much more. As "the abode of God" (K 32), the body itself gains "a halo of illumination" (K 71). The body is perfected, not left behind.

Third, Lalleśwarī actively preaches against harsh asceticism, which only stifles the processes of perception and pulls one away from one's true nature. She scolds others for harming the body: "You have cut your own skin and fastened it with pegs / What have you sown to reap a rich harvest?" (K 16). By contrast, she advises, "Let it not suffer from hunger or thirst; / Take care of the body" (K 34). She also criticizes those who roam afar to find what is closer than themselves:

> The wandering *sannyasin* goes from shrine to shrine
> seeking Him who abides within his own self.
> Knowing the truth lose not the way, O Mind,
> when from the distance you see the turf look green.
> *(K 107)*

Because the Self is within, it is futile to seek it in the places of others. Instead, she gives the advice to "stay as you are" (K 108).

Finally, her teaching of *sahaj* fosters practices of moderation. Attention to the genuine needs of the body is the best course: "Only such clothes are helpful as ward off cold. / Such food alone is beneficial as can appease hunger" (K 33). She elaborates:

> Eating too much will lead you nowhere,
> not eating will make you conceited.
> Be moderate in eating and you will become even minded.
> Because of moderation the gates will be unbolted to you.
> *(K 27; cf. K 25)*

If one fails to care for the body, all other religious observances are for naught. Instead, practices should accord with our nature, which is rooted in divine consciousness. For the flowers used in traditional Hindu ceremonies, therefore, one should simply offer heart, will, and faith (K 69); and for the water, one should pour out contemplation of the self (K 120).[21] In sum, "He who ... constantly meditates on Śiva with devotion / . . . That is the natural [*sahaza* (O 84)] form of worship" (K 67).

Contrary to Odin's reading, then, Lalleśwarī is fully in line with her Kashmir Śaiva tradition, which sees no reason to deny pleasures such as eating or sexual relationships, because all of these desires mirror the movement of ultimate consciousness. As difficult as it can be to realize the Self within the self, it is as close as the breath or the flicker of thought. *Sahaj* is the rule for discovering the nature of the Self. Natural physical needs and desires are windows into our very nature and so should not be suppressed. Heroic abstention only increases attachment to the false self and snuffs out the very processes that reveal the Self in us: thought, language, perception. Hedonistic indulgence feeds the delusion that the body is all that we are (cf. K 60). The antidote to both unhealthy obsessions is not mortification of the body, but a view that simultaneously elevates it and removes it from the center. Lalleśwarī summarizes her teaching on the body: "O embodied one, should you be too much obsessed with your body, / . . . / of this body not even ashes will endure" (K 31).

Lalleśwarī's legacy repels charges of unhealthy mind-body dualism. Not only is her anthropology radically plural rather than dualistic, but her practical teachings aim for moderation. She recognizes the human temptation to identify solely with outward name and form; but instead of rejecting those markers, she elevates the body by employing them in practices conducive to liberation. Seekers must look inside, not suppressing the workings of mind and body, but observing them as a model of the Self's dynamic activity. Religious disciplines are, therefore, not only a means of transcendence; they also become miniature enactments of the activity of divine consciousness in the world.

MECHTHILD'S PRACTICES

If Lalleśwarī proves to be not much of an ascetic after all, Mechthild's case is more difficult. One of my colleagues, a scholar of medieval Christian women, often comments to me how miserable Mechthild seems, and how much of her misery appears to derive from her ascetic practices. Mechthild writes of their effects: "In twenty years the time never came that I was not weary, weak, and sick—mostly from repentance and suffering, but also from holy longing and spiritual toil and, in addition, many a difficult day of sickness from my nature" (*FL* 4.2). She prescribes an ascetic regimen, advising that under his regular dress a good cleric "should wear coarse clothing to combat the various pleasures he has received in his skin" and keep "two switches next to his bed to chastise himself upon awakening" (6.2). Mechthild is undeniably an ascetic; we must, therefore, inquire whether her asceticism entails a derogatory view of the body.

A deep mistrust of physical nature seems to be behind Mechthild's austerities—in one hyperbolic passage, she narrates her journey in terms of collecting weapons to employ against the body (4.2). Upon examination of her reasoning for her ascetic lifestyle, however, we see that she has in view a deeper problem: passions or spiritual habits such as anger and lust that enthrall the soul. For example, she observes retrospectively that anger "consumed our strength and dried out our flesh, and . . . wasted our valuable time when we should have been serving God" (7.3). So intractable are these unholy attitudes that, Mechthild teaches, it can become necessary to "do violence to yourself" in order to drive them out (7.3). It feels like violence to wrench ourselves away from the passions that consume us; yet it is the only remedy if we want to return to health.

In these disciplines, Mechthild is not advocating punishment of the body but the purification of the whole person. In fact, she often shows concern for the body's well-being. She directs religious superiors to ensure that the community has plenty of good food: "For a starving cleric does not sing well. Also, a hungry man cannot study with concentration" (6.1). Moderation balances penance. She advises the cleric with the switches next to his bed to retain modest comforts such as woolen blankets, pillows, "simple, comfortable clothes," and "honest servants in proportion to his rightful needs" (6.2). Overly scrupulous individuals can become addicted to discipline; Mechthild wants Christians to employ it to its proper end, and no further.

Despite Mechthild's relative moderation and laudable spiritual goals, my colleague is correct in noticing the strikingly central role of suffering in Mechthild's view of the Christian life. Mechthild goes as far as to comment, "That suffering is very profitable which a person *inflicts upon himself* for the love of God after seeking counsel" (5.2, emphasis added). Before we chalk this statement up to a strange religious masochism, we must locate it within Mechthild's rather extensive analysis of the sources of suffering in the Christian life.

At one level, suffering *is* self-inflicted. It comes, in part, with the consequences of one's actions: Mechthild writes, "In all that I suffer I am guilty" (2.24); and in her descriptions of hell and purgatory, the punishment always fits the crime (3.21). The other part of self-inflicted suffering consists of active practices of purgation such as the restriction of pleasures like food, sleep, and sex. It can be painful to uproot harmful habits, and our natural aversion to pain impedes such disciplines. But the difficulty we experience, Mechthild tells us, is beneficial: it "purifies a person of his many sins, . . . protects us from a future fall, . . . [and] "makes us worthy to receive God's favor" (5.2).

The soul's love relation with God is a second source of distress. As discussed in chapter 2, Mechthild's experiential cycles run from ecstasy to abasement and back again, for neither body nor soul can survive the overwhelming divine presence for long. The burning love of God purges the powers of the soul in preparation for union. After being caught up to the third heaven like Paul, Mechthild expresses surprise that she could yet "remain a living person" (2.24). God avers that the line between rapture and death is rather delicate:

> No matter how softly I caress you,
> I inflict immense pain on your poor body.
> If I were to surrender myself to you continuously, as you desire,
> I would lose my delightful dwelling place on earth within you.
> For a thousand bodies cannot fully satisfy the longings of a soul in love.
> *(2.25)*

Rapture feels like death to the body, and the unquenched longing arising from divine absence intensifies the soul's pain (3.10; 7.8). These themes follow the tropes of the courtly love poetry of Mechthild's day, in which a knight suffers and longs for his lady from afar. Dangerous liaisons, death from loving, deathlike parting—the lover experiences passion as anguish at every turn. Although with time and purification Mechthild becomes more at home in these states, she knows both agony and ecstasy until she dies (see 7.63).

A third type of suffering, innocent suffering from persecution by human or diabolical others, enables the soul to identify with the innocent suffering of Christ. Mechthild encounters her fair share of opposition in her life as a beguine. Comparing this with the first type of suffering (from oneself), she writes:

> But that suffering is much nobler and more useful which God inflicts upon us by means of his enemies or his friends, since he is nobler than all tormentors. Christ did not redeem us with the pain that he inflicted upon himself; rather, he taught us how we should serve him in toil and suffering. (5.2)

Christ's suffering was primarily, for Mechthild, the result of human resistance to his message. Here she subtly departs from a tradition claiming that the Father directly willed the excruciating death of the Son as a means to redemption. For her, Christ's mission was completed not with his execution, but with the postmortem piercing of his heart that unblocked the flow of divine love to humanity (6.24). Suffering is a fact of existence in this world, which neither he nor anyone else could avoid. Christ's example enables Mechthild to make sense of experiences of persecution, loneliness, and anguish. There is no need for her to seek out opportunities to struggle. She *already* suffers, and she gains solace in finding her Beloved in that very place. She can persevere in difficult practices with the confidence that even the negative responses of others are part of the process by which God conforms her to Christ's example.

Ultimately the three types of suffering fit under the rubric of the imitation of Christ. Mechthild's ultimate goal of union with Christ places her asceticism in continuity with other bodily practices such as her devotion to the Eucharist, which also unites her with God's body (see 2.4 for a remarkable vision born of her longing to attend mass when ill). She eagerly treads the "path . . . that God himself trod" (1.25) in every aspect of her religious life: she is "brought to trial in confession, struck blows by penance, . . . crucified in voluntary withdrawal from all things, nailed to the cross by the holy virtues," and so on (1.29). In all of these practices, Mechthild meets Christ in his passion.

All of Mechthild's physical disciplines participate in a trajectory that returns to the heart of God. The bodies of Christ and Mary initiate this return and embody the restorative stream of life to the soul. In a vision that places the flowing breasts of Mary together with Christ's wounded side, she writes:

> Both his wounds and her breasts were open.
> The wounds poured forth.
> The breasts flowed.
> The soul was invigorated and completely restored
> As he poured the sparkling red wine
> Into her red mouth.
>
> *(1.22)*

Christ's wounds give birth to the soul, but Mechthild praises Mary for nursing each Christian according to their need: "the hearts of martyrs with strong faith, the ears of confessors with holy protection, the virgins with your chastity, widows with constancy, married people with kindness, and sinners with patient hope" (1.22). Such physical disciplines are integral to the rising and sinking journey of the soul to God, which is accomplished through the agency of flowing *bodies*.

Mechthild is clearly an ascetic insofar as she curtails her physical pleasures and seeks out ways to suffer with Christ, yet her somatic theology pushes beyond common characterizations of Christian asceticism as world- and body-denying. Mechthild's God is always becoming flesh. Humanity exists in the second person of the Trinity for all eternity. Christ took on a particular body, and this incarnation elevates embodied humanity above the angels in the cosmic hierarchy. Bread and wine become the body of God, to mingle with our bodies in the sacrament. God is madly in love with lovers with bodies and transforms their senses to better take in the divine presence. Despite human limitations for absorbing the divine flow in this life, bodies have a great capacity for divinity, and they expand those powers through concrete practices. Far from utterly devaluing the world and punishing the body, Mechthild longs to praise God with and for them, even beyond what they can sustain in this life.

Mechthild and Lalleśwarī clearly have differing approaches to the role of the body in religious practices. They both employ disciplines that help them reach their physiospiritual goals; but while Lalleśwarī eschews extreme deprivations, Mechthild sustains a genuine (and to many contemporary readers, troubling) ascetic program. This is not a mere difference of opinion, and I suggest that the deeper sources of the discrepancy can be found if we attend to their theological metaphors of fluidity. To this point, their currents of procession and return have run alongside one another: God overflows into worldly creation, and selves that bear the divine image or nature can flow back to their source. When we reach the juncture of their religious practices, however, their fluid imagery divides: we shall see that Mechthild courses on with watery metaphors, while Lalleśwarī converts to airy metaphors of breath. These subtle differences in their fluid theologies invite multiple ways of negotiating the tensions inherent to a somatic theology.

NARRATIVES OF THE BODY: *JĪVANMUKTI*

Both narratives of the body begin with conflict and move into a period of training through spiritual practices. What do all these practices accomplish? In the end, do body and soul *dis*integrate from one another, as we suspected? The techniques we have surveyed demonstrate keen attention to the capacities of the body and a concentrated effort to develop these faculties beyond their initial, conflictual state; but such practices might still be oriented against the body if they aim to leave the physical state behind or if they equate it symbolically with suffering. When we pick up the women's narratives and follow them through to the end, we find that the practitioner is destined not for disintegration but for a perfected state that Hindus know as *jīvanmukti* and Christians as divinization.

According to legend, when Lalleśwarī reached old age, she visited the newly born saint Nund Rishi. The infant was refusing to nurse. She scolded him: "You were not ashamed of coming into the world; why do you shy away from sucking your mother's breast?"[22] Even as a baby, the saint was wise; but in his infancy he grasped only half the truth. He knew that the deluded ego can become falsely identified solely with the body and its birth, death, thoughts, and senses. A mature point of view would realize the other half of the truth about the body: the world, the body, and its needs are nothing to be despised. If a saint thinks he is too pure to nurse from his mother's breast, he still has much to learn.

Lalleśwarī teaches that the untrained mind and body cannot fulfill their potential. She employs several striking metaphors to impress upon her pupils the necessity of instruction:

> For a wooden bow I got an arrow of rush grass, and
> an unskilled architect for this royal mansion.
> In the midst of a market place I became a shop without [a] lock.
> I am left without a preceptor, who can realize my plight?
>
> *(K 4)*

Without the means to tie, build, lock, or firm up its faculties, the body loses its inherent integrity. But the practices she proposes—attention to the breath, chanting the Oṃ syllable, moderation in all things—avail the seeker of the means to attain *jīvanmukti*, liberation (*mukti*) while living (*jīvan*).²³

For Lalleśwarī, "Those who have experienced the bliss of consciousness / and the light of knowledge are liberated while alive" (K 118). Knowledge that one *already* shares the nature of Śiva is all that one requires to become liberated while alive and thereby escape the bondage of birth and rebirth. Thus she can claim, "No one will die to me and to none shall I die. / Alike for me are life and death" (K 104). One need not wait for liberation at the point of death to abandon limited identification with name and form and to be freed of the fetters of separation and transmigration.

How can this be, given the role of the body in perpetuating separate identities? Andrew Fort unravels the paradox of embodied liberation by clarifying that "ignorance, not . . . the body," binds souls to transmigration: liberation is a way of viewing the self, not the absence of a body.²⁴ Paul Muller-Ortega traces the development of *jīvanmukti* as a Kashmir Śaiva concept, including a detailed explanation of seven stages of the soul's experience as the individual rises through the various cosmic points of view (*tattva*s) from a liberated perspective.²⁵ We have seen that because the individual consciousness (*cit*) expands to realize its share in Śiva's own awareness (*caitanya*), Lalleśwarī is able to view the world from many degrees of subject-object duality. *Jīvanmukti*, then, refers to a number of stages of realization of unity and difference, through which Lalleśwarī moves fluidly. For the *jīvanmukta* in her tradition, the sole advantage of death is that the last traces of karma, which tie a person to an individual body, finally run their course. After complete merger with Śiva, one possesses the entire universe for one's body.

Lalleśwarī's realization of the unity of all consciousness—"I am that and that and that and that" (K 73, my trans.)—underpins her teaching of *sahaj*, the simple and natural life in which every act becomes religious ritual:

> Whatever I did became worship of the Lord,
> what my tongue pronounced became mantra.
> Whatever the body experienced became [Tantric practice]
> leading to the realization of . . . Śiva.
>
> *(K 138)*²⁶

> Laughing, sneezing, coughing, yawning,
> always bathing in holy waters,
> roaming naked throughout the year,
> He is within easy reach, recognize Him.
> *(K 84)*

Commenting on a similar passage in *Vijñānabhairava Tantra* 118, Jaideva Singh explains that in sneezing (or as Lalleśwarī adds, coughing, yawning, or laughing), "the ordinary normal consciousness receives a sudden jolt or shock, [and] it is thrown back to its inmost depth and comes in contact with *spanda*, the pulsation of the deepest consciousness, the source of his being."[27] Sudden involuntary acts like laughing alert the practitioner to the dynamic flow of consciousness that is always present, even in ordinary activities.

The results of Lalleśwarī's practices shower down upon the entire person, renewing both body and mind (K 137). According to commentators on the *Spanda Kārikās*, self-realization "preserves the body beyond its normal life span" so that "yogis are free of wrinkles and gray hairs and (their) body is firm."[28] Legends attribute supernatural powers such as unconstrained knowledge, control, and mobility to Lalleśwarī and other accomplished practitioners. The ordering of mind and senses conveys the freedom to do seemingly impossible things (K 55, 63). As the senses open up to the full expanse of consciousness, they perceive everything, directing their awareness anywhere they wish and projecting the occurrences they desire into the objective world.[29]

In the end, when Lalleśwarī has fully trained the mind and senses through her yogic practices, she does not abandon them. These faculties need not be transcended if one recognizes that *every* body is rooted in the power of consciousness. When Lalleśwarī states that this body is known as the Supreme Self (K 32), she proclaims that it is nothing less than divine.

NARRATIVES OF THE BODY: DIVINIZATION

Lalleśwarī provides a vivid sense of the body's potential for manifesting the powers associated with divine consciousness. The Christian tradition on divinization, *theōsis* in Greek, offers parallels insofar as the human being increasingly participates in God.[30] Mechthild's narrative of the estrangement and reconciliation of the body is a basic narrative of creation, fall, and redemption that begins with the creation of the first human beings and concludes in the eschaton. This narrative constructs the framework for ascetic practices; fasting, penance, and hardships contribute to the divinization of the body. Mechthild's visions of the saints in heaven give the clearest picture of the end and goal of the body's narrative in her work. Although full perfection awaits her at the end of time, in the eschaton, the earthly body is not excluded entirely from the soul's progress.

In Mechthild's visions, Mary's body is a promise of the physical divinization promised to all the saints. She bore divinity in her body as no other, and the powerful presence of God in her enabled her to experience pain as but a "shadow" (*FL* 3.4). When the angel appeared to announce her pregnancy, "her senses became full"; and the eternal fire of the Trinity "passed through her whole virginal body into the fiery soul of her devout will, placed itself in the open heart of her most pure flesh, and united itself with all that it found in her" (5.23). Notice that Mary's entire being—soul, body, flesh, and senses—participates in the growth of the incarnate divinity within her. Mechthild writes that "the longer she carried him, the more radiant, beautiful, and wise she became" (5.23); ordinary Christians, too, increase in wisdom and grace until the last day. Divinization is a process that gradually engulfs the whole person.

Bodies are undoubtedly important in Mechthild's narrative. They persist into eternity, marked with the narrative of their return. For instance, Mechthild envisions Jesus in heaven, with "open wounds bloody and unbandaged" that flow "as long as sinning continues on earth" (2.3). The incarnate God will always have a body; but his wounds will heal after the last day, marked with scars like red rose petals that "will never fade" (2.3). The saints, too, retain physical marks of their individuality, bearing like badges the signs of their martyrdom and wearing crowns and cloaks symbolizing the virtues they cultivated on earth.[31]

The bond between body and soul provides for the good of both. For the soul, the body's limitations foster the crucial virtue of humility. Physical asceticism integrally employs the body to remove obstacles to the process of divinization. Sensory reception of "God's body" in the Eucharist further enables "the Holy Spirit [to] make his dwelling in our faith" (4.8). In addition to the spiritual blessings of the body-soul connection, the body benefits as well: "the body gain[s] its share" as "love . . . dissolves through the soul into the senses . . . so that it is refined with respect to all things" (5.4). As love permeates the human person, it trains even the physical body to respond positively to what first feels like deprivation. Thus Mechthild can write toward the end of her book, "when you touch me with your most sublime sweetness that permeates my body and my soul utterly, then I fear that I can draw to myself all too much of your divine pleasure" (7.50). No longer does the body complain of the fire of divine love; instead, it actually fears the vice of overindulgence.

Mechthild's visions constantly evoke sensory experience, describing the appearance, fragrance, and sound of what she encounters therein.[32] By the end of her narrative, her treatment of the senses blurs the distinction between body and soul. Bernard McGinn explains that men and women who used the love poetry in the Song of Songs as a template for the religious life

> stressed the necessity for full human experience, both carnal and spiritual, in the path to union with God [so that] . . . the sensual language of the Song begins to be used more as the referent for what eventually appears as a single "set" of senses, a sensorium, or general activity of sensation, which was to be progressively spiritualized in the mystical life.[33]

In effect, Mechthild's religious practices develop a spiritual sensorium in which not just the eyes and ears *of the soul* but the *physical* senses as well become attuned to God. Although Mechthild occasionally distinguishes between the spiritual and physical senses in order to defend herself against critics who find her visions too carnal (see 6.36), her text as a whole indicates a single sensorium that can develop, expand, and focus on various objects. "The five senses have the power to determine which way they turn" (7.46). When the faculties become impure, crass, and lazy, they shut out spiritual realities and lose the taste for God's sweetness (4.2; 6.4). But when purified and focused in the spirit, God's love "dissolves through the soul into the senses" and refines them "with respect to all things" (5.4).

This sensory matrix takes time to develop. As long as the external senses are overwhelmed in the presence of God, the soul "guides the senses as one with sight guides a blind person" (1.26). Eventually, however, body and soul perceive the same thing. Mechthild calls sensory visions and orations a "second heaven" because they allow sensory access to God's love, but in an inferior manner to the direct contemplation in the "third heaven" that the soul really desires (2.19). At this intermediate stage, she cannot *see* but

> Rather she tastes an indescribable sweetness
> That permeates all her members.
> She hears as well a voice speaking of certain things
> That she really wants.
> For she is still joined to her earthly senses.
>   (2.19)

The soul knows there is more beyond these sweet sensations, and she begins to *see* the light of God when she progresses to the third and highest heaven (cf. 2 Cor. 12:2).

The early strife between soul and body yields to reconciliation in the end. Mechthild ends her work with these conciliatory words: "Ah, dearest prison in which I have been bound, I thank you especially for being obedient to me. Though I was often unhappy because of you, you nevertheless came to my aid. On the last day all your troubles will be taken from you" (7.65). After the body progresses through purification in this life, it temporarily becomes separated from the soul at death, but the body ends with reunion and reward in eternity. The soul then speaks to the body:

> Rise up, my dearly beloved, and be healed of
> All your sufferings,
> All your days of pain,
> All your humiliation,
> All your sadness,

All your loneliness,
All your wounds,
And all your toils.
. . . .
In the past my whole well-being depended on you;
Now all your consolation depends on me.
. . . .
Eternal day has arisen for us.
Now we receive our reward.

(6.35)

From beginning to end, the body-soul nexus *is* the human being. This union is precious to Mechthild, even as she feels its strain during the exile of waiting for its eternal reward at the last day.

Mechthild diverts charges of practical dualism with her incarnational view of the human being, her holistic concept of practice, and the central place she accords to the body in the next life. Mechthild's practices are not means of escaping the body but tools that expand the entire physiospiritual sensorium to participate in the divine life.

COMPARISON: FLUIDITY AND EMBODIMENT

Although diverse cultures interpret bodily experiences in diverse ways, bodily experiences are not entirely determined by these interpretations. Descriptions and analyses of pain and limitation may differ, but these basic unavoidable realities are common to all embodied subjects and provide common ground for cross-cultural conversation. Lalleśwarī and Mechthild can speak to each other, and to us, because they speak to somatic experience. Comparison of their fluid itineraries illuminates two important theological features of embodiment. Where they diverge in their fluid images of breath and water, Lalleśwarī explores the body's capacity for divinity, while Mechthild teaches that somatic suffering is integral to the divine flow of love.

As we have seen, Lalleśwarī flows easily to her divine source once she cultivates yogic practices of the breath. She transposes the terrifying expanses of water that separate her from the Lord into the rivers of the body, the *nāḍīs*, which channel the breath. For Lalleśwarī, divinity is immanent in the devotee. An analysis of this shift from water to breath will draw out its implications for a theological treatment of the body.

For Lalleśwarī, although the cosmos and self flow directly from Lord Śiva, who is an ocean of bliss (K 130), the water metaphors stagnate at the point of the self's return to the divine. Going back to Śiva is like crossing a vast ocean or lake.

> I came by the highway, by the highway I returned not.
> The day failed me midway on the embankment.
> My pockets I searched, not a *cowrie* could I find.
> Ah me! what shall I pay for the ferry fee?
>
> *(K 5)*

Having come from God, the heart longs to cross and go home, but a wide expanse of water separates her from her goal. Lalleśwarī has, apparently, taken the wrong path: the bridge-embankment she has chosen to follow has ended, and it is getting dark. None of her deeds or preparation is sufficient to pay the boatman. She realizes how futile her efforts have become:

> With a rope of untwisted yarn
>   am I towing my boat on the ocean.
> Would that God heard my prayer and
>   ferry me across safely.
> Like water in unbaked plates of clay
>   my efforts are going to waste.
> How I wish I would reach home!
>
> *(K 1)*

In her longing, Lalleśwarī invokes divine grace: *she* cannot pull herself to the other shore, but God has helped others across in the past.

Lalleśwarī surmounts this impasse when she learns to follow her breath. Now the return metaphor straightens out and the flow is restored: "Straight I came and straight shall I return. / . . . / I was known to Him at the very source" (K 26). In the end, the ocean of life proves not to be an obstacle to God, but the very flow of the divine within her. Instead of crossing, towing her boat, or finding the correct bridge, Lalleśwarī finds that lake, boat, and bridge are all inside:

> In the midst of being lost, I lost the sense of being lost[.]
> After being lost I found myself in this worldly ocean[.]
> Laughing and playing, I attained the all-pervading Self[.]
> This philosophy became a part of me.
>
> *(O 29)*

Lalleśwarī's imagery shifts with her experience of the "melting," "dissolving," "mixing," or "merging" of God, world, and self in experiences of union (*mīlith*; K 76, 88, 89, 90, 91, 125, 130). She becomes immersed, merged, or part of (*lay karmas*) Śiva himself (K 99, 102, 130, 133) through practices of the breath.

An ability to transcend suffering follows this shift. Early in her search, she suffers in mind and body due to her estrangement from the divine source

(K 128); but through yogic practice her suffering ceases. The mind trained by yoga can slake the stirrings of hunger and thirst along with "all pairs of opposites such as pleasure and pain, heat and cold, etc. in addition to cravings for sense and pleasure."[34] Lalleśwarī reflects that she could have "cut the bonds of sorrow . . . / Had [she] known how to control the cluster of the *nadis* [*sic*] with the mind" (K 80). She recommends:

> [One] who can control the mind after inhaling
> will not be troubled by hunger and thirst.
> [The one] who can do this up to the end
> is born to create a name in the world.
>
> *(K 51)*

For Lalleśwarī, yogic practice eradicates the suffering imposed by false identification with the bare trappings of bodily existence. In lower states of consciousness, pleasure and pain obscure the purity of consciousness by creating desire and aversion; but the one liberated while alive (*jīvanmukta*) no longer fixates upon such sensations or the injuries inflicted by others (cf. K 40, 42). As a perfected *yoginī*, Lalleśwarī appears to take a rather stoic stance on the suffering body.

Meditation can powerfully reorient a person toward pain; yet spiritual, physical, and environmental conditions render many people unable to transcend pain in this way. In light of such experiences, Mechthild supplements Lalleśwarī's account with an intensely responsive account of physical frailty, mortality, and pain. Mechthild's images never stop flowing because suffering is a major tributary in the flow of redeemed humanity. We have seen that suffering has many causes for the beguine. Like Lalleśwarī, Mechthild teaches that the body suffers because of "the weakness of its external senses, because it has not yet been transformed by death"; but she adds the further insight that these pains humble the soul so it will be "fully grown in virtues and holiness" (5.4). Though she, too, undertakes physical disciplines, she teaches that the difficulties of practice and of embodied existence in general constitute a participation in the flowing love of God.

Mechthild views suffering as integral to the patterning of the flow of risk, relation, and reconciliation. Both consolation and suffering, blissful meetings with God and painful periods of separation—these are necessary parts of the economy of flow. For her, as inevitable by-products of the soul's relationship with God and others, days of suffering are as valuable as moments of bliss. Mechthild illustrates this with a vision in which God offers two chalices, one filled with "the red wine of suffering," and the other with "the white wine of sublime consolation" (2.7). The blessed develop a palate for the bitter as well as the sweet.[35]

The flow of love in *all* of its moments, its rising and its sinking, draws humanity into the divine life. Mechthild phrases this dynamic as through paradoxes:

> The less she becomes, the more flows to her.
> ....
> The greater the distress in which they part, the more he bestows upon her.
> *(1.22)*

The embodied soul imitates the divinity that flows downhill:

> God knows, this is what happens to the soul and also to the body. The soul, rich in love, sinks downward under the pull of profound humility and constantly retreats from what God does to her out of love. . . . The body, too, sinks far down when it serves its enemy, obeys without complaint, and avoids its friends to God's honor. (5.4)

Mechthild does not identify the body's functions of sense and perception with those of God as Lalleśwarī does, but she does believe that the physical body participates in the experience of redemption. Despite the suffering of the body, the process of training body and soul benefits both, and both body and soul gain their full reward in eternity as they flow to their final destination.

In their diverging streams of water and breath, Mechthild and Lalleśwarī offer two approaches to the suffering inherent to the human condition: water flows through suffering, while breath sublimates it in a higher reality. Here it is not my intention to set up a new dualism. Suffering should not become the polar opposite of health or well-being. Both theologians acknowledge the lived realities of the embodied condition. Furthermore, neither theologian divides the experience of pain from the realm of divinity, for Mechthild's God takes up this experience directly, while Śiva perceives it alongside all other movements of consciousness. When we consider the implications of these patterns for a contemporary theology of the body below, we must remember that theologies rooted in somatic experience are currents that flow over, around, and through the givenness of embodied reality in diverse ways.

BODY THEOLOGY BEYOND MODERNITY

Today the old hierarchical pairings of soul/body and spirit/matter are being leveled, if not reversed. In reaction to the Cartesian *cogito* (I think) and all of its fallout in modernity, many philosophers and theologians eagerly reclaim the body as inherently good, integral to praxis, and a locus of contact with God. They deny the harmful dualisms that denigrate the material realm and, by association, bodies, women, and others who have been set apart from "rational" humanity. Previously dismissed as inferior to elite men in their traditions, women like Lalleśwarī and Mechthild have much to offer to this conversation.

Accusations of mind-body dualism routinely miss distinctions integral to the practitioner, but a comparative orientation helps to skip the grooves of critiques routinely leveled against religious traditions. Thomas Kasulis notes that the mind-body distinction in the West is not, as many have come to assume, commonsensical: it is a conceptual distinction without a clear ontological basis, which is not shared in many Eastern systems.[36] We are only beginning to reacquaint ourselves with the correlation and overlap of mental and physical events, such as the interplay of mind and body in perception or the somatic effects of strong emotions like fear.

Mechthild and Lalleśwarī resist any anachronistic and overdetermined charges of Cartesian dualism through their plural categories for what today we reduce to mind and body. For Mechthild, human beings can "both ... lose or win" by means of "our natural faculties" (4.3). Soul, body, and senses all exist within a single sensorium that together may participate increasingly in the love of God. Lalleśwarī associates mind with the other physical and mental senses but expands her map of the human faculties to mirror many more levels of divine consciousness. These grammars and narratives of the body offer alternative frameworks for discussion about the capacities of the body.

Critics of asceticism, the discipline of mind and body for a specific (here, religious or spiritual) goal, often locate its motivation in hatred of the body. Mechthild, however, has shown that ascetic practices can signal an intense concern *for* the body and its range of capabilities rather than its mortification. Contemporary theologians are unlikely to prescribe a return to all medieval Christian religious practices, but the positive valuation of the body in such practices opens the door for new embodied ways to experience the divine. Stephanie Paulsell, for example, has offered bathing, exercising, and resting as spiritual practices that respond to contemporary stresses on the body.[37]

Beyond their attentiveness to the body's capabilities, Mechthild and Lalleśwarī push the body to *exceed* its apparent limitations. In particular, Lalleśwarī's expansive concept of the body unites all beings as the Self so that through meditation one may see one's "body as comprising the whole cosmos" (K 72). She attends to the processes of her body and finds Śiva manifest there. Her emphasis on control and restraint of the faculties contains no dichotomization of mind and body: Śiva's consciousness in the individual must be brought under control, just like the mind or heart and the senses. All the faculties are a continuum, reflecting Śiva's manifestation as the increasingly condensed layers of the cosmos. Yoked together through moderation and meditation, the body's components unblock and channel the flow of divine consciousness. Luce Irigaray's retrieval of yogic practices of breath offers one demonstration of the contemporary relevance of these themes.

Although such positive visions of corporeality can augment current theological work on the body, a powerful critique of this renewed celebration of the body has emerged from the standpoint of persons with disabilities. An uncritical affirmation of the good of embodiment can, according to Jackie Leach Scully, "be naïve, oppressive and harmful. Not all embodiment is good." Theology that celebrates disabilities as "gifts," she says, becomes offensive in the face of persons who will have only a brief and obscenely painful lifespan or who will never develop the reflective capacity to appreciate their condition as a gift.[38] The body's potential is not limitless. Incapacitating pain, failure of organs, loss of limbs, and periods of depression are inescapable realities for a significant portion of the world's population. Even the most "healthy" of bodies has limits and will eventually deteriorate and decay.

Theologians engaged in an enthusiastic discursive rehabilitation of the body are often uncomfortable with such reminders. For a movement like feminist theology, which emphasizes wholeness and empowerment, disabled persons

> embody all that the blossoming feminist does not want to be.... Feminists have struggled so long to shake off the association of defilement . . . that they have needed to disassociate and seek independence from aspects of the body and mind which threaten to return them once again to self-negation and disempowerment.[39]

If theologians overlook certain embodied conditions, they will likely arrive at narrow and unrealistic standards. This optimism lends itself to the old model that places blame for disease or disability, either "as punishment for a form of sinful individual behavior, such as poor diet or willful exposure to risk, or sinful collective behavior, such as environmental pollution."[40] Such critiques call for sensitive and inclusive theological treatment of bodily realities.

PREMODERN RESONANCES

Despite their premodern locations, Mechthild and Lalleśwarī exemplify some of the paradoxes of "the body" in discourse that tries to move beyond Cartesian dualism. Unique religious parameters—the suffering Christ in Mechthild and the yogic body in Lalleśwarī—give shape to their wisdom about the body. A comparative approach to these two theologians of embodiment has yielded a complex interplay of somatic possibilities and ambiguities.

Theologians of the body will benefit from apprenticeship to the practices and teachings of Mechthild and Lalleśwarī as alternatives to modernity. In framing this comparison around the imagery of fluidity within parallel patterns of the soul/self's origination and return, differing approaches to pain appear in greater relief. As we have seen, their systems diverge at the point of their metaphors of water and breath. In her desire to imitate Christ, her suffering lover, Mechthild teaches that somatic suffering is integral to the divine flow of love. Informed by Śaiva wisdom relating to the flow of consciousness, Lalleśwarī by contrast cultivates the breath in order to *overcome* suffering and connect with the divine. This point of tension highlights fundamental differences that zealous apostles for the body might otherwise overlook. Comparison might also enable contemporary scholars of embodiment to attend to their exclusions and presuppositions and lead to fruitful interchanges with scholars of disability.

Mechthild affirms the givenness of suffering and uncovers its constructive role in spiritual formation. For her, difficulties are not primarily obstacles but part of her participation in God. Contemporary scholars have similarly proposed that bodily ambiguities can help human beings "to accept our limits and live responsibly within them," to discover "mystery in limits," and to appreciate the diversity within the human community.[41] Lalleśwarī's experience of suffering parallels Mechthild's, both in her social isolation and in her frustrated longing to merge with God, but she is not as willing to accept limits or the differences created by physical constraints. In the idea that yogic practice can end a person's suffering, her teaching resembles the "conflicting message of condemnation, compassion, and incipient Pelagianism" that disabilities scholars identify in contemporary body discourse.[42] Her rather heroic vision transcends suffering and teaches others to do so as well: through praxis one should be able to eliminate pain or at least find the mental fortitude to bear it. Where Lalleśwarī finds obstacles to overcome, Mechthild offers a more inclusive vision that sees all kinds of difficulties as part and parcel of the rising and sinking of desire.

If Mechthild offers a more sensitive diagnosis of the symptoms and causes of the body and soul in pain, Lalleśwarī may be the more skilled physician. Mechthild's views of the profound limitations of the body leave many of its capacities unexplored. The body's worth shines through the figures of Christ and Mary, yet human participation in incarnation and divinization is for her overwhelmingly mired in suffering in this life. By contrast, Lalleśwarī's attention to body and breath helpfully suggests practices that unblock and channel the divine flow. The structure of breath and mind reveals the divine nature. Lalleśwarī says,

> I stopped my breath in the bellows pipe;
> the lamp of knowledge shone bright for me, and
> revealed to me my true identity.
>
> *(K 98)*

In attending to the movement of breath, she observes how life flows through the body. As an advanced practitioner, she realizes that simple (*sahaj*) processes like breath, thought, and sensory perception are none other than the activity of divine consciousness in and through her. In answer to Mechthild, Lalleśwarī assures us of the goodness of the rhythms of the body. She invites us to find our divine source in and through such processes—in short, through our experience.

Together the gifts of these women to each other—Mechthild's careful attention to the reality of suffering of all sorts, and Lalleśwarī's tending of the body as the locus of the divine breath—suggest routes toward a theology that values the body while still taking account of its capacity for pain. Specific contributions from each thinker may supplement one another as gifts to contemporary theologians.

Lalleśwarī's positive configuration of embodied human faculties in relation to the absolute might help comparative readers extrapolate how, as Mechthild writes, the divinized senses "gain . . . [a] share" (*FL* 5.4) of the soul's bliss. In Mechthild's Christian vocabulary, because the soul is the image of God's desire, our experience *is* in some way analogical to God's experience, as the breath mirrors the divine rhythm in Lalleśwarī. The divine link to our suffering is not only the human passion of Christ, but also the Spirit's concomitant perception and comprehension of our experience. We are, in Śaiva parlance, the bodies of the enjoying subject. In our perceptions—be they external, internal, pleasurable, or painful—we experience something of what God experiences in relation to this world; and through humanity, God experiences the creation. Mechthild once wrote, "Lord, between you and me there goes unceasingly an imperceptible breath in which I come to know and see many marvels" (2.24). In response to Lalleśwarī, theologians might work anew with Mechthild's image of "God's breath," which "must draw [us] effortlessly into itself" (4.12) as the *embodied* matrix of the relationality of God and self. The marvel of the divine in common experience, as close as the breath, moving within the body and into the world, might provide the antidote to the world- and body-denying tendencies that worry contemporary readers.

In her attention to suffering, Mechthild keeps our gaze unflinchingly on embodied experience, despite the temptation in Lalleśwarī and many others today to transcend it. Her perspective tempers all uncritical celebration of physicality. The healthy may blithely extol the goodness of the body, the comfortable may easily embrace the environment, and the powerful may profess their respect for women; but the sick, poor, and oppressed *feel* the inconsistencies and blind spots of those who construct these orthodoxies. They know that even salutary beliefs do not always translate into salutary relationships in the world. Eventually everyone comes up against physical limitations. Finitude brings with it sickness, loss, and death—what Rita Gross calls "an irreducible suffering . . . that is simply a constituent of being human."[43] Mechthild's otherworldly longing gives voice to the dissonance between her relation to divinity and the world's forceful denial of it; she validates the longing in Lalleśwarī's verses without hoping to escape hardship.

These two women buttress their divergent solutions to the difficulties of embodied existence with differing emphases on divinity and humanity in the body of the practitioner. The figure of Christ illustrates for Mechthild how God's experience intersects with *human* experience. In his suffering, we recognize ours. Lalleśwarī's religious heritage affirms that the "impurities" (*malas*) in the individual are nevertheless the material form of the *divine* body. Lalleśwarī's teachings can help those in Mechthild's tradition to see more clearly that embodiment itself is divine insofar as divine consciousness and love flow through it. Lalleśwarī expresses the body's divinity through a technical vocabulary of the yogic body that is lacking in Christianity. Even so, Mechthild's tradition can make more room for the divinization of the body through bliss as well as hardship. Together these theologians illuminate how the body and its suffering are caught up in the flow connecting humanity to God, and how the body itself is the site of procession from and return to divinity. Their fluid theologies negotiate a tension between the facticity of pain and the horizon of desire that remains acute in discourse on the body today.

CONCLUSION

When we move past a dualistic view of the human person, we discover that the world's religious traditions contain complex, often multilayered views of the human faculties. Medieval Christianity and Kashmir Śaivism fashion a range of physical, mental, and spiritual capacities that shade into one another while remaining immersed in the divine. Contrary to the Cartesian paradigm, at no point in these thinkers does the mind take precedence: for Lalleśwarī, mind is but one of the sensory faculties; for Mechthild, the soul and its senses are always embodied. If we take this wisdom seriously, we might revise the binary categories of mind and body that seem so natural to us in modernity. We might begin to catch ourselves when we habitually employ this pairing.

Perhaps we ought to coin new terminology that reflects *more* than two components and that represents distinctions as well as the overlap between them.

For Mechthild and Lalleśwarī, the flow of divinity to the human being is all-pervasive; yet together these theologians honor the many ways the flow can be blocked. Hence, moving beyond dualism to a range of differences opens up new pitfalls, including the possibility of an uncritical celebration of the body that alienates some people. As Nancy Eiesland observes, "The corporeal is for people with disabilities the most real."[44] If the body is to become more than a discursive construct, theologians must listen to people with all kinds of bodies. The next chapter takes up the importance of human difference in the context of the lived effects of dualism on people on the underside of dualistic hierarchies such as race, class, gender, sexuality, and ability.

5

Flowing Out to Others

> You are me, I am you; I did not understand this meeting.
> Who are You, who am I? I have doubt.
> *Lalleśwarī of Kashmir (K 129, my trans.)*

> ... *in the beginning*, I am my relation to you ...
> *Judith Butler*[1]

None among us is one. As I write this chapter, another life is taking shape inside me. My pregnant body is one-becoming-two.[2] In a fluid exchange of blood, water, and nutrients, I in-fluence this fetus and it in-fluences me: *This is my body; this is my blood.* The astonishing primary relation in which we all begin does not end with our birth. We remain fundamentally part of one another through myriad patterns of influence.

That I exist in *this* body, at *this* place and time, is one of the fundamental ways I receive my identity from outside myself. I did not choose my race or gender, and I cannot control the meanings and expectations that society places on these identity markers. I do not will any abuse or trauma that might befall me, but it too becomes part of who I am. Psychoanalysts have theorized how even some of the most basic drives and desires are imprinted in infancy.[3] If so much of who and what I am is determined by others, then whatever my self is cannot be spoken of in isolation from these others.

In light of this radical interconnectedness, Judith Butler has suggested that rather than base ethics in the notion of the individual, rational subject, we instead begin from "a difficult and intractable, even sometimes unbearable relationality: . . . a common vulnerability, a common physicality and risk."[4] We saw in the last chapter that the vulnerability of body-soul links us all.

Dualistic habits—the longing for heaven over earth, the neglect of the body for some "higher" faculty, the severance of one from relation to the other—all try to overcome this vulnerability. Instead, they cut off the vital flow of relation. Racial segregation, gender apartheid, hate crimes, and genocide are only some of the more stunning ways human beings try to shore up themselves against our common fragility. In this chapter, we shall inquire of our premodern interlocutors whether they can offer more salutary patterns of relationship.

The theological issues examined in the previous chapters derive their urgency from the lived experience of dualistic self-other relationships. Scholars grapple with the metaphysical and practical implications of binary thought patterns because God's symbolic alliance with spirit, mind, and the masculine appears to authorize the subordination of matter, body, and the feminine. Most historical oppressions can be traced to dualistic thought patterns through what Val Plumwood calls "linking postulates," "assumptions normally made or implicit in the cultural background which create equivalences or mapping between the pairs."[5] Ecological, gender, and class dualisms do seem to share a common and interrelated pattern of binary logic. We shall have to ask not only how intractable the links between various dualisms are, but also whether there might be some other logic. Need difference between God and the world, for example, imply the subordination of body to mind or of women to men? And as we pursue a more fluid logic of relation, must we refrain entirely from recognizing and evaluating differences altogether? Must we embrace, as the only alternative to a separative logic, a slippery, soluble mode of dependency that prevents persons from developing fully as agents?

The lives of persons on the margins can be the basis for thinking differently about difference. Pamela Sue Anderson has argued that the practice of retelling such stories inspires new imitations and performances of their challenge to dominant norms. The knowledge we gain when we "think from the lives of the marginalized others" engenders the "imperative—to reinvent ourselves as other."[6] As I discuss below, one response to reading self-other relations from the margins through the lives and teachings of Lalleśwarī and Mechthild is to think with, act like, and become more receptive to such others.

LALLEŚWARĪ ON THE MARGINS

Kashmiri legends preserve a good deal of what people found remarkable about Lalleśwarī, even if they cannot grant unobstructed access to her experience. We may read them for points of disjunction between the human relations she sought and those she experienced.

Although the earliest legends say nothing of Lalleśwarī's upbringing or her family of origin, contemporary hagiographers make a special point to insist that her father's home was a place of learning and piety, in which she "had gained a fair measure of publicity even before she had married."[7] This narrative strategy helps to integrate Lalleśwarī into the Kashmir Śaiva mainstream by placing the blame for her later rejection on her husband's family. Some even posit that "her husband was a follower of the left-handed [tantric] order, . . . in which wine and flesh were freely made use of," and that Lalleśwarī opposed these practices.[8] Her opposition to difficult and extreme means to liberation in some of her verses (cf. K 89–90) is taken as the context for her difficulties in her marital home, so that the majority of "right-handed" practitioners effectively escape scrutiny in the hagiographies (but see K 68–70, 78).

What is certain is that Lalleśwarī faced opposition in her husband's home. She was ill-treated by her mother-in-law, who starved her by giving her only a stone covered with a thin layer of rice. Each day, without complaint, Lalleśwarī ate her rice and washed and returned the stone.[9] The older woman also insinuated to her son that Lalleśwarī's long periods of meditation were actually spent in infidelity. One morning, when she was returning from her morning devotions at the river, the jealous husband became so enraged that he struck the pitcher of water she carried on her head. It shattered, but the water miraculously stayed in place until she calmly poured it into the household vessels. When she threw the rest out, it pooled to form a famous lake.[10] At this turning point, she left her home for good, to wander nude as a renouncer in search of God. Although many scorned and abused her, others remembered her teachings in form of pithy vernacular sayings (*vaakh*s).

This basic narrative indicates at very least that Lalleśwarī was at odds with parts of her religious tradition. Her early devotional experience culminates with being thrust—by choice forged of necessity—outside the threshold of the Kashmir Śaiva household. Kotru attributes her renunciation to all the attention she gained because of the water miracle. She could no longer hide her spiritual powers and "did not like to make an exhibition" of them.[11] Indeed, Lalleśwarī views people who are attached to exercising such powers as frauds (K 112); but it is odd that the hagiographies gloss over the dangers to her person. The violence of her home setting points to the crucial way in which her pursuit of Kashmir Śaiva ideals as a woman paradoxically puts her on the margins of her tradition.

Lalleśwarī's departure from her home is all the more striking because of Kashmir Śaivism's distinctive relationship to the household. Unlike the Vedic pattern of four stages of life in which the last is the abandonment of all ties to family and society (*sannyāsa*), in the Kashmir Śaiva tradition of liberated sainthood, this renunciation is unnecessary. By Lalleśwarī's time, Kashmir Śaivism had become the practice of householders rather than wandering ascetics.[12] Lalleśwarī affirms that regardless of one's external situation, one can remain awake to one's true identity, "even if attending worldly affairs night and day" or engaging in the "householders' active life" (K 110, 111). There is no contradiction for an adept to carry out social, familial, and even Vedic ritual duties if he or she views all things in light of the ultimate consciousness of Śiva.[13]

Despite this orthodox norm, the option of remaining within the household is not available to Lalleśwarī. Theoretically, Lalleśwarī should have been able to reconcile her life as a wife and devotee like the male householders; but she is unable to live out her ideal of liberated relations in a situation where her mother-in-law torments her, her husband vents his anger violently, and her parents' home is no longer open to her. After the water miracle, it cannot be clearer that there is no place for her intense piety and meditative practice within the household system. She leaves her husband's home to wander unkempt and naked, like the renunciants her tradition eschews.

Paradoxically, Lalleśwarī's disruption of the householder life as a female renouncer, though unorthodox, offers a window into an undercurrent of ambivalence toward social institutions in her tradition. Gavin Flood cites a "truly creative dynamic in which Śaiva values are embedded in social institutions, such as caste and kingship, while simultaneously undermining those values." In keeping with the iconoclasm of Śiva's mythology "as family man and vagabond, as form and formless, and as transcendence and immanence,"[14] Lalleśwarī's mastery of her tradition puts pressure on its gender, religious, and class boundaries.

In terms of gender, the householder life enjoyed by most male practitioners in this tradition is untenable for her. She also eschews another religious option open to her, the intensified rituals of Tantric initiates involving "left-handed" rites. The initiation and rituals outlined in Tantric texts require a specific set of obligations and abilities (*adhikāra*) designed for the *male* practitioner. Female practitioners (*yoginīs* or *dūtīs*) appear almost exclusively as conduits of the goddess to a male partner in esoteric sexual rites of the Kaula branch of the tradition. Lalleśwarī may have been qualified to be such a partner,[15] but her verses reflect a view that the difficulty of such rituals distract from a simpler (*sahaj*) path and the higher goals of Śiva consciousness (cf. K 60–61, 89).

Beyond her transgression of the gender roles open to her, Lalleśwarī pushes specifically religious boundaries when she passes along her teachings in the vernacular. She fits comfortably nowhere in her religious milieu; and while she *may* have undergone initiation into Śaiva doctrine and ritual after cultivating the appropriate yogic disciplines, she certainly does not view insider status as necessary for liberation. Initiates "would certainly not approve [that] she spoke of the secret doctrine and its disciplines to all and sundry, disregarding the strict injunctions in behalf of *adhikārabheda*, in the vulgar tongue of the unlettered masses."[16] She liberally dispenses knowledge to everyone, regardless of their qualifications.

The intersection of class and gender appears in Lalleśwarī's particular choice to wander as a *nude* renunciant. When she leaves, she rejects the comforts of a stable home. Outside of these constraints, her bare physicality threatens male social control of her circumstances. Popular Śaiva traditions in the south of India, affirmed in a commentary by the Kashmir Śaiva theologian Kṣemarāja, state that demons attack people in vulnerable situations such as

> women when naked, who have bathed after menstruation, who are filled with passion, intoxicated, pregnant, or prostitutes. . . . That is, possession happens to those who are or are potentially outside of social control, as women's sexuality was perceived to be by the male-oriented Śaiva Brahmanism.[17]

Women's bodies and sexuality are perennially problematic for religious traditions, and Lalleśwarī's behavior forces this confrontation.

That Lalleśwarī's self-attested nakedness distresses commentators is evidenced by exegetical attempts to "cover up" her body. J. L. Kaul creatively interprets her statement "Naked I began to dance" (K 21; O 15): he would translate the word *natsun* (to dance) as "to wander," and read *nangay* (naked) as a corruption of the word for "mountain flower."[18] Her transgressions are literally covered over in twentieth-century artistic depictions. In one, Lalleśwarī's naked body modestly covers itself: her hair covers her breasts, and her stomach sags downward to cover her pubic area (one etymology for her name is related to *lal*, stomach[19]). In another rendition, excerpts from her own text are plastered over her midsection from neck to knees. Thus, when her admirers look at her, the wisdom of her *vaakh*s, not her body, is her defining feature.[20] The concern to cover up Lalleśwarī's body suggests that her dissent in relation to gender, religion, and class remains on the margins of her tradition even now, when she herself is incorporated as a saint.

LALLEŚWARĪ'S TEACHINGS ON RELATION

Given Lalleśwarī's dissent regarding social hierarchies of gender, class, and religion, one might assume that she advocates and practices absolute equality in her relationships with others. Several aspects of her teaching support this assumption. Lalleśwarī describes the definitive moment in her life as the moment when she turned away from certain external circumstances, including "social decorum and external appearance," as Kotru puts it, toward her inward search:[21]

> My guru gave me this one precept:
> "Withdraw your gaze from without,
> and concentrate on the self within."
> That became the turning point in Lalla's life,
> and naked I began to dance.
>
> *(K 21)*

What Lalleśwarī finds within her changes the nature of her relationships with others. She sees "the one inside fellow beings" (K 58). All are one body (*yekuy deh* [O 22]): "You are [me] and I am you, and both are one" (K 129).

Because she is an accomplished *yoginī* with the ability to remember past lives, Lalleśwarī has special insight into the threads connecting people. One legend relates that when in a previous life she gave birth to a son, she posed a riddle to the family priest: "How is the newborn baby related to me?" When the priest responded that it was her son, she told him that she would soon die and be reborn in a certain village as a horse with certain marks. He was to seek her there after a year and learn the true answer. When this happened, she told the priest that she soon would be reborn as a dog in a certain place. This pattern continued for six births, and in the seventh she was reborn into her original family. She grew up, and at her marriage she whispered to the priest: "The boy who was born to me in a previous birth . . . is the bridegroom here." Lalleśwarī's new husband had been her son in a previous life.[22] The legend offers a big-picture view into the deep and enduring connections between human beings: we are related and connected at deeper levels than we know.

Beyond these abiding ties, all human beings are equal in their nature as Śiva. Her encouragement to see "the one inside fellow beings" troubles the exclusions of gender, class, and religion discussed above: if the one Self resides in all, she asks, "What then is the inhibition in eating" with people from different backgrounds (K 58)? Religious boundaries have proved to be particularly challenging since the advent of Islam in Kashmir in the mid-fourteenth century, but for Lalleśwarī, it matters little how one names the divine. She prays, "*Śiva, Keśava, Buddha*, or the lotus-born Lord—whatever the name—may he cure me of the sickness of birth and death" (K 73). She ranks the Islamic faith alongside other paths to God:

> Śiva abides in all that exists anywhere.
> Do not discriminate between a Hindu and a Musalman.
> If you be wise recognize your true self;
> that is the true knowledge of God.
>
> *(K 57)*

Although the Hindu and Muslim communities would become more polarized in later generations, Lalleśwarī's inclusive attitude remains a countervailing force for those who remember her.[23]

The interconnectedness and equality of all human beings do not negate the embodied differences upon which daily life depends. Equality in essential nature does not dictate sameness in society. Human differences can be corralled and put to use for the good of all. This is a second meaning to Lalleśwarī's saying:

> Alas! the five, the ten and the eleventh
> scraped this pot and went away.
> Had they all come and pulled the rope together
> why should the eleven have lost the cow?
> *(K 6)*

Śiva's differentiated consciousness that "I am this" creates the possibility for relatedness at the level of human community. Just as the gross elements, the sense organs, the organs of action, and the mind can be harnessed in meditation, society can possess the "cow" of mutual flourishing, which escapes when members work at cross-purposes. When each regards "others as [one's] own self" (K 132) in relationships rooted in mutual recognition of the flow of divine consciousness, persons overcome greed and pride and do good to others (K 34, 36).

NOT ALL HIERARCHY IS DUALISM

The mutual recognition of Śiva's nature in everyone challenges the dualistic hierarchies of gender, class, and religion that would deny this principle; yet people are not "equal" in every way. Lalleśwarī's reverence for the guru-disciple relationship illustrates how some hierarchies can be helpful.

Lalleśwarī attests, "O my guru, you are to me . . . the Supreme Lord" (K 95). You may recall that her tradition carefully orders the many layers of Śiva's self-differentiation in the universe from the subtle to the material, and that each of these layers (*tattva*s) can be an important vantage point from which to understand reality. The accomplished practitioner, like Śiva himself, masters the wisdom of each gradation of the cosmos and teaches it to others. In this capacity, the guru "becomes the embodiment of tradition, reveals the supreme, liberating truth (*tattva*) to the disciple, . . . and reveals the structure of the hierarchical cosmos."[24] Thus, even as guru and disciple come to realize one another as forms of the same divine consciousness, a degree of hierarchy based on this mastery endures in the teaching relationship.

Lalleśwarī moves by phases from elementary tutelage to full recognition. At first, when she has difficulty holding on to the guru's teaching, she feels like a shepherdless flock with a propensity to stray (K 23). Only this particular teacher can give her the guidance she needs:

> The flesh of my soles wore away on the roads . . .
> The one showed me the way to the One.
> Lalla chose one word out of a hundred. . . .
> (K 87)

In the beginning of their relationship, there is a clear sense of difference between the enlightened teacher and the disciple; but "at the highest level of practice the Master infuses this awareness into the disciple directly and he [sic] rises in an instant to the recognition that he and the Master are one."[25] The guru's advice for Lalleśwarī to look inside herself leads her to find universal consciousness as well as her own voice.

Liberated relations make hierarchies fluid. When Lalleśwarī masters the teacher's insights, she becomes a guru to others: "I preached to others and practiced myself" (K 47). On occasion she even instructs her own guru. According to the hagiographies, Lalleśwarī's guru once returns from his bath to find her scrubbing the outside of a pot filled with dirt—an object lesson for him on the folly of washing the body when the inner self is impure. Another time, having glimpsed the direction of his thoughts during meditation, she chides him for letting them stray.[26] The hierarchy of guru and disciple is that of the fully conscious teacher to one who has yet to discover one's own consciousness; it is a gift of relation that empowers the recipient to give in return.

Lalleśwarī's position as a woman indicates, however, that even the guru-disciple relationship, the most salutary relationship for someone seeking liberation, faces gender constraints. Because the Kashmir Śaiva tradition places great stock in tracing the spiritual genealogies of each of its teachers to the founding of the tradition, one might expect to have more information on Lalleśwarī's guru and disciples.[27] The bulk of such attempts are of fairly recent date. Kotru names Lalleśwarī's preceptor as Siddha Śrīkantha, a man "descended in direct lineage from Vasugupta, the founder of Kashmir Śaivism in its present form."[28] However, Lalleśwarī does not name him or any other member of her or his spiritual genealogy. Contemporary scholars cannot agree about who belongs to "the line of disciples" connected with her, especially when Sufi figures are concerned.[29] Her spiritual genealogy is largely missing.

In addition to uncertainty about her precise lineage, Lalleśwarī may be all the more set apart from her tradition due to the nature of her initiation (*dīkṣā*). Alexis Sanderson describes three modes of initiation: a lengthy program of contemplative worship, a higher path of "sudden enlightenment" through the use of mantras, and the most immediate means, in which "the goal was believed to be attained without any instruction, either spontaneously or through some non-verbal stimulus such as the guru's glance."[30] Most interpreters assume that Lalleśwarī's initiation must have been the third type, the instantaneous result of a single encounter. When Lalleśwarī recalls that her guru told her only "one word" (K 21), she seems to support an interpretation that surpasses human institutions.[31] Rather than sitting at the guru's feet for extended expositions of the Śaiva Tantras, her contact with her guru (whoever he or she might have been) may have been limited to a single meeting in which the guru imparted a single teaching that she transmitted to others. While this interpretation obviates the gendered problem of her engagement in protracted study in a lineage of (male) teachers and disciples, it also removes her from one of the most fulfilling relationships still available to her.

As Lalleśwarī's life and teachings indicate, beneficial hierarchies like the guru-disciple relationship can intersect with dualistic ones. The theory of spiritual equality is not always equally applied. When Lalleśwarī, a woman, attains enlightenment, she is ejected by the patriarchal family. After she leaves, she continues to disrupt dominant religious scripts through "oral transmission" of Kashmir Śaiva teachings, "a subversive act to resist the written discourse to which she and other people did not have access."[32]

Today, now that Lalleśwarī is safely in the past, she can be reincorporated into the tradition. Pamela Sue Anderson's reading of the Rajasthani saint Mirabai demonstrates how "female dissent slowly becomes read according to a male bias," and women's dissenting practices are spun as "consent to familial religious devotion."[33] We have seen Lalleśwarī posthumously reintegrated into the patriarchal framework despite her dissent: when her husband's family abuses her, her piety is attributed to her *father's* family. Her transformative power lies in her dissent from dominant structures, but the dominant reading of her devotion neutralizes its potency.[34] Even if her story reminds us that relational ideals straining the boundaries of institutions do not always succeed in changing them, her memory continues to challenge dualistic structures.

EVALUATING LALLEŚWARĪ

Given the gender constraints that exclude her from mainstream Kashmir Śaiva society, we may now ask how well Lalleśwarī lives out her own ideals of self and other as one body. How much does she actually challenge the religious status quo?

We have seen that Lalleśwarī rejects the expectations placed on her as a woman when they stand in her way of spiritual progress. In her teachings, she takes a long view on social and gender roles. She reminds her listeners that human beings play many different roles across lifetimes: "However many roles I played on the stage of life, . . . / yet I am the same Lalla" (K 115; cf. K 81, 123, 124). Essentially "colorless," we take on the "color" of different names and forms (cf. K 123). She weaves the process of becoming a gendered self that distinguishes self from others into a *vaakh* twice its usual length:

> I, Lalla, set forth in the world
> hoping to bloom like a cotton flower, but
> the cleaner and carder came to give me hard blows.
> Spun into fine yarn I was hung on the weaver's loom.
> Then the washerman thrashed me on the thrashing stone,
> and rubbed me too much with soap.
> When the tailor applied his scissors piece by piece[,]
> then only did I, Lalla, attain the highest state.
>
> *(K 105)*

Odin interprets this utterance in light of the socially constructed nature of gender roles. She explains that despite coming into the world with "potential and possibilities intact," society sees Lalleśwarī's raw material as something to be "hung on the weaver's loom to be turned into cloth. Her social self is the creation of others to be used by others."[35] Lalleśwarī's liberation comes by deconstructing this conditioning. She is washed and cut into pieces through realization of the Self: "Lalla the daughter, Lalla the daughter-in-law, and Lalla the wife are simply torn into shreds and her true identity emerges."[36]

For Odin, Lalleśwarī does not go far enough in her deconstruction because the self she comes to accept is still constructed according to patriarchal ideals. In place of the passive, familial woman, she takes instead the persona of the autonomous, detached self. She says, "Now I shall die while alive; what can the world do unto me?" (K 130). Although this model of detachment purports to be gender-neutral, it represents the flip side of a well-entrenched gender dualism. Odin reads Lalleśwarī's renunciation in light of a male-defined model of the separative self: "In order to find a space for herself, . . . she was compelled to make a break with the social as well as family relations," adopting "a mode of existence that was outside the patriarchal social and religious arrangements at one level, but intimately tied to it at another."[37] She criticizes Lalleśwarī for falling short of the full gospel of Kashmir Śaivism: "By focusing on transcendence, Lalla follows the patriarchal discourse, casting the world in a conflictual stance, wherein the self must transcend the other."[38] Indeed, Lalleśwarī does become aloof to the opposition of the people around her.[39] For example, when a supporter angrily chases off the children who are taunting Lalleśwarī, she asks him for a piece of cloth. She cuts it neatly in two, and all day she ties a knot in one half for every kind word and a knot in the other half for each insult. At the end of the day she asks her friend to weigh the two ropes: of course, they weigh the same.[40] This tale functions to demonstrate her assimilation to the transcendent ideal.

Odin's critique of the separative and masculinist nature of the renunciant ideal demands the best of the Kashmir Śaiva vision for the *jīvanmukta*, the one who lives liberation within society. For Odin, Lalleśwarī's detachment and her images of merging and nothingness fall too much on the side of identity rather than relation. Continual absorption in Śiva prevents full involvement in worldly relations: "The insights that she gains in the spiritual realm do not in any way enrich her life in the material realm in terms of allowing her to live a fulfilling and creative life. The two realities remain separate because of the contradictory position she occupies."[41] One would hope to see, instead of this bifurcation, concrete societal changes go hand in hand with her inner liberation.

Odin's critique finds a wider target beyond Lalleśwarī's poetry insofar as readers of the tradition have failed to notice the tension between the fully relational ideal of the *jīvanmukta* and the masculinist model of selfhood in the renouncer. Some of Lalleśwarī's interpreters even see the transcendence of name, form, and gender as enough to strike "a blow at the prevalent patriarchy."[42] On their reading, Lalleśwarī's nakedness signifies scorn for the external appearances that differentiate men from women. If transcendence of difference becomes a permanent stance rather than one phase of relation, however, there is little impetus to rectify structures that devalue persons who differ from oneself.

Lalleśwarī's evident struggle to find a mode of relation correlative to her spiritual knowledge prompts me to temper Odin's criticism of her. I see Lalleśwarī's hopes for society expressing her vision of unity-in-difference, although her experiences of society fail to realize these hopes in full. Odin herself notes that Lalleśwarī discovers a "third space" beyond simple unity or duality, which empowers her "in her spiritual life, even as she is an outcast in her social life."[43] The move from theology to praxis is always tricky, especially as egalitarian ideals collide with habituated hierarchies. In the cotton flower verse, the tailor's cut brings about a new identity; yet one must construct this liberated identity within the fabric of one's given location in the world. Liberated relations become possible through the interplay of inner vision and outer manifestation, even though receptivity to the other can be inhibited by the ways in which particular differences are constructed in society.

Lalleśwarī teaches a liberated form of consciousness of subject-object duality with implications for all aspects of interhuman difference. For her, all beings share the same nature as expressions of Śiva's divine consciousness, and all have the capacity to experience this unity by viewing differences in society from the higher perspectives within the cosmic hierarchy. Unity and duality are two poles of a single reality that encompasses a fundamental connection between all human beings in their "diverse roles" (K 127) in society. The ideal is that the *jīvanmukta* becomes an integral though nonattached part of society.

Nonattachment differs in crucial ways from detachment. Lalleśwarī does not completely detach or separate from those around her. Her patience in the face of her mother-in-law's abuse is both a pragmatic and an enlightened response. Pragamatically, if her husband or his father should learn of the situation, the older woman could make matters worse. The young wife takes the opportunity to practice equanimity, which better approximates the ideal of nonattachment. She learns to face both hardship and well-being with a "stability of mind" (*Śiva Sūtra* 3/40) that pervades all experiences and perceptions. This is not just a survival strategy of the abused. She enacts "the practice of a realized soul," which she describes as acting foolish though knowing, blind though seeing, dumb though hearing—in short, not being attached to a concept of self that can be perturbed by offense (K 40). Being able to remain calm or even laugh at the jeers of others signals her nonattachment to name and fame. Unlike in the realm of bodily discipline, Lalleśwarī concedes a lack of control over her social circumstances and uses them as an opportunity to practice holding firm to her liberated view of the self. She confidently asserts:

> Let good and bad come to me.
> My ears will not hear nor eyes see.
> When the inner call comes up in the mind[,]
> my lamp will be lighted even by the storm of adversity.
> (K 42)

In her nonattachment to external circumstances, Lalleśwarī keeps faith in herself and the inextinguishable power that wells up inside her.

Duality is most palpable in the social realm. In addition to the dissonance that is to be expected for a woman trying to follow a path designed for male practitioners, Lalleśwarī's isolation from others can also be understood from a metaphysical point of view, as a by-product of the obfuscations of *māyā* in phenomenal experience. Each person travels a unique path: some may still be lifetimes away from realizing difference-in-relation, and even a *jīvanmukta* cannot force the will of another. As long as others retain their propensity for attachment, hatred, and all other kinds of obstacles to community, the new vision of the liberated cannot in and of itself end their resistance.

Lalleśwarī's teachings on how to encounter diversity and conflict are in accordance with Kashmir Śaiva religious devotion, but they do not cease to dissent from the oppressive power dynamics she experiences around her. Viewing praise and blame equally and seeing the One in her enemies,

Lalleśwarī does not excuse their ill-treatment of her. She has no qualms about calling them fools (K 16, 18, 19, 59) when they neglect the deep relatedness of self and others. She almost despairs of teaching such people: "I might be able to drain the ocean, . . . but it is beyond me to teach a fool" (K 19). Hers is not a philosophy of gritting her teeth and walking into the wind, or of passively condoning injustice. Rather, given the hardships that life brings, Lalleśwarī finds that the best approach is to tame her mind so that it will not drown in hatred. Lalleśwarī retains her agency and the ability to speak and act. Most strikingly, when the opposition of her family and society become great enough, when her husband physically strikes out at her because of her devotion, she physically leaves them.

Thus, for Lalleśwarī, relationships naturally strain because of our sense of separateness and genuine differences of perspective. Relationships break when these limitations lead to cruelty. In all such situations, Lalleśwarī says, "I patiently faced the storm of adversity / and remained devoted to God" (K 25). Many of her verses evince a feeling tone of alienation, isolation, and heartbreak that stems from human relations in the world. This longing is rooted more deeply in her longing for the Self. It is difficult to live as "one body" in society because not everyone recognizes the inherent connectedness with others to the same degree. From her abusive home situation to the sectarian strife of the religious community, she sees more examples of the failure of community than its flourishing. We do not know whether Lalleśwarī eventually found acceptance in a community of disciples; but we can be certain that, as a renouncer, Lalleśwarī retains at least a "partial bond with society, . . . though only as a social critic and teacher."[44] From all indications, Lalleśwarī could only yearn for the kind of community she taught; but this yearning disrupts dominant configurations insofar as her life exposes ruptures between religious ideals of relation and the translation of these ideals into concrete situations.

In Lalleśwarī's case, the disjunction between liberating knowledge and her experience of society contains an element of tragedy. We see similar tragedy in the experience of Mechthild of Magdeburg, who continually deals with opposition and eventually gives up her participation in her unique way of life as a beguine. Mechthild's tactics for navigating the fraught waters of spiritual authority will help us to discern her principles for self-other relation.

MECHTHILD ON THE MARGINS

As with Lalleśwarī, Mechthild placed herself on the margins of her religious tradition through both her way of life and her teachings. Like Lalleśwarī, Mechthild was a renouncer: at an early age she deprived herself of the class privilege of her noble upbringing. She set out to embrace the apostolic ideal of poverty touted by the new mendicant orders, the Dominicans and Franciscans (*FL* 4.2). The women's branches of these orders were not permitted to practice absolute poverty because they were required to stay in the cloister and, therefore, to own property; but the ideal of service in the world proved so popular that laywomen called beguines began to live together for this purpose. After leaving her hometown and the comforts of family and friends, Mechthild likely lived in a beguinage alongside other such women. For about one hundred years, beginning with the papal approbation of Marie d'Oingt's beguine way of life in 1215, beguines pursued lives of contemplation and service in society without the official protection of a monastic order. They were neither wives nor nuns, but a new, third option.

The rise and fall of this relatively independent women's movement played out during Mechthild's lifetime. The beguine way of life was on the margins because it departed from women's traditional options—and the new lifestyles of other such groups like the Waldensians was enough to earn them the label of heresy. Her path became doubly marginal when the beguine movement came under scrutiny. Most beguinages were incorporated into existing cloistered orders. Mechthild herself decided to take refuge in the convent of Helfta, perhaps due to a combination of ill health and mounting opposition such as the 1261 Magdeburg Synod that issued a decree to control the activities of the beguines.[45] Within decades of Mechthild's death, the beguine Marguerite Porete was executed as a relapsed heretic (1310), and the Council of Vienne (1311–12) ruled to prohibit the beguine way of life.

Beyond the beguines' fall from institutional favor, Mechthild's writing also put her in danger of marginalization. Her bold claims for her book's inspiration and its role in God's redemption of the church caught the attention of critics. Mechthild's authorship was particularly problematic for the "Pharisees" (2.24; 3.1) around her, people who looked to discredit her by twisting her words. One such critic objects to her vision of John the Baptist presiding at mass because he was not an ordained priest (6.36; cf. 2.4). Elsewhere, when Mechthild calls God "my Father by nature" (1.44), her accuser suspects heretical aspirations to personal deification by one's "own efforts or by way of a metaphysical similarity of nature with God."[46] Perhaps in order to circumvent this allegation with regard to her claim to witness the counsel of the Trinity in 3.9, she explicitly criticizes those who purport to "be so holy [as to] enter into the eternal Godhead" (7.47). Neumann believes the charge to be directed at the so-called *homines perfecti*, a heretical group in the nearby Ries, whose claims of perfection led them to reject spiritual guidance and the laws of the church.[47] Heresy is a serious charge and poses a grave potential danger for the beguine.

In the face of opposition, Mechthild defends herself with theological acuity, invoking sophisticated concepts such as a distinction between the fleshly and spiritual senses (6.36) and the necessarity of cooperation between nature and grace (6.31). She also does not mince words. For example, after clarifying that her vision was not of a physical nature, she replies to the outrageously trivial objection to John the Baptist's lack of ordained priesthood by saying, "Neither pope nor bishop nor priest can ever speak so perfectly the word of God as did John the Baptist. . . . Was this man really a layman? Prove me wrong, you who are blind!" (6.36).

Mechthild's most adamant rebuttal comes in response to the charge of personal perfection. Her insistence on strict spiritual discipline may reflect suspicions about the unclear parameters of the beguine way of life. She decries the heretics' false sense of sublimity as an "evil beyond all sins" that "I never had anything to do with" and which "enrages me in my whole soul and in my whole body and in all my five senses and in my whole heart" (7.47). If anyone really had such intimate knowledge of the Trinity, it would lead not to self-exaltation but humility in the knowledge that "one cannot be perfect in the sight of God" (7.47). Some might view her hyperbolic description of the soul's intimacy as antinomian, as when she writes, "And so you must cast off from you / Both fear and shame and all external virtues" (1.44); but her constant emphasis on humility and the virtues as "half gifts from God and half our own doing" (6.30) puts this unique statement in its proper place.[48] In these examples, Mechthild fights for her way of life and for her teachings from the margins of the church's institutions.

Despite the specific instances of conflict and marginality above, Mechthild, like Lalleśwarī, has been posthumously removed from the margins. Sara Poor meticulously documents how the transmitters of Mechthild's book over the centuries neutralize the problematic of her female authorship. By posthumously designating her as an instrument of divine authorship, the earliest German translators circumvent her unique authorial voice. When her texts are reproduced in devotional anthologies for female readers in the fifteenth century, Mechthild's name is simply removed from the text. The Latin translations of the work edit her criticism of the clergy and her erotic imagery; and by the seventeenth century these texts are subsumed under the name of another Mechthild, Mechthild of Hackeborn, whose saintly reputation outlived both of them. When rediscovered in the nineteenth century during a revival of German vernacular literature, Mechthild's texts become examples of an essentially experiential and feminine mode of writing. Although each of these modes of incorporation makes her authorship safe for the patriarchal tradition, Sara Poor hesitates to encourage literary scholars who would reclaim Mechthild's text "based on concepts of dissent, unconventionality, or nonconformity." In her assessment, Mechthild's "dissent turns out to be theologically conformist."[49] Yet, elsewhere Poor's interrogation of the role of the vernacular in Mechthild's work helps to uncover a subtle form of sociopolitical resistance in her urban context.

In the late twelfth and early thirteenth centuries, Magdeburg's position on the Elbe River made it a prime center for the missionizing, commerce, and warfare of the Northern Crusade begun in 1193.[50] In this context, Mechthild lays claim to a broad audience by writing in Middle Low German rather than having a scribe write her book in Latin for her, as did Hildegard of Bingen and Elisabeth of Schönau before her. Through the local dialect, Mechthild could appeal to the populace of her northern locale, while her courtly metaphors resonated with her neighbors to the south. She may also have supported the Dominican mission to the outlying frontiers of Christendom and intended the vernacular to reach that audience as well.[51] Despite the wide reach of her authorial ambition, Wendy Farley points to a major ideological departure from the crusaders' imperial project. Mechthild's personification of Lady Love embodies God's own "renunciation of authority" in a "divine kingdom . . . run by an entirely different logic from the kingdoms of the world."[52] For all the courtly trappings of her poetry, Mechthild charts a radical reversal of lordly systems of domination in favor of mutuality and humility. We must follow her vision of flowing love to discover in greater detail how, like Lalleśwarī, her relational wisdom opposes oppressive hierarchies.

MECHTHILD'S TEACHINGS ON RELATION

Mechthild's challenge to religious, gender, class, and imperial norms is undergirded by her theology as well as by her beguine way of life. None of these hierarchies can withstand the outflow of divine love. God models the desire and the mutual surrender that makes room for the other. God says of the soul:

> I cannot be completely intimate with her unless she is willing to lay herself in utter repose and nakedness in my divine arms, so that I can take delight in her. For it was for this that I surrendered myself into her power—like a child, poor, naked, bare, scorned, and finally into death—that she alone—ah, if she desires it—might be my closest, my dearest companion. (5.25)

Mechthild's God is neither self-sufficient nor self-contained but risks scorn and death for intimacy with the human soul.

As we saw in chapter 2, the metaphor of fluidity characterizes relations between God and the soul. Mechthild's watery divinity promises that the soul "shall ever more in soul and body soar about and play to her heart's content in my Holy Trinity and drink herself full like the fish in the sea" (5.25). Mechthild experiences this fluid connection within herself as the "melting" of the heart (3.1) into a "full exchange" with God: "you give God everything that is yours, both inwardly and outwardly, and he truly gives you everything that is his inwardly and outwardly" (4.15). Even as giving oneself over to the divine other forfeits the security of a self-contained identity, however, Mechthild does not go all the way with other medieval authors to a total union with God that negates the self. For Mechthild, more important than becoming one is the nature of the relationship between herself and God. This is a relationship that requires two; it requires difference. Difference is never completely annihilated through relation: the integrity of the self is a good not to be overcome in union with God—or in relation to others.

The self that sinks and soars in relation to God experiences a parallel dynamic in relation to human others. For Mechthild, human beings image the Trinity insofar as they flow outward to others:

> To the extent that we love mercy and practice constancy we are like the heavenly Father. . . . To the extent that we suffer poverty, humiliation, rejection, and pain here we are like the true Son of God. . . . To the extent that we here flow outward with all the abundance of our heart to give our possessions to the poor and to spend our lives in the service of the sick we are like the Holy Spirit, who is an abundant outpouring of the Father and the Son. *(6.32)*

Christian love flows downhill. The mendicant orders and beguines embraced the ideals of voluntary poverty and the apostolic way of life, and their uncloistered status allowed many of them to serve the poor and sick in the cities. In this ideal, the marginalized in society are the best recipients of the love that flows through the church.

Mechthild's practice of the virtue of humility is, perhaps, the richest place to observe how flowing love functions in her self-other relations. On the one hand, Mechthild's humility is a form of assent to Christian ideals, as this virtue was especially expected of women. On the other hand, her humility has several subversive functions: it authorizes her theological speech as a woman, and it dissents from theologies of domination by calling for the uplift of the downtrodden.

FLUID HIERARCHIES

The Christian virtue of humility relativizes the notion of authority: paradoxically, the most qualified leaders of the Christian community should be those least interested in wielding such power. As the First Gospel puts it, "The last shall be first, and the first last" (Matt. 20:16 KJV). For Mechthild, leadership is founded on mutual submission and respect, with give-and-take appropriate to the communal goals of perfecting one another in the Christian life. Priors and prioresses should have the humble attitude that "though unworthy of anything good, . . . unfortunately, however, I have authority over you and send you forth." They should "be very careful not to use . . . [their] authority contrary to the will of the brethren or the community, for that is a source of much dissension"; and they should take action only after seeking the advice of the brothers and sisters (6.1).

The ideal of humility, rooted in Christ's example, has the potential to subvert worldly hierarchies, but historically it has suffered from unequal application. Women and marginalized men have been encouraged to stay in their places as a way to imitate Christ. They must bear their cross, not complain, and never challenge the unjust structures that bind them. Any such challenge would only prove their *lack* of humility; self-assured behavior, on the part of the oppressed, appears uppity at best and dangerous at worst to those in power. Individuals in the classes repeatedly reminded of their inferiority often internalize these messages and come to believe in their worthlessness. This is not true humility but the tragic result of unjust uses of power. Mechthild herself often seems to have interiorized her own inferiority when she refers to herself in self-denigrating terms: "lowly crow" (2.4), "foul puddle" (2.4), and "helpless puppy" (7.1).[53] Mechthild seeks out the most shockingly abject position she can imagine in pursuit of "sinking humility," which

> chases her [the soul] up into heaven and drags her down again into the abyss. It leads the soul to all creatures one by one and says: "Now look, all this is better than you are!" And it brings her then to the spot where she can go no further: under Lucifer's tail. If, in her desire to honor God as she would want, she could remain there, she would prefer nothing better. (5.4)

Feminist readers cringe at the apparent self-abasement of Mechthild and her medieval female counterparts.[54] Because it is all too easy to suspect that humility is only a tool of the patriarchy, we must look very closely at how it functions in Mechthild's writing.

As I have discussed elsewhere, the role of humility in Mechthild's text is quite complex.[55] Humility resonates within the literary context of courtly love poetry as well as with beguine spiritual virtues. For women not ordinarily authorized to speak with religious authority, performance of the humility topos often counterbalances claims of divine favor. Sara Poor describes the paradox: "Attempts to avoid making authoritative claims produce strategies that make authoritative claims."⁵⁶ Mechthild highlights her humility, in part, as a way to reverse many of the hierarchies that had calcified within the Christianity of her day.

Mechthild draws attention to her triply marginalized status when she wonders whether God might receive more honor from her book if its author were a "learned religious man" (2.26). She cannot communicate in Latin like the learned scholars of her day, including some nuns educated in centers like Helfta. Unattached to an established religious order, her beguine way of life is particularly vulnerable to attack. And as a woman, she lacks the authority to teach. After someone warns her that her book might be burned, the statement sets the stage for God's direct authorization of her work. God then assures her,

> No one can burn the truth.
> For someone to take this book out of my hand,
> he must be mightier than I.

Her book even has quasi-scriptural status because God is its true author:

> It flows continuously
> Into your soul from my divine mouth.
>   (2.26)⁵⁷

God chooses her precisely because she is *not* a learned religious man.

In Mechthild's model of revelation, the flow of divine teaching, so often mediated by "wise men" from "famous schools," actually runs most directly to the humble. God prefers the humble by nature:

> By nature I have acted accordingly many a day.
> Wherever I bestowed special favors,
> I always sought out the lowest, most insignificant, and most unknown
>   place for them.
> The highest mountains on earth cannot receive the revelations of my
>   favors
> Because the course of my Holy Spirit flows by nature downhill.
> One finds many a professor learned in scripture who actually is a fool in
>   my eyes.
> . . . .
> . . . It very much strengthens Holy Christianity
> That the unlearned mouth, aided by my Holy Spirit, teaches the learned
>   tongue.
>   (2.26)

What is true in the God-soul relationship holds true in the church as well: the humble receive God's favor and are, therefore, the best teachers.

Mechthild's principles find communal application in her prayers for the clergy, her practice of confession, and her advice to beguines and nuns, all of which are only comprehensible within the hierarchy of the church on earth. For Mechthild, the present life is a microcosm of the hierarchically ordered universe: thus she prays for popes, bishops, clergy, and religious orders. She has special affection for the Dominicans and offers intercessions for their well-being in gratitude for their administration of the sacraments of confession and Eucharist. Counsel or spiritual direction is essential: she shudders to hear people say, "No, I am beyond the need for human counsel. I intend to live according to God's counsel" (5.5). Mechthild places herself below the authorities in the church, but she takes on an advisory role toward other beguines (5.11). At one time she may have been the head of a beguine community, as evidenced by the instructions she gives to priors, prioresses, canons, and prelates about judgments, chapter meetings, and the like (6.1–2; 6.7). For everyone within the church hierarchies, following Christian counsel with an obedient heart is an elementary form of humility that no one can surpass, no matter how great their revelations from God.

A dynamic of mutual criticism with other Christians flows both with and against the traditional hierarchy. Mechthild submits to her confessors in Christian humility, but this does not prevent her from exhorting others in turn. To be sure, it is more dangerous for the beguine to voice criticism of the clergy than the other way around; and she has no shortage of persecutors. But because God seeks out "the lowest, most insignificant, and most unknown place" to impart revelation, the humble may challenge the authority of clerics tempted to resist their witness: the "unlearned mouth . . . teaches the learned tongue" (2.26). Her visions of hell and purgatory give her ample opportunity to caution against the corruptions she has witnessed in the religious life. She even speaks with God's voice in criticism of the clergy, claiming to have overheard God's speaking to the pope in his prayers (6.21).

No one is exempt from the scourge of her pen—least of all herself—but she has special words for those who fail to develop the purity and humility that are the goal of spiritual vocations: lazy nuns and beguines (2.23), those who make false claims to special experiences (7.47), those who doubt the existence of such experiences (2.19), "imperfect" religious persons (2.24; 3.24; 4.16; 5.8), Dominican preachers who are reluctant to preach and hear confession (3.1), priests who lack purity and humility or abuse their power (5.14; 6.21), the lustful canons she calls smelly "billy goats" (6.3), priors who hold office with the wrong attitude (6.1), a beguine still attached to the court (4.17), those who do not submit to their spiritual directors (5.5; 6.7), those who are more attached to transitory outward things than their inner life (5.8; 5.11; 6.13), and those who contemplate but neglect good works (6.30). Her purpose is always to urge others, even her enemies, toward greater perfection in this life: "I pray to God for all who slander me or revile me, that God preserve them from sin" (6.26).

Principles of humility and authority complement each other in Mechthild's negotiations within the ecclesial and social hierarchies. For her, hierarchy is a given: like the cosmos, church and society are ordered by God to draw the community toward greater perfection through the gifts of all its members. On the one hand, persons under the authority of others should receive confession and spiritual direction as gifts rather than restraints; on the other hand, humility is a prime qualifier for such spiritual authority, and those in office must not only rule but also defer to others when necessary. Mechthild is well aware that the church on earth is corruptible: its hierarchy rarely mirrors the celestial hierarchy of the saints and angels. Although those on the margins of institutions like the beguines have little status in this life, they often have the clearest perspective and offer the best direction. Heaven rewards their purifying role. For Mechthild, all are not "equal"; but each plays a unique role in the loving work of correction and direction. Alongside great responsibility and the great risk of harming others lies great reward in participating in the divine flow of humility and authority.

EVALUATING MECHTHILD

Humility empowers the meek to teach the powerful. How does this principle work in practice? As with Lalleśwarī, we can look into Mechthild's wider teachings, especially those on gender and class, to imagine the extent of the reversals she envisioned in church and society.

Mechthild's life as an unattached woman in medieval Europe speaks volumes about her resistance to customary gender relations: women need not be confined to the cloister or the court but can act fully as agents of Christ in the world. The few instances in which she addresses her gender in her writing serve a particular rhetorical function. Just as her comment that she is not a "learned religious man" gains God's reassurance, Mechthild again references her gender in the passage that contains her strongest earthly endorsement, the command to write from her confessor: "He commanded me, a frail woman, to write this book out of God's heart and mouth. And so this book has come lovingly from God and does not have its origins in human thought" (4.2).[58] When Mechthild cites her gender, it is with the purpose of demonstrating her earthly and divine authorization to write.

Mechthild rarely underlines her status as a woman outside of these authorizing contexts. Elsewhere she departs from patriarchal gender stereotypes. She celebrates the nobility of the soul, imaged as female, as the bride of Christ, while resisting the misogyny of some of the depictions of the female soul that appear in writers like Bernard of Clairvaux. Bernard writes that the depiction of the soul as female "means people who are sensual and worldly, people devoid of manliness, whose conduct lacks both fortitude and constancy, people who are entirely superficial, soft and effeminate in their lives and behavior."[59] Although Mechthild shows familiarity with the trope when she invokes associations of the body with evil as she defends her writing (4.2), she does not employ the common correlation of women with the flesh and sin that pervades the writing of medieval men. She correlates vices, if at all, with both sexes: Eve with vanity and Judas with betrayal (7.50). Her hell is populated almost exclusively by men, with the exception of only "exalted ladies who here love all kinds of sins just as their husband lords do," thus indicating that in her view class outweighs gender in making one susceptible to sin (3.21).

Mechthild's attitudes toward gender and social class suggest a vision for a just society, but Ulrike Wiethaus worries that Mechthild does not live her ideals as thoroughly as one might hope. Wiethaus's critique from a psychological angle finds Mechthild "still engaged in the process of personal psychosynthesis" because of her apparent lack of interest in "work for the sake of the community." She concludes that Mechthild viewed such works as duties rather than acts of love: "Her capacity for love appears to be developed only toward God, and the majority of her fellow human beings are excluded."[60]

Mechthild does appear to stop short of full affirmation of lowliness as the precondition for revelation when she ranks the voluntary poverty of the beguines and mendicant orders over involuntary poverty. Her rationale—if the involuntarily poor "had an abundance of earthly things, they would not care to return my [God's] love. . . . And so I [God] must win them by being very hard on them" (3.19)—sounds dangerously like divine endorsement of the status quo rather than the full force of love flowing to the margins. For Mechthild, although the fluidity of relation impels service to the community, contemporary readers might like to see more concrete liberating efforts on behalf of the oppressed. Her point is that God reveals Godself to those whose hearts are radically empty and open to the other, and so she focuses on how service produces spiritual effects for the serving individual rather than on any material improvements for the one receiving help.

In contrast to our contemporary worries about a spiritualization of poverty that neglects real structural change in society, Mechthild worries about the opposite problem: that service will not be grounded in the appropriate dispositions. Poverty and lowliness are primarily states of the soul; social disadvantage (being unlearned, nonreligious, a woman) can prepare the way for this condition. She wants her readers to experience the spiritual poverty that opens one to the divine outpouring. It is all too easy to neglect inwardness in favor of activity, as when religious malingerers avoid intimacy with God because they "can be of much use in external matters" (6.13). Mechthild brooks no excuses for neglecting the inner spirit, the source from which outward works flow. The contemplative should attend to the spirit's guidance regarding action: "Give it time and room in you; . . . It shall melt you so deeply into God that you know what his will is concerning how long you should pursue his intense caressing of you, and when and how you should . . . attend to the needs of each and every person" (6.13). Service must be rooted in its divine source, which regulates when and how much to flow out to others.

The role of hierarchies in Mechthild's thought will be distasteful to a modern hermeneutic suspicious of the power of religion to underwrite oppression. One of the fundamental differences between Mechthild's presuppositions and our own is that, unlike her, many contemporary readers assume that the social structures causing poverty can be changed. For her, humility has the potential to elevate those oppressed by hierarchies of gender and class in terms of *spiritual* authority, but it may not actually change their material lot in life. In light of these differences, Mechthild's writing might still inspire her readers to find new and subversive ways of attending to the disempowered in society. Readers might begin to notice what scripts—whether based on humility or some other way to massage the powerful—strategically authorize persons on the underside of hierarchies today. Mechthild might also inspire those in subordinate positions to develop novel tactics as they negotiate their unique settings. Both the privileged and the disinherited can work to change the social and religious structures that have made such tactics necessary, so that these structures become fully responsive to the authority of diverse kinds of wisdom.

The flow of empowering love does not only find a place alongside other visions of power, as when women's supposedly greater empathy is valued in today's (otherwise patriarchal) workplace. It also lures Mechthild's heirs toward less-hierarchical models of authority. Mechthild accepts the existence of hierarchies and differences of authority; but by grounding humility and flowing love as the main supports of the system, she radically destabilizes the flow of power within those hierarchies. Her principle that divine love flows downhill finds an alliance with the preferential option for the poor in Latin American and African American liberation theologies and the critical principle of women's flourishing in feminist theology. The mutual empowerment that these visions engender has been an effective lure to many seekers of justice and solidarity.

MODELS OF SELFHOOD IN RELATION

If the lives of persons on the margins can help us to "reinvent ourselves as other," as Pamela Sue Anderson suggests, Lalleśwarī's and Mechthild's stories invite us to inhabit alternative models of selfhood. The prevalence of fluidity in their relational visions calls us away from separative models of the self and toward selfhood in relation. We already exist in relation to many others; a fluid theological orientation calls us to embrace that relation, to flow out to others, and to view all as one body. We must inquire whether, in these women's departure from the ideal of the autonomous individual in dualistic "self-other" and "us-them" relations, they migrate too far in the opposite direction. Is their fluid alternative a self with no boundaries at all?

Catherine Keller insightfully diagnoses this dichotomy as the separative and the soluble. She observes that men are often socialized into a separative model of selfhood, whereas women's relational patterns tend toward "merger and self-dispersion."[61] When women's cultural function is to foster the separate selfhood of their fathers, husbands, and sons, it can be difficult for them to maintain a sense of identity or value outside these relations. Furthermore, in a context in which the autonomous model is the ideal, to suggest the value of connectivity is to provoke fears of "slid[ing] into a soft, undifferentiated slime of emotional dependencies."[62]

In light of such fears, Keller argues that denial of our fundamental interconnectedness is a fundamentally sexist, gynophobic stance. As an alternative to the separative/soluble dualism, she offers a paradigm of the "connective self" that calls for "not less but more (and different) relation; not disconnection, but connection that counts."[63] She also chooses fluid images for the connective self: "Fluidity and interpermeability, long associated with the monstrous and feminine, show themselves to be the character of every being: every entity in the universe can be described as a process of interconnection with every other being."[64] The self is neither a unitary, immutable substance; nor does it dissipate completely.

One need not choose between the freedom of transcendence and the intimacy of immanence. Keller proposes that transcendence and immanence need not be opposed if transcendence is defined in terms of "activity and creativity in an open world," and immanence "is the way relations are part of who I am."[65]

Transcendence and immanence also coexist in relation for our medieval interlocutors. Neither woman is reduced to the relations that surround her. Each asserts her agency to overcome constraints of gender, class, and religion. Yet each also seeks out new and better patterns of relation with others. Lalleśwarī longs to overcome the separateness she experiences between herself and human others. As a *jīvanmukta* she can see the inherent connectedness of the Self in all selves. Although human beings must play different roles across lifetimes, Lalleśwarī challenges us to overcome separateness by seeing all as one. Mechthild's Trinity is constituted as a fount of love flowing between them: they are three persons who both maintain their integrity and act together in the generation and redemption of the world. The flow of divine love creates others with whom to be in relation. It courses "downhill," empowers the powerless, gives voice to women, and destabilizes the hierarchies of this world. Human beings become like God to the extent that they too flow outward in service to others, but if they fail to attend to the flow of love between them, they sink and drown in the swamp of sin.

Fluidity as a theological metaphor neither washes the many into the whole nor merges two into an indistinct One. Even as Mechthild melts and flows in love, she does not dissolve completely. And when others try to break the vessel of Lalleśwarī's selfhood, her true identity remains intact. The soluble and separable adhere together. Mechthild and Lalleśwarī desire the permeability of the self with the divine, and they long for radical mutuality between persons that differences too often divide. Their fluid imagery illustrates the depth of their desire for this sort of solubility. However, they also struggle to find a discrete sense of self that will support an authoritative voice. Each remains separately embodied and values embodied difference: service is possible only through genuine recognition of the concrete particularity of others. Desire calls one to the other, but the self does not simply dissipate in the desires of the other.

DUALITY, HIERARCHY, AND TRAGEDY

The lives and voices of two women on the margins of religious institutions have suggested a surprising role for hierarchy in a theology of difference: *metaphysical hierarchies can subvert rather than support unjust social relations*. Difference, and even hierarchy, between God and the world does not necessitate the subordination of body to mind or of women to men. In fact, it can create an appreciation for duality and difference that challenges customary social hierarchies.

This bit of wisdom from Mechthild and Lalleśwarī should give pause to a society in which hierarchies are ideologically repugnant, and where democratic ideals of equality actually serve to mask the hegemony of the rich, the light-skinned, the masculine. We cannot assume that equality and mutuality guide institutions in the so-called first world when separative notions of the self actually govern our actions. In the face of the liberal assumption that as democracy marches forward, hierarchies of gender, race, and sexuality will dissipate with freedom for all, Lalleśwarī and Mechthild suggest that what we need is not the total utopian absence of hierarchy, but difference-in-relation that constructs fluid and life-giving structures of authority.

Divine consciousness and love ramify into a rich multitude of beings; and from this hierarchy of creator and creation, hierarchies of spiritual realization give rise to the teaching relationship. Mechthild reveres her confessors and the saints, and Lalleśwarī venerates her guru and aims to become a *jīvanmukta*, for those who have progressed along the liberating path have the authority to teach and correct. Women may attain this position as well as men. Gender is no bar to Lalleśwarī becoming a guru in the grand scheme of Śiva's consciousness. Women like Mechthild gain authority within Christian hierarchies because of the paradoxical reversals of revelation: God flows "downhill" and lifts up those whom society deems to be of little value. Hierarchies can be fluid and dynamic, constantly unsettling communities in the direction of greater consciousness and love.

The tension between the hierarchies structured by love and consciousness and those structured by ordinary power relations retains a tragic dimension. Despite the relational visions of persons on the margins, their metaphysics and the practice of broader society often fail to align. One might be destined to join the highest choirs of heaven like Mechthild and yet receive nothing but contempt and abuse in this life. One might view life's diversity from the perspective of the highest *tattva*s like Lalleśwarī and yet bear the scorn of others who cannot see the unity she sees. Both find themselves historically situated within striated hierarchies, where there is little chance of the poor becoming rich or of women becoming bishops, or where a community's religious ideals fail to accommodate female householders or low-caste individuals.

Mechthild and Lalleśwarī present two different responses to less-than-ideal social situations. Mechthild moves within the worldly hierarchies and does her best to subvert them; Lalleśwarī apprehends the unity between all people but is shut out by society and consequently turns away from it. In this life neither fully realizes the kind of community she desires, or that contemporary readers would hope to find in them. Both renounce their original contexts. Although Mechthild settles in communities of women, her experience demonstrates that one cannot participate in flowing love without opposition, doubt, and distress. Lalleśwarī roams alone; with the possible exception of her guru, she never experiences a society that harnesses the unity of consciousness for the common good. She can only long for a society free of ignorance and abuse. The attainment of salutary relations, hierarchical or otherwise, too often remains painfully elusive.

Whence this tragedy? Many of the spiritual adepts of the world's religions testify that periods of deep disappointment are a fact of the spiritual life. Frank Tobin connects Mechthild's experiences of abandonment by God to the "dark night of the soul" in St. John of the Cross; I would add that abandonment by coreligionists contributes to the sensory (the "dark night of the senses") as well as the spiritual experience of alienation.[66] The saints offer much counsel about these painful times, advising monastic subjects not to despair and still to trust the imperceptible work of God occurring within them. Mechthild's security in the memory of God's love helps her become "so content that she considers everything good that estranged souls feel as pain" (4.15). Lalleśwarī, as in her approach to bodily suffering, adopts an attitude of nonattachment to all kinds of loneliness, abuse, and scorn: "Take it, dear, and contentment will reach you on its own" (K 28, my trans.). In moments of absence, one can give up hope, regard previous experiences as deception, and distrust the security of divine love; or one can allow the experience to deepen the virtues and lead to an even more intimate level of relation.

Contemporary feminist and womanist theologians caution that the suggestion that suffering serves a good is dangerous ground for women, who tend disproportionately and to their own detriment to embrace suffering as redemptive. This wariness toward the prescription to bear oppression highlights a dimension of holy women's suffering for which the explanatory power of the dark nights of the soul and the senses is inadequate. Beverly Lanzetta identifies the "dark night of the feminine," an additional phenomenon that occurs when women embark on the purgative life of the spirit. Women's experiences of exclusion and betrayal by religious institutions can create a serious impasse for faith. To realize their deepest nature, women have to interpret their reality through language structures that often belittle or silence them. The memory of this oppression lingers in the body, mind, soul, and emotions.[67]

The societal forces that block the divine flow in communities intensify the desolation and self-doubt of women and marginalized men. In addition to the usual spiritual obstacles mapped by their traditions, they must navigate their devaluation and exclusion in the dark. Although they might inscribe alternate routes that correspond to the terrain of their experience, in this unstable cartography, the view from the margins is tragic insofar as the margins remain.

Further tragedy derives from the double-edged means of surviving the onslaught of the dark night. Prescriptions of nonattachment or humility, while useful for the fully liberated, can crush the spirit of persons still on their way. What are the hidden effects of bearing the scorn of others through spiritual nonattachment? Is it truly possible to flourish while steeling oneself against abuse? The complexity of Mechthild's use of humility tropes is a fine example of how the connective self can parody or slip into the soluble self when negotiating the relations of worldly hierarchies. Lacking authority within unjust structures of the world, she and her contemporaries use gendered humility tropes to their advantage. Yet her culture's characterization of women and the persecution she experiences pose real temptations for her to denigrate the self and forget the noble radiance of the God-beloved soul. The fluidity that overturns hierarchies must be channeled with care lest it simply capitulate to relations of domination.

The realities of embodied difference also contain an inherently tragic dimension. Bodies and skin quite literally separate one from the other. Figuratively, they can divide entire communities when differences of sex, sexuality, race, and ability emigrate from the realm of self-other duality into the dualistic realm of us-versus-them. As Lalleśwarī discovers, individuals as discrete centers of consciousness cannot be coerced to see their essential interrelatedness. Her advice about bearing opposition is therefore realistic, for even the most spiritually accomplished person will experience the loss of unrealized relation.

The tragedy inherent in embodied difference compounds when oppressions blind their victims to the plight of persons inhabiting *other* margins. Mechthild's struggle for the poor in spirit, for example, keeps her from seeing the plight of the materially poor. Today we have similar difficulty holding in mind the complex relations of race, class, gender, and other differences. Repeatedly and often painfully, liberation movements must come to terms with the interplay of these dualities: white feminists must learn to hear the voices of their sisters of color, race activists need to confront the sexism and homophobia of their movements, and the able-bodied must attend to the insights of the aged and disabled. The liberating strands of religious wisdom continually unsettle communities.

As the *mujerista* theologian Ada María Isasi-Díaz so aptly puts it, "*La vida es la lucha*": life *is* the struggle to achieve liberating relations.[68] Those on the margins must struggle, minimally, to survive, but also to resist the denial of their humanity. Those at the center will struggle in refusing the temptations of self-interest and domination. Love and consciousness of the other impels the powerful to cede their privilege and to see those on the margins, and the outsider within, with new eyes.

CONCLUSION

The institutional exclusions that Lalleśwarī and Mechthild bring into view are all too often the reality in the world's religious traditions. Egalitarian societies based on viewing the other as self remain the stuff of prophecy and hope. When those on the underside of power relations proclaim a reversal of values, it is a delicate business, fraught with peril. The brevity of the beguine movement demonstrates how short-lived gains can be. Liberating hope migrates to new and ever different loci. There are also costs to such efforts: while Mechthild maintains a tenuous balance between her authority and the church hierarchy, Lalleśwarī may have been pushed out of the family and religious hierarchy altogether. Many who raise their voices in oppressive scenarios suffer worse fates still.

Though today women and men of spirit build networks for themselves, new life-giving relationships may never completely soothe the loss of their original familial and religious communities. The regret that loved ones have forfeited the beauty of unity-in-difference remains, even as hurt and resentment fade. Yet Lalleśwarī's husband and mother-in-law and Mechthild's "Pharisee" detractors tread their own paths to God: reconciliation was and never is beyond hope. Sometimes streams part, only to reunite again downstream.

Careful assessment of what can be accomplished within the real constraints of social expectations is an important tactic for the survival and flourishing of those on the margins. How much should a person risk for what seems impossible? Some may choose to leave the chokehold of a family of origin or the ashes of a marriage to create community anew; others may find grace in committing to such relations in the face of great odds. Some may yearn for solitude and inner communion with God; others may find fulfillment only in working, living, and breaking bread with others. Desire shifts as we taste fulfillment or slam into walls of frustration. Risk and self-protection work together in various degrees to nourish the desire for community.

The relational horizons of Mechthild and Lalleśwarī arise out of the divine activity in the human person. Even if they do not reach these horizons, we can follow the lure of the relational divinity toward them. Mechthild calls on us to overturn the hierarchies of value through the erotic flow of love to the lowest place. Lalleśwarī counsels us to clear the self from the Self and see others as equal; and she encourages the development of a consciousness that acknowledges our limited, situated, individual perspectives but can move between the universal and the particular with wisdom and ease. Their lives are, in the words of Pamela Sue Anderson, "actual, socially significant cases of yearning which have given expression and place to both female desire and outsiders within," and which call us who come after them to "reinvent ourselves as other."[69]

Anderson would have us "become" these marginal subjects in various ways in order to move toward ever more encompassing apprehensions of truth.[70] Persons on the margins can imitate these women's dissent as they negotiate their own hierarchies of gender, race, class, sexuality, and so on. In imitation of Mechthild and the beguine movement, some might build alternative institutions within their religious traditions. The Women's Ordination Conference, for example, arranges for Catholic bishops to ordain women as priests, deacons, and bishops. In the absence of top-down reform, and without the approval of Rome, this group fiercely defends its fidelity to Catholic Scripture and tradition. The threat of excommunication looms over those who openly declare their support for this movement.[71] Such risks attend any challenge to dominant values, and many persons on the margins are pushed out of the very structures they wish to change. Others, like Lalleśwarī, claim the freedom to opt out of institutions when they demand compromise on core values. Many women have left the religious communities in which they were raised in the face of prolonged and deadening gender oppressions.

The question of whether to work for change from within or to leave for reasons of health does not apply only to religious institutions. Our human hierarchies are all-too-often bastions of the separative self. Women in male-dominated fields must weigh carefully the risks to their careers of advocating for policy changes related to such issues as maternity leave, breastfeeding, and child or elder care. A woman at one educational institution, when confronted with policies that prevented her from carrying her nursing infant during off-site excursions, elected to withdraw from leading a program abroad rather than accept the implied dichotomy of the teaching mind and the mothering body; but many do not have the luxury of abdication and must find other ways to live with integrity. Too often, direct advocacy must be postponed for a level of job security that might never arrive.

For their part, those in power can reconstruct themselves in light of the wisdom gained from the encounter with the other. By voluntarily taking up positions of marginality, those on top of hierarchies can become responsive to the other. For example, white people can come to terms with their own racism and enter into solidarity with racial minorities, as in the churches in the American South that have become sites of ongoing dialogue about the effects of slavery and Jim Crow. Groups once excluded can attend to exclusions that remain. As new issues of justice arise, such as the ordination of gay and lesbian members in the Presbyterian Church (U.S.A.), we must use intention and care while conducting dialogues between persons of different races, social classes, sexual orientations, and approaches to Scripture.[72]

What, then, happens if communities take to heart the insights of human unity and flowing love? The tensions that are straining relations might not disappear, but factions might learn to see apparent dualisms as differences to explore or relations to heal. The strength of relations forged—such as that between the guru and student, or the sisterhood of nuns with whom Mechthild finds refuge—might prove powerful enough to melt the resistance of others into mutuality. Women and men, black and brown and white, rich and poor—all might embody the flow of love and recognition necessary for entire communities to flourish. Though oceans seem to separate us and a styptic something seizes the source of our love, the divine movement of desire softens our hearts, and they begin to flow out to one another.

6

Fluid Relations in a Dichotomous World

The previous chapters have argued that relations between God and self, God and world, self and body, and self and other are better conceived as dualities than as mutually exclusive dualisms. Duality or difference is only "dualism" in the sense criticized by contemporary opponents if (1) it is hierarchical, and (2) hierarchical metaphysical arrangements are linked to social hierarchies. These four types of duality are dynamic relations, and as such they need not succumb to the dualistic patterns that have proved to be so damaging for women and the natural environment.

Hierarchy does not necessarily support oppression—some social hierarchies, such as teacher-student or parent-child, can be salutary relations—yet the reverse is almost always true.[1] The theologies of Mechthild and Lalleśwarī contain metaphysical hierarchies with mechanisms that prevent them from devolving into oppression. For Mechthild, that mechanism is the subversive role of humility. In Jesus' principle that the last shall become first, those the world considers of no account are commissioned to challenge worldly authorities with an ideal of humble leadership. For Lalleśwarī, cosmic hierarchy itself denaturalizes hierarchical dualisms. The universe emanates from the divine subject into degrees of differentiation, and human subjects can view reality from each of these perspectives. As Mark Dyczkowski puts it, "All these views are correct insofar as they correspond to an actual experience. . . . *Dualism is not an incorrect view of reality although it corresponds to only one of the levels within the absolute.*"[2] When we locate hierarchical dualisms within a range of possible approaches to unity and difference, we relativize their power over our experience of duality and our relation to difference.

Dualities are relations with specific spheres of operation. Hierarchies attaching to these relations are not linked in any necessary way. There is no inherent reason that differences must devolve into dominance and subordination. Theology needs alternative metaphors—such as the metaphor of fluidity in the work of Mechthild of Magdeburg and Lalleśwarī of Kashmir—if the dominance of humanity over nature, or men over women, will no longer appear as the natural order of things.

REPRISE: FLUIDITY IN THE THEOLOGIES OF MECHTHILD AND LALLEŚWARĪ

It is worth pausing to reflect just how systematically the logic of fluidity structures the thought of the two women we have been reading. We have explored the significance of differences between them; here we may step back and recall the overarching framework in which these particularities occur. The very title of Mechthild's book, *The Flowing Light of the Godhead*, signals the importance of fluidity for her thought. While Lalleśwarī uses the overt vocabulary of flow (Sanskrit-Kashmiri root *vah*) in only two of her verses (K 10, 96), the concept is no less central to her schematic of emanation and return to Śiva via the ocean of life.

In each of the previous chapters, a major theological relationship takes form amid dualities that flow. We witnessed a parallel dynamic of procession and return of the individual soul or self and the divine that breaks down dichotomous views of Eastern and Western spiritual goals. Love flows between the persons of the Trinity and spills over into creation, and Śiva's nature as consciousness flows forth into objects for perception, so that even before the end of time, human beings can retrace this stream to its divine source. We also encountered obstacles to this return. Lalleśwarī cites the *malas*—obscuring forces of individuality, karma, and bewildering diversity—that choke the channel of our consciousness before it reaches its goal (K 106). Mechthild cites sin as the primary blockage to the flow of divine grace (3.21; 5.1) or, alternately, as the swamp in which sinners drown (7.27). Both women refuse to ascribe ultimacy to the obstacles they encounter. For Lalleśwarī, the self is by nature a jar "brimming over with wine" (K 99); for Mechthild, the soul sinks and soars by nature in the divine breath.

Not only the individual soul but also the entire cosmos is caught up in the divine flood. For Lalleśwarī, the individual self is but one of the objects that arises in the unfolding of divine consciousness. The cosmos emanates into various tiers of subject-object duality that the individual can navigate through meditation and, eventually, realize as a place of delight. Mechthild imagines all things flowing forth from God as an eternally burning fire (6.29). Human beings can participate in heaven and hell, even in this life, because of the fluidity of the cosmos.

The body, too, flows toward divinity. In Lalleśwarī's yogic practice, the *nāḍīs*, channels of the breath in the body, replicate the coursing of divine consciousness. Attention to the breath unites the practitioner to her source. In Mechthild's case, ascetic practices employ the body in eliminating obstacles to the flow of grace; it too participates in the soul's reward. Finally, all of this attention to relational flow gives shape to their treatment of others: as coparticipants in Śiva's consciousness, all are one body; and Christians are called to flow outward in charity to one another.

Fluidity structures a way of being in the world, but this structure can be difficult to verbalize, especially in a comparative context. How is it possible to suggest that two thinkers from such diverse settings, and with such different religious vocabularies, share so many foundational assumptions? In the face of challenges posed by the comparative endeavor, I suggest that conceptual metaphor theory offers a basis for bringing together diverse religious perspectives on the common ground of embodied experiences of relation.

METAPHORICAL MAPPINGS

The theologies of Mechthild and Lalleśwarī are comparable insofar as their metaphors are rooted in the basic somatic experiences that condition all human cultures. The metaphor of fluidity, which has roots in the spiritual traditions of the world's religions as well as in embodied experience, offers clues for a contemporary theology of difference. This metaphor arises out of tactile experiences of water and air. Its concreteness communicates across contexts as diverse as thirteenth-century Germany, fourteenth-century Kashmir, and twenty-first-century North America. In each of these settings, we grasp the significance of the application of fluidity as a metaphor for theological relations.

As George Lakoff and Mark Turner explain, metaphors work by mapping the structure of a "source domain" onto a "target domain" to open a variety of understandings that would not otherwise exist. For example, in the conventional metaphor *life is a journey*, our knowledge of journeys structures a view of life. The *journey* metaphor is composed of basic slots such as the traveler, the starting point, motion, and the destination, which are mapped onto the target domain (*life*). A metaphor transfers relations in the source domain such as the traveler's reaching the destination, properties of the source domain such as the traveler's strengths and weaknesses, and basic knowledge including what a dead end is and how to deal with one. The *journey* metaphor evokes other schema that can be combined with this basic structure. For example, because it implies motion toward a destination, it can be elaborated in terms of a path or stream, obstacles in the path, speed, intensity, and so on. Seemingly disparate images cohere within the metaphorical system. Although life need not be viewed as a journey, the metaphor is persuasive because of its power to structure and evaluate the target domain.[3]

Lakoff and Turner's analytic categories may assist in parsing the fluidity metaphor. In *divinity is a fluid*, fluids are the source domain, and divinity the target domain. The fluid schema has three primary slots that are mapped onto divinity: a container, a fluid, and how the fluid enters or leaves the container.[4] We fill in the slots to articulate a concept of divinity by using knowledge of this schema, and the power of this metaphor is in the conceptual options it opens. The container can be a person or being such as Śiva, the Trinity, or a human being; and the divinity or divine attribute that flows between containers can alternately be imagined as being, love, consciousness, or bliss. Images of water, air, blood, and milk serve as the vehicle for conveying that attribute. These images have ramifications for the metaphor's third compartment: the relation between container and fluid. Depending on the form of the fluid (river, ocean, rain, puddle, waterfall, air current, circulatory system), it will flow, seep, trickle, evaporate, pulse, pour, dissolve, or flood into its container.

Metaphors always have an "is" and an "is not" quality, and this is especially true of metaphors for divinity.[5] The sixth-century Syrian theologian Pseudo-Dionysius is known for his contribution to negative (or apophatic) theology, which posits that God is beyond all human language and concepts. His book *Mystical Theology* ascends through material, human, and intellectual categories to contemplate a Being beyond being: God is not literally a rock, a loving father, or the Idea of the Good. The negative theological move belongs in any constructive Christian theology as a reminder that divinity cannot be reduced to the limited categories and perspectives of created beings. It stands guard against hubris and opens Christians charitably toward other perspectives. This move provides a necessary check on all constructive or affirmative theologies, but it does not prevent the naming of divinity. On the contrary: in the work *Divine Names*, Pseudo-Dionysius also discusses how God *can be* described as a rock, a loving father, and goodness, wisdom, and so forth.[6] The back-and-forth movement revels in the tension between speech and mystery. A spirit of poetry that uses words inappropriately breaks us out of comfortable, habituated modes of thought through epiphanies of unseen relations. *Divinity is a fluid* encourages a vision of God *as* a fluid entity without equating God with material substances. It provides a salutary schematic for viewing reality without claiming to represent that reality finally or definitively.

One of the most important ramifications of *divinity is a fluid* is how it structures views of the human person. In the Christian tradition, as in the Kashmir Śaiva, human beings bear the reflection of a divine being who is not set apart from the world but permeates it through the activities of creation, sustenance, and inspiration. In the Śaiva system, human consciousness is a microcosm of the pulsing awareness of divinity. The Christian tradition affirms this resemblance through the doctrine that humans are *imago dei*, in the image of God. If God is imaged as the ecstatic outpouring of love rather than a detached and transcendent being, this outward flow is what constitutes authentic human relation as well. *A person* is not only a *container*, demarcated from others by a body, but a *fluid* as well. Quite literally, our weeping, wounded, nursing, menstruating, excreting, and aroused bodies flow. Metaphorically, our relations exhibit qualities of an overwhelming flood or a life-giving stream, of the dissolution of boundaries or the coagulation of healthy identities. We can feel polluted or refreshed, parched or nourished, by others. All of these streams mingle with the divine waters in a matrix of divine, human, and worldly relations.

Divinity is a fluid does not yet function as a basic or conventional metaphor in our society the way that *life is a journey* does; yet it composes, extends, and elaborates the human experience of relation in fruitful ways and therefore deserves theological attention. Fluidity lends to theology a powerful internal logic that can be applied to holy mystery. In its ability to structure ways of being and doing in the world, the metaphor creates something for us that might not exist in its absence. For example, we know from observing rivers what happens when there is an obstacle placed in its path: it finds another way toward its destination, diverts in new directions, pools behind a dam, or gradually erodes the obstacle until it is no blockage at all. We can borrow patterns of inference from this common natural event to think about relation. We might discern how divine love flows over and around blockages of injustice and hate and how, in its persistent efficacy, love softens and dissolves even the most intractable obstacles. We might ponder how energies applied to an excessively resistant project might find more productive outlets elsewhere. We might attend to the difference of bodies from one another in order to determine appropriate boundaries for the flow of relation.

The fluidity metaphor carries with it implicit criteria for evaluating relations. These criteria transfer from the source domain (air, water, etc.) to the target domain. Fluids in the natural realm are good if they are unpolluted: water and air are better without contaminants such as oil spills or automobile exhaust. Fluids should also be present in a moderate amount and velocity, for both wind and rain are destructive in absence or excess. The permanent severance or blockage of anything that ordinarily flows (rivers, blood, breath) signals harm. People disagree over their preferences for a natural or a controlled flow. The channeling of rivers for irrigation and the control of breath in meditation can be salutary; but big dam projects—in India, for example—touted as a marker of progress in modernity, have dislocated millions of India's tribal people, disrupted ecosystems, and effectively killed off the rivers downstream.[7] The quality of the flow of relation can be evaluated through a conceptual transfer of evaluative judgments such as these.

The evaluative power of metaphor suggests how a fluid relational scheme is preferable to other, more dualistic schemes. Dualism, based on the experience of two things that are external to one another—separate bodies, hard surfaces, unrelated entities—is metaphorical as well. Its logic follows an either-or pattern: we can identify either with God or the world, with the soul or the body. The age, sex, and race of our bodies often predetermine these associations. The evaluative pattern of dualisms mandates the subordination, control, and maintenance of these distinctions. In dualistic systems, human beings must rise above fleshly, earthbound fetters; by virtue of likeness to a transcendent God, we must discipline and control these unruly and unspiritual forces. Dualism wields enormous power to structure experience, but from the perspective of fluidity, it stunts genuine relation. Its either-or patterns of inference do not reflect life's complexity. The hierarchical evaluations of one and the other carry over into the target domains of gender, race, sexuality, age, ability, and species in oppressive and highly problematic ways.

Furthermore, dualism is unfaithful to how we actually experience ourselves in relation. Our very language indicates that we are not disconnected and unaffected by others. The already-familiar metaphor of *a person is a container* arises out of embodied experience. For example, Lakoff and Turner discuss the metaphors *life is a fluid in the body* and *death is loss of fluid*:

> In the *life is a fluid* metaphor, the body corresponds to a container (a cup, a grape), and the life of the body corresponds to the fluid in the container. The intensity of life corresponds to the amount of fluid in the container. When the container breaks or is broken, the fluid escapes and the amount of fluid diminishes. Metaphorically, life diminishes. Death corresponds to the total absence of fluid in the container.[8]

Life can drain out of a person; it can also be crushed out. Like physical breath and blood, life flows within and out of the body. The metaphor further maps onto the effect that we have on the quality of others' lives. Relations can be life-giving or death-dealing; they can drain or restore creative and energetic capacities. Relations to divinity follow the same pattern, as reflected in prayers and hymns: "Spirit of the living God, fall fresh on me. Melt me, mold me, fill me, use me" (Daniel Iverson). Dualism closes the container; it shuts off the human person so that nothing flows in or out.

Contrary to the primary metaphor of the self as an individual to whom relation is external, tactile experiences of fluids such as air, water, milk, and blood lend themselves to other models of self and society. Fluidity has just as much power as dualism to structure our lives. It is just as available in terms of embodied experience—if not more so, because it better reflects the body's basic permeability. Its patterns of inference account for dynamism and responsiveness between living entities. Fluidity offers more options for relation, for its hierarchies are not rigidly inevitable. It also offers a mode of evaluation: relations of mutuality are good because they flow, and relations of dominance are harmful because they block life-giving streams.

FLOWING RELATIONS

The history of Western thought can be told as the story of the suppression of fluidity and connection. As Catherine Keller recounts, the watery goddess Tiamat was quite literally killed off in the creation myths that feed into Genesis. Tiamat's memory endures as the deep (*tehom*), over which the spirit broods before creation; but in Genesis as in the original myth, the patriarchal god separates earth from sky and puts this watery chaos in its place. Aristotle gives further expression to these ordering instincts with the notion of the individual as a self-subsistent, independent substance. Connections are severed, relations made external or "accidental" to the subject. Keller traces the ramifications of this anthropology through Augustine, Thomas Aquinas, Descartes, and Hume. The great mythological monsters—Tiamat, Medusa, the Furies, and Jung's Terrible Mother—become expressions of the monstrous connections to bodies and nature that adhere to women and others who deviate from the norm of the separate self.[9]

Unsurprisingly, a fluid theology wells up from the undercurrents in society. It does not flow from the elites but survives in the legacies of women such as Mechthild and Lalleśwarī. We may witness the flow of creation from the spring of Mechthild's flowing Trinity or plumb Lalleśwarī's abysmal void to find deep affinity with our source. Feminist theologians, who claim women's experience as source and norm, have begun to reclaim the watery matrix of becoming. Laurel Schneider takes a cue from Keller's tehomic metaphysics and reads the Christian tradition for the "aspects of flow, partiality, or change in the nature of the divine" that theologians eventually consolidated in a self-enclosed deity.[10] The dualistic "logic of the One" that came to govern Christian theology makes clear distinctions between truth and falsity, God and not-God.[11] Fluidity, by contrast, denotes multiplicity at the very heart of divine being and becoming:

> Divine multiplicity is characterized by fluidity, porosity, interconnection, temporality, heterogeneity, and a-centered relation. But divine multiplicity actually flows, bodes, and bodies in spite of all of those abstractions; it is utterly there and so impossible to abstract, after all. It is incarnation, again. After All.[12]

Embodied multiplicity, including the diverse embodiments of variously colored, abled, and aged women and men is the expression—nay, incarnation—of the flowing multiplicity of divinity.

The powerful taboos that adhere to bodily fluids may derive from the fear of chaos that the blood and waters of birth evoke, yet a fluid divinity prompts a graced mode of being that "lies not in escaping the watery chaos but in moving with its currents."[13] We need not drown in life's turbulence, but neither should we flee it to some fixed and unchanging higher ground. Experience itself has a fluid structure: we encounter the world in a moment-to-moment flow, and only later do we bundle our memories into neat little packages.[14] Human relations are aptly described in terms of influence, "the flow of me into your experience, of you into mine, by which we consciously and unconsciously affect one another."[15] This flood of relation can be gentle and healing or damaging and invasive—but in a fluid idiom we understand that we were created to be anything but isolated.

A fluid theology overturns unjust hierarchies such as that of the one over the many. Once seen as the natural state of things, rigid hierarchies and intractable dualisms are unmasked as an extremely limited subset of the many possible metaphorical options for understanding difference. Persons traditionally on the underside of dualisms have recourse to undercurrents of divine empowerment and human solidarity. I would like to draw out some of the implications of a renewed orientation toward fluidity for our relations with three kinds of others: the ecological other, the human other, and the divine other.

TOWARD AN ELEMENTAL THEOLOGY

The natural world offers paradigms for relating to divinity and to the world. We rely upon the elements of nature. Water, fire, earth, and air are material yet beyond our control—"sensible transcendentals," to borrow Luce Irigaray's apt phrase.[16] Ellen Armour experiments with these pre-Socratic elements as nonpersonal metaphors for divinity, which call humanity to acknowledge its location within and responsibility for nature. These images retain the twofold character of affirmation and denial essential to all theological language: "The elements 'are not' a God, properly speaking, yet they 'are' that in which we 'live and move and have our being.'"[17] I would like to pick up this elemental impulse for ecology in response to the idioms of breath, air, wind, and water in my sources.

Earth, water, fire, and air are all connected to one another and, in some sense, fluid. Earth is not impermeable. Solids are not solid. At the atomic level there is far more empty space than mass. Geologically, fire and water contour land masses. Rock liquefies in the fiery flow of lava. Seeping water filters through dense layers of stone, carves underground caves, and deposits rich minerals. The permeability of the soil is essential to the flourishing of life; without it the earth would be barren. The reified solidity of dualistic thinking sinks its foundations in shifting sands.

The interconnectedness of all life is nowhere more evident than in ecology: whatever enters the air and water affects us all. Studies by the (U.S.) Environmental Protection Agency have demonstrated that pharmaceuticals processed by the human body make their way into the rivers, groundwater, and drinking water.[18] Fish, plants, and mammals ingest these contents. Higher concentrations of the hormones in birth control pills in our water, for example, have been linked to mutations in the sex characteristics in fish, earlier menstruation for girls, and the development of breasts in men. Hormones injected into the beef and dairy cows that supply much of the meat and milk on the grocery shelves appear to have similar effects. We have come to realize the broader ramifications of pharmacological solutions to our problems.

The causes and disproportionate effects of global warming further illustrate our interconnectedness. Industrialized nations and large corporations are responsible for most of the deforestation and burning of fossil fuels that exacerbate the accumulation of carbon dioxide in the atmosphere. Yet as glaciers melt, ocean levels rise, and heat waves and severe storms intensify, the poor—who cannot simply turn on the air conditioning or relocate their livelihood—suffer the most. Growing seasons have been altered, and climactic zones have shifted. Entire species of animals are threatened with extinction as their habitats change. Many of the costs of a high standard of living are paid by others than those who enjoy the comforts of the modern world.

Can a renewed appreciation of this interconnectedness translate into more responsible ecological actions? Sallie McFague has argued that we need new metaphors of God's relationship to the world in an ecological age. She suggests "the world as God's body" as one alternative to remote, dominating monarchical models.[19] As scholars of Indian religion have noted, however, symbols that seem to value the earth do not always result in ecofriendly action. The Earth and her rivers are goddesses in the Hindu symbolic world, but a distinction between the concepts of physical cleanliness and the eternal purity of the goddesses allows pollution to go unchecked.[20] Women who revere the Earth as Bhu Devi through early morning *kolam* rituals also use a mechanism Vijaya Nagarajan calls "intermittent sacrality" to rationalize the heaps of trash they throw on the ground later in the day. One woman explains:

> Oh, what we believe does not have to rule at all times and at all places. Just because one place is made sacred at one particular time does not necessarily mean that it remains special throughout the day.... It is understood that we are human and that we need to live too. So, there is no expectation that we need to care for everything that is sacred all the time. We could not do it. We could not live. We have human needs and we must fulfill them.[21]

Worshipers invite divinities to be present for the period of worship but then ask them to leave graciously so that daily life may go on. These mechanisms—intermittent sacrality, the bracketing of ritual and material cleanliness—create dualisms that sever the interrelatedness implied by other theological categories.

Similar mechanisms guide individuals and communities who are otherwise well informed about ecology. Our essential relatedness is, indeed, an "inconvenient truth" that we set aside when it is most convenient to us. Why walk to the recycling bin when there is a garbage can right here? Why carpool when I could come and go as I please in my own vehicle? Overcoming a sense of individual exception is a real challenge. It is extraordinarily convenient to blame someone else: the large corporation with its enormous carbon footprint, the automakers that avoid tighter fuel efficiency standards, or the Hummer driver whose ecological sins are so much worse than mine. How significant can my individual choices really be in the face of such large-scale irresponsibility? I reason my way to a personal exemption because the "real" problem lies elsewhere.

A metaphorical economy of fluidity can help to dissolve the practical dualisms we habitually construct. Dare we dream of a time when this metaphor will become one we live by—when we will systematically adopt it, and when our initial impulse will not be the truncated sense of self-interest that permits individual and corporate exceptionalism but will become a radical sense of interrelation? Everyone and everything is connected, but a theology grounded in any of the dichotomies examined here will never equip us to live in accordance with this fundamental reality. A fluid schematic equips us not only to imagine divinity in line with this elemental connectivity, but to *experience and enact* our everyday relations with ourselves, our bodies, our communities, and our environment as part of the same matrix of becoming.

FLUIDITY AND THE OTHER

I have proposed that we follow Mechthild's and Lalleśwarī's fluid metaphors to a less-solid view of persons and entities. Having flowed out of the heart of the Trinity, Mechthild flows out in charity to others. Lalleśwarī longs to mingle and dissolve into the void of Śiva-consciousness, where she cognizes all beings as one. Fluidity assaults the adamantine boundaries of the ego. Our worry is that in abandoning the old, individualist model of selfhood, persons will become vulnerable to the abuse of their newly permeable selves. For all her eagerness to swim and float in the breath of God, Mechthild perceives the divine benediction "May your heart dissolve" as a loving but vaguely threatening "curse" (1.7). The line between union and nonbeing is thin indeed. For women tempted less toward pride than toward a dangerous self-negation, permeability to the influx of the needs and desires of others is hardly empowering.[22]

If we are to take the fluid ontology to heart, we will have to overcome the false dualism of what Catherine Keller calls the separable and the soluble selves. She asks, "Need differentiation imply separation? Need connection imply merger? Or can a richly differentiated self after all evolve on the basis of connection, never outgrowing its permeable ego boundaries?"[23] Boys are usually socialized to differentiate from the mother, while girls are encouraged to identify more closely with the world around them; however, there is nothing innate or "natural" about this difference. From the field of psychology, Keller reclaims the pre-oedipal phase of human development as the "empathic continuum from which we emerge."[24] Rather than severance, maturity for men *and* women entails the gradual differentiation and extension of this continuum.

Let us test the waters of relation for their capacity to sustain difference. The originating relation we share with our parents begins amid fluidity: seminal and cervical fluids that facilitate conception, the amniotic fluid that suspends and protects during gestation, the waters of birth that break forth into the world. Adrienne Rich writes powerfully of the mother-daughter bond that begins in pregnancy and continues as "the flow of energy between two biologically alike bodies, one of which has lain in amniotic bliss inside the other, one of which has labored to give birth to the other."[25] Not every person will create another human life in this way, but every single person who has ever lived shares the experience of being nurtured and born amid the life-giving flow of bodies. Self-other relations begin here, with connection. Fluidity facilitates the becoming of unique persons even as it connects them materially with others.

These generative waters have long been used to interpret humanity's most meaningful connections. Divinity creates amid watery chaos. The waters of baptism birth Christians anew into the community of the church. Karen Baker-Fletcher, who develops her pneumatology from a womanist perspective, describes divine spirit as "the all-encompassing, inclusive force in which God/Creator, Jesus, and all of creation are inextricably enwombed." Drawing on African theologies, she argues that spirit "is like the amniotic fluids—the waters of the womb—that encompass a child before it is born and accompany it, flowing out with it, as it makes its way into the world as we know it."[26] Human beings actively image the divine when we create, birth, and sustain the lives of others. We join the divine matrix of relationality not only as biological mothers, but also whenever we love, feed, encourage, teach, and struggle alongside another.

Our bodies and our skins ensure that we never become so identified with another that we cease to exist as unique, embodied individuals. The fluids of intercourse denote the ecstatic union of persons who literally and spiritually flow out to one another. Christians imagine Christ as wed to the church, and Mechthild's melting dissolution into God also evokes sexual intimacy, because sex rivals birth for the greatest intensity of self-other relations. Our union with others—both sexual and nonsexual—touches our deepest desire and calls us more fully to be ourselves. Neither divine nor human union destroys selfhood. It does not break the skin, as it were; and when it does—when our bodily or spiritual integrity is violated—we know that something is seriously amiss.

The wounded body of the other calls us back to our common humanity. Blood flows in our enemies' veins as well as our own; their wounds hurt as badly as ours. The vulnerable presence of a body in pain unmasks the lies we tell to mask their humanity. For Wendy Farley, the power in the blood of Christ lies in its ability to call us back to our own woundedness, both as individuals and as a species: "We hide these wounds from ourselves, burying them in recesses of mind and hiding the mass graves of history where we have massacred and tortured each other. Because Christ shows us his wounds, we can begin to show him ours."[27] Divine solidarity washes our wounds; compassion moves us to do the same for others.

The metaphorical fluidity of our "influence" on one another is rooted in bodily flow. Christian theologians need not seek metaphors that transcend touch, for the incarnation encourages us to look to the body as a source of revelation. For the fourteenth-century theologian Julian of Norwich, no bodily experience is so unedifying as to be off limits for contemplation:

> A man [sic] walks upright, and the food in his body is shut in as if in a well-made purse. When the time of his necessity comes, the purse is opened and then shut again, in most seemly fashion. And it is God

who does this, as it is shown when he says that he comes down to us in our humblest needs. For he does not despise what he has made, nor does he disdain to serve us in the simplest natural functions of our body, for love of the soul which he created in his own likeness.[28]

A fluid theology transgresses taboos surrounding the body, subverting patterns of thought that demarcate purity from impurity. This subversion has social ramifications, for it flows against systems of Untouchability, whether in explicit forms as in India's caste system, or in its countless implicit forms elsewhere. If divine love flows downhill, then the abject, the marginalized, and the impure become the recipients of long-awaited justice.

A fluid model wells up in a long lineage of women theologians, but in none of the above meditations has difference been eradicated. A "fluid bondedness"[29] shifts and widens human connection; a bounded fluidity ensures the integrity of body and self. As our fluid metaphors lap away the boundaries created by dualistic thinking, we move beyond the dualism of self and other toward difference-in-relation. This interplay of union and difference is a function of bodies and of desire, both of which are rooted in overflowing divinity. We conclude, therefore, where we began: with icons of divinity in flowing relation.

FLUIDITY AND DIVINITY

This book's comparative methodology has focused upon theological metaphors of fluidity from specific Hindu and Christian contexts. In contrast to the blanket denunciation of dualism in much contemporary literature, the notable differences between Kashmir Śaiva and Western Christian ways of talking about twoness have impelled us to critically evaluate which entities we juxtapose in our dualisms and how they relate to one another. The interplay of the texts and lives of Mechthild and Lalleśwarī has drawn us more deeply into a fluid dynamic that deserves greater prominence in Christian theology, but we need not travel far to find it. The fluid relation to divinity also wells up in embodied experiences of devotion.

In my observations of Hindu worship, I am struck by reminders of the life-giving flow that pools in the Christian baptismal font. *Abhiṣeka*, the ritual bathing of the deities, offers a vivid living portrait of the outpouring of gifts. Using ritual substances, the priests repeatedly douse the image (*murti*) that has been installed in the temple to embody the god or goddess. Liberal pitchers of water, milk, yogurt, ghee, honey, and even orange juice are prodigally poured over the deity's form. My stingy twinges of Protestant iconoclasm

("That's enough milk to feed a family for a month!") give way to fascination at the shifting beauty of the statue. Worshipers line up on either side of the enshrined goddess to witness the event. Water gushes down. Milk trickles more slowly. Yogurt clings to the face and arms of the goddess, enhancing her features through contrast. Ghee and honey make her face shine. Orange juice turns the flowing image golden. After each ritual dousing, a priest circles a flame around the image and then toward the crowd. Worshipers wave the light from the flame to their eyes, gratefully receiving the sacred sight (*darśan*) and illumination from the deity. The flow goes two ways: offerings shower down upon the *murti* as blessings shower down from divinity. In some temples, sacred substances trickle continuously from the womb of the inner sanctum (*garbagṛha*) to the exterior of the temple, for devotees to touch and drink after these substances come into contact with the deity.

The sacredness of flowing things in India—the life-giving cow, the cleansing river—keeps holy fluidity ever in the mind's eye. Every river is a goddess. Pilgrims travel to the city of Varanasi to bathe at the ghats on the edge of the holiest of rivers, the Ganges. Descending these stairs, they enter the water that is said to convey salvation and wash away sin. At temples all along the river, from its source to its end, visitors are offered this sacred water to drink. Many gather water in pots and jugs that they will bring home for those unable to make pilgrimage. At dusk, as the Ganges ripples orange, rose, and silver in the sunset, worshipers sing and wave their lamps in circles, lighting the face of the Goddess. Many place in the water offerings of candles bedded in flowers, and the flames dance off down the river.

In Rishikesh, at the bend in the river where the evening offerings take place, stands a lovely image of the dynamic interplay of divinity with itself. A tranquil white statue of Lord Śiva in lotus position faces the ghats just offshore, with Ganges herself swirling and glinting on the rocks all around him. As the story goes, to spare the world the full impact of the river's forceful descent from heaven in ancient times, Śiva invited her to fall upon his head and flow to Earth through his hair. They are one in divinity and in love, yet one or the other becomes more prominent as the light shifts. In the daylight, the powerful river attracts the eye. The colors become more subdued and the illuminated image of Śiva more prominent as the sun sets, until only Śiva is visible; yet the river is still there, flowing silently around him. The faces of the divine are alternately two, one, masculine, feminine, personal, and nonpersonal.

In this play of light on water, a counterpoint to the evening songs of praise arises from the memories of our two medieval theologians. We hear the rich strains of Mechthild of Magdeburg, who praises the flowing light of the Godhead:

> O you pouring God in your gift!
> O you flowing God in your love!
> O you burning God in your desire!
> O you melting God in the union with your beloved!
>
> *(1.17)*

The mystery of the holy Trinity, that "playful flood of love" (7.45), submerges our desire to reify the three and the one.

The power of rivers, of water, as symbols or even incarnations of divinity strikes nearly simultaneously with the memory of polluted beaches and nonpotable water. Lalleśwarī now takes up her chorus, strains of longing in the sweet soprano of Indian classical training: "Would that God heard my prayer and ferry me across safely. . . . How I wish I would reach home!" (K 1). Although Lalleśwarī knows she, like this holy river, has flowed from God, she feels cut off from the flow. The distance and the darkness are prohibitive. We could cultivate the flow within us, but instead we stop it up with the detritus of our paltry and myopic concerns. We forget our innate connection to the land, air, and rivers. We cut ourselves off from one another through violence and indifference. Into this quagmire, divinity breathes.

What is the relation of the divine to itself? Divinity mixes with divinity. What is the status of the world to the eternal? It flows from it and returns there again. How does the individual soul experience this return? It mingles while remaining whole—but not before it flows out to others, whose bodies also flow, in all their differences. Relation oscillates, defying dualism. Three-in-one. Two. None. And two again, in relation.

Notes

Introduction

1. Aristotle, *Metaphysics*, in *The Basic Works of Aristotle*, ed. Richard McKeon (New York: Random House, 1941), 986a.22.
2. These narratives have become somewhat stock-in-trade. See Grace Jantzen, *God's World, God's Body* (Philadelphia: Westminster Press, 1984); and Rosemary Radford Ruether, *New Woman, New Earth: Sexist Ideologies and Human Liberation* (New York: Seabury Press, 1975). Val Plumwood gives a critical survey of the use of Plato and Descartes in these narratives in Val Plumwood, *Feminism and the Mastery of Nature* (New York: Routledge, 1993).
3. Among her many works on this subject, see Sallie McFague, *Models of God: Theology for an Ecological, Nuclear Age* (Philadelphia: Fortress Press, 1987).
4. Gillian McCulloch, *The Deconstruction of Dualism in Theology: With Special Reference to Ecofeminist Theology and New Age Spirituality* (Cumbria: Paternoster, 2002), 2–3.
5. Ibid., 209.
6. Lance Nelson levels insightful feminist and ecological critiques of these trends in "Reading the *Bhagavadgītā* from an Ecological Perspective," in *Hinduism and Ecology: The Intersection of Earth, Sky, and Water*, edited by Christopher Key Chapple and Mary Evelyn Tucker (Cambridge, MA: Harvard University Press, 2000).
7. John J. Thatamanil, *The Immanent Divine: God, Creation, and the Human Predicament* (Minneapolis: Fortress Press, 2006); Milton Scarborough, *Comparative Theories of Nonduality: The Search for a Middle Way* (London: Continuum, 2009), 2.

Chapter 1: What to Do about Dualism?

1. Scarborough, *Comparative Theories of Nonduality*, 6.
2. Plumwood continues, "Dualism is a relation of separation and domination inscribed and naturalized in culture and characterized by radical exclusion, distancing and opposition between orders constructed as systematically higher or lower, as inferior and superior, as ruler and ruled, which treats the division as part of the natures of beings construed not merely as different but as belonging to radically different orders or kinds, and hence as not open to change." Plumwood, *Feminism and the Mastery of Nature*, 47–48.
3. Ibid., 60.
4. Ibid., 67.

5. Ibid., 58.
6. One classic work that weaves together these strands beautifully is Catherine Keller, *From a Broken Web: Separation, Sexism, and Self* (Boston: Beacon, 1986).
7. The six systems, or *darśana*s, are Sāṃkhya, Yoga, Nyāya, Vaiśeṣika, mīmāṃsā, and Vedānta. Sāṃkhya teaches an irreducible dualism between material creation and the highest principle, and Yoga bases its system of meditation upon Sāṃkhya metaphysics. Vedānta philosophy includes dualist, nondualist, and qualified nondualist varieties.
8. See, for instance, Lance E. Nelson, "The Dualism of Non-Dualism: Advaita Vedanta and the Irrelevance of Nature," *Purifying the Earthly Body of God: Religion and Ecology in Hindu India*, ed. Lance E. Nelson (Albany: SUNY Press, 1998).
9. For some of the ambiguities surrounding this history, see Hugh Nicholson, "Comparative Theology after Liberalism," *Modern Theology* 23, no. 2 (2007).
10. See Jonathan Z. Smith, "In Comparison a Magic Dwells," in *Imagining Religion: From Babylon to Jonestown* (Chicago: University of Chicago Press, 1982).
11. Jonathan Z. Smith, "The 'End' of Comparison," in *A Magic Still Dwells: Comparative Religion in the Postmodern Age*, ed. Kimberley C. Patton and Benjamin C. Ray (Berkeley: University of California Press, 2000), 239. Two works that follow Smith's methodological suggestions with admirable results are Lee H. Yearley, *Mencius and Aquinas: Theories of Virtue and Conceptions of Courage* (Albany: SUNY Press, 1990); and Barbara A. Holdrege, *Veda and Torah: Transcending the Textuality of Scripture* (Albany: SUNY Press, 1995).
12. Francis Xavier Clooney, *Hindu God, Christian God: How Reason Helps Break Down the Boundaries between Religions* (Oxford: Oxford University Press, 2001), 163.
13. Francis X. Clooney, *Theology after Vedanta: An Experiment in Comparative Theology* (Albany: SUNY Press, 1993), 187.
14. Smith, "The 'End' of Comparison," 239.
15. Patricia Hill Collins, *Black Feminist Thought: Knowledge, Consciousness, and the Politics of Empowerment*, Perspectives on Gender Series 2 (Boston: Unwin Hyman, 1990), 5.
16. I consider the importance of this category at greater length in Michelle Voss Roberts, "Gendering Comparative Theology," in *The New Comparative Theology: Voices from the Younger Generation*, ed. Francis X. Clooney (New York: Continuum, 2010).
17. Peter Feldmeier, *Christianity Looks East: Comparing the Spiritualities of John of the Cross and Buddhaghosa* (New York: Paulist Press, 2006), 6, emphasis added; cf. 117–18.
18. Ronald Inden, *Imagining India* (Oxford: Basil Blackwell, 1990), 117.
19. Ibid., 119.
20. Jai Lal Kaul, *Lal Ded* (New Delhi: Sahitya Akademi, 1973), 61.
21. The first text to mention her is Bābā Dāwūd Mishkātī's Persian chronicle, *Asrār-ul-Abrār* (The Secrets of the Pious) in 1654. Bābā Nasīb-ud-dīn Ghazi's *Nūrnāma*, a seventeenth-century hagiography of Nund Rishi, is perhaps the earliest Kashmiri text that mentions her. For a list of biographical references to Lalleśwarī, see Kaul, *Lal Ded*, 1–5.
22. For theories on the origins of the term, see Elizabeth A. Andersen, *The Voices of Mechthild of Magdeburg* (Oxford: Peter Lang, 2000), 61–64, 67, 78. For a broad historical analysis of the connections between heresy and medieval

women's movements, see Herbert Grundmann, *Religious Movements in the Middle Ages: The Historical Links between Heresy, the Mendicant Orders, and the Women's Religious Movement in the Twelfth and Thirteenth Centuries, with the Historical Foundations of German Mysticism*, trans. Steven Rowan (Notre Dame, IN: University of Notre Dame Press, 1995).
23. For essays on this connection, see Bernard McGinn, ed., *Meister Eckhart and the Beguine Mystics: Hadewijch of Brabant, Mechthild of Magdeburg, and Marguerite Porete* (New York: Continuum, 1994).
24. Hans Neumann, "Mechthild von Magdeburg," in *Die deutsche Literatur des Mittelalters: Verfasserlexikon*, ed. Kurt Ruh (Berlin: Walter de Gruyter, 1987), 260.
25. Frank J. Tobin, *Mechthild von Magdeburg: A Medieval Mystic in Modern Eyes* (Columbia, SC: Camden House, 1995), 2.
26. Bernard McGinn coins the term "vernacular theology" to classify medieval women's writings alongside scholastic and monastic models. Bernard McGinn, "Introduction," in *Meister Eckhart and the Beguine Mystics*, 1–14.
27. Frank J. Tobin, "Introduction," in Mechthild of Magdeburg, *The Flowing Light of the Godhead*, trans. and intro. Frank J. Tobin (New York: Paulist Press, 1998), 3.
28. Ursula Peters, however, cautions against lassoing Mechthild into the general stereotype of the "endangered beguine." Ursula Peters, *Religiöse Erfahrung als literarisches Factum: Zur Vorgeschichte und Genese frauenmystischer Texte des 13. und 14. Jahrhunderts* (Tübingen: Niemeyer, 1988), 59–67.
29. See Sara S. Poor, *Mechthild of Magdeburg and Her Book: Gender and the Making of Textual Authority* (Philadelphia: University of Pennsylvania Press, 2004), 203.
30. Ibid., 201.
31. Tobin, "Introduction," 7.
32. The earliest documentation on Lalleśwarī (the *Asrār-ul-Abrār* and *Nūrnāma*) is from the seventeenth century, almost three hundred years after Lalleśwarī's lifetime. Other than a mention of Lalleśwarī's renunciation of her marriage home in *Asrār-ul-Abrār*, tales connected to Nund Rishi in *Nūrnāma*, and much later traditions about her birth and her relationship to other saints (cf. Kaul, *Lal Ded*, 2–5), most Lalleśwarī legends first appear in writing in the early twentieth century. The first English language testament I have found for most of the stories is Anand Koul, "Life Sketch of Laleshwari—a Great Hermitess of Kashmir," *Indian Antiquary* 50 (1921): 302–8; he does not name his sources. Contemporaneous scholarly treatments—Sir George Grierson and Lionel D. Barnett, *Lallā-Vākhyāni: The Wise Sayings of Lal Děd, a Mystic Poetess of Ancient Kashmīr* (London: Royal Asiatic Society, 1920); and Richard Carnac Temple, *The Word of Lalla the Prophetess* (Cambridge: Cambridge University Press, 1924)—do not seem to know the legends that Koul relates. S. S. Toshkhani is of the opinion that their source lies in "oral lore" and that they were first written down for the *Indian Antiquary* (personal correspondence, June 30, 2006).
33. Kaul, *Lal Ded*, 7.
34. Temple, *The Word of Lalla the Prophetess*.
35. Grierson and Barnett, *Lallā-Vākhyāni*. Also see the foreword of B. N. Parimoo, *The Ascent of Self: A Reinterpretation of the Mystical Poetry of Lalla-Ded* (Delhi: Motilal Banarsidass, 1987).

36. Jaishree Kak Odin, *To the Other Shore: Lalla's Life and Poetry* (New Delhi: Vitasta, 1999), ix.
37. S. Bhat, "Lal Ded: Her Spiritualism and Present Scientific World Order," in *Lal Ded: The Great Kashmiri Saint-Poetess*, ed. S. S. Toshkhani (New Delhi: APH Publishing Corp., 2002), 25.
38. Those who classify Lalleśwarī as a *bhakti* saint or compare her with others in the "movement" include David Kinsley, "Devotion as an Alternative to Marriage in the Lives of Some Hindu Women Devotees," *Journal of Asian and African Studies* 15, nos. 1–2 (1980); Nil Kanth Kotru, *Lal Ded, Her Life and Sayings* (Srinigar: Utpal Publications, 1989), xi–xii; Odin, *To the Other Shore*, 39–44; and the scholars featured in *Lal Ded: The Great Mystic Saint-Poetess*, ed. S. S. Toshkhani (New Delhi: APH Publishing Corp., 2002).
39. Gavin Flood, "The Śaiva Traditions," in *The Blackwell Companion to Hinduism*, ed. Gavin Flood (Oxford: Blackwell Publishing, 2003), 213. Jaishree Odin outlines Lalleśwarī's position within the Trika tradition, along with her familiarity with the Tantric schools of yoga (such as the Vijñānabhairava Tantra) in *To the Other Shore*, chap. 5.
40. See Alexis Sanderson, "Śaivism and the Tantric Traditions," in *The World's Religions: The Religions of Asia*, ed. Friedhelm Hardy (London: Routledge, 1988).
41. Lance E. Nelson, "Foreword," in *Self Realization in Kashmir Shaivism: The Oral Teachings of Swami Lakshmanjoo*, ed. John Hughes (Albany: SUNY Press, 1994), xxxvi.
42. Kaul (*Lal Ded*, 33) believes that "whatever education Lal Ded might have had would be in Sanskrit," but he does not offer evidence that she was actually afforded such an education.
43. Lalleśwarī's *vaakhs* were first made available to English-language audiences in the 1920 study of Sir George Grierson and Lionel Barnett, *Lallā-Vākhyāni*, based upon transcriptions from Kashmiri pandits. Between 1921 and 1933, Anand Koul supplemented this collection with an additional 60 verses through installments in *Indian Antiquary*. See Koul, "Life Sketch of Laleshwari"; "Some Additions to the Lalla-Vakyani," *Indian Antiquary* 59 (1930); "Lalla-Vakyani," *Indian Antiquary* 60 (1931); "Lalla-Vakyani," 61 (1932); and "Lalla-Vakyani," *Indian Antiquary* 62 (1933).
44. The word "mysticism" is fraught with a history that tends to preclude women's religious authority. Grace Jantzen explains that, in particular, William James's influential definition of mysticism as an intense, emotional, private, ineffable subjective state has effectively barred the women "mystics" from authority in the public sphere. See Grace Jantzen, *Power, Gender and Christian Mysticism* (Cambridge: Cambridge University Press, 1995).
45. For an excellent study of the term *darśana* in relation to European philosophy, see chap. 15 of Wilhelm Halbfass, *India and Europe: An Essay in Understanding* (Albany: SUNY Press, 1988).
46. Despite the differing and overlapping terminology for the spheres of religion, theology, and philosophy in Indian traditions, some Hindu scholars today accept the title of theologian. See, e.g., Parimal G. Patil, "A Hindu Theologian's Response: A Prolegomenon to 'Christian God, Hindu God,'" in *Hindu God, Christian God: How Reason Helps Break Down the Boundaries between Religions*, ed. Francis Xavier Clooney (Oxford: Oxford University Press, 2001).
47. As possible sources for this imagery, in addition to biblical precedents, Neumann ("Mechthild von Magdeburg," 263–64) identifies Pseudo-Dionysian

emanation and return, the role of light in Neoplatonic metaphysics, and Judeo-Christian images of revelation.
48. James C. Franklin, *Mystical Transformations: The Imagery of Liquids in the Work of Mechthild von Magdeburg* (London: Associated University Presses, 1978).
49. Nancy G. Siraisi, *Medieval and Renaissance Medicine: An Introduction to Knowledge and Practice* (Chicago: University of Chicago Press, 1990), 105. For the importance of bodily fluids in medieval spirituality, see chap. 6 in Caroline Walker Bynum, *Fragmentation and Redemption: Essays on Gender and the Human Body in Medieval Religion* (New York: Zone Books, 1991).
50. George Lakoff and Mark Johnson, *Metaphors We Live By* (1980; Chicago: University of Chicago Press, 2003), 18.
51. Ibid., 57.
52. Ibid.; cf. 257.
53. See, famously, Judith Butler, *Gender Trouble: Feminism and the Subversion of Identity* (New York: Routledge, 1990).
54. James Egge, "Theorizing Embodiment: Conceptual Metaphor Theory and the Comparative Study of Religion," in *Figuring Religions: Comparing Ideas, Images, and Activities*, ed. Shubha Pathak (Albany: SUNY Press, forthcoming).
55. Edward Slingerland, "Conceptual Metaphor Theory as Methodology for Comparative Religion," *Journal of the American Academy of Religion* 72, no. 1 (2004): 13.
56. Lakoff and Johnson, *Metaphors We Live By*, 29.
57. Ibid., 145.

Chapter 2: Duality in Union with the Divine

1. Richard King, *Orientalism and Religion: Postcolonial Theory, India and "the Mystic East"* (London: Routledge, 1999), 209.
2. Although this is a standard reading of Advaita metaphysics, vigorous defenses that Śaṅkara does not dismiss the phenomenal world as an illusion have emerged in recent years. See, e.g., Sara Grant, RSCJ, *Śaṅkarācārya's Concept of Relation* (Delhi: Motilal Banarsidass, 1999); and Anantanand Rambachan, *The Advaita Worldview: God, World, and Humanity* (Albany: SUNY Press, 2006).
3. These terms are often treated as interchangeable with reference to Indian traditions, in part because of the difficulty of applying nonnative terms. *Monism* denotes the unity of all realty, *pantheism* emphasizes that all that exists is divine, and the *mystical* has a long and complicated history, which I shall discuss shortly.
4. Rudyard Kipling, "The Ballad of East and West," in *Rudyard Kipling's Verse: Definitive Edition* (Garden City, NY: Doubleday, 1946), 233.
5. Thatamanil, *The Immanent Divine*, 4–5.
6. See, e.g., chap. 82 of Marguerite Porete, *The Mirror of Simple Souls*, trans. Edmund Colledge (Notre Dame: University of Notre Dame Press, 1999), 107.
7. Meister Eckhart, "Sermon 48," in *Meister Eckhart: The Essential Sermons, Commentaries, Treatises, and Defense*, trans. Edmund Colledge (New York: Paulist Press, 1981), 198.
8. Meister Eckhart, "Sermon 22," in ibid., 194.
9. Porete, *The Mirror of Simple Souls*, 145–46.
10. Rudolf Otto, *Mysticism East and West: A Comparative Analysis of the Nature of Mysticism*, trans. Bertha L. Bracey and Richenda C. Payne (New York: Collier Books, 1962), 216.

11. Thatamanil, *The Immanent Divine*, 19.
12. Ibid., 143.
13. J. C. Chatterji, *Kashmir Shaivaism* (Albany: SUNY Press, 1986), 1. Kashmir Śaivism has also been called "'realistic idealism,' 'monistic idealism,' 'idealistic monism,' and 'concrete monism." See Mark S. G. Dyczkowski, *The Doctrine of Vibration: An Analysis of the Doctrines and Practices of Kashmir Shaivism* (Albany: SUNY Press, 1987), 51.
14. B. N. Pandit, *Aspects of Kashmir Śaivism* (Srinagar: Utpal Publications, 1977), 45.
15. Dyczkowski, *The Doctrine of Vibration*, 37; here Dyczkowski cites the great Kashmir Śaiva theologian Abhinavagupta as saying in *Mālinīvijayavārtika* 1/628 that the "if [duality and oneness] were in fact [to contradict each other], they would clearly be two [distinct realities]."
16. See Edward W. Said, *Orientalism* (New York: Vintage Books, 1978); Mrinalini Sinha, *Colonial Masculinity: The "Manly Englishman" and the "Effeminate Bengali" in the Late Nineteenth Century* (Manchester: Manchester University Press, 1995), 181; Jane Miller, *Seductions: Studies in Reading and Culture* (Cambridge, MA: Harvard University Press, 1991), 118–22; and, for an exception that attends to women's contributions to Orientalism, Reina Lewis, *Gendering Orientalism: Race, Femininity and Representation* (London: Routledge, 1996), 4.
17. Grace Jantzen, "'Where Two Are to Become One': Mysticism and Monism," in *The Philosophy in Christianity*, ed. Godfrey Vesey (Cambridge: Cambridge University Press, 1990), 164.
18. Ibid., 166.
19. King, *Orientalism and Religion*, 28–29. This strategy also gave "an easy 'monistic' target for Christian missionaries . . . By characterizing Hinduism as a monistic religion, Christian theologians and apologists were able to criticize the mystical monism of Hinduism, thereby highlighting the moral superiority of Christianity" (132).
20. Jantzen, "Mysticism and Monism," 166.
21. Jaishree Kak Odin, *To the Other Shore: Lalla's Life and Poetry* (New Delhi: Vitasta, 1999), 84.
22. For a discussion of how the *malas* contract the powers of Śiva, see Gavin D. Flood, *Body and Cosmology in Kashmir Śaivism* (San Francisco: Mellen Research University Press, 1993), 62–66.
23. Ibid., 161–68.
24. The Bhagavad-Gita famously teaches that "abandoning attachment to fruits of action, always content, independent, [one] does nothing at all even when he engages in action. He incurs no guilt if he . . . performs actions with his body only." *The Bhagavad-Gita: Krishna's Counsel in Time of War*, trans. Barbara Stoler Miller (New York: Bantam, 1986), 4.20–21.
25. This traditional argument appears in Rājānaka Rāma's *Spandavivṛtti*. See Mark S. G. Dyczkowski, trans., *The Stanzas on Vibration: The Spandakārikā with Four Commentaries*, translated with introduction and exposition (Albany: SUNY Press, 1992), 75.
26. Cf. Kaul, *Lal Ded*, 1 n. 1. Kotru renders the term as "simple" in his translations of K 50 and 67.
27. "Self-awareness" (K 76), "Self-knowledge" (O 81), "Self" (Kaul, saying 76), and "God" (Koul, "Life Sketch of Laleshwari," 305) are among the various attempts to translate this rich term.

28. The *Spanda Kārikās* use the terms *jīva* (individual soul), *svabhāva* (one's being), or *svasvabhāva* (one's very own being). The Trika school refers to the *anu*, "point" or individual center of consciousness, as a counterpart to the divine Śiva and Śakti. Lalleśwarī uses the term *svatmas* in K 49 (O 80), a technical philosophical referent for soul or self that is eternally united with its divine source (related to *ātman*, the Sanskrit term used in the *Śiva Sūtras*). She also uses the common Kashmiri word *pan*, "oneself," which includes the mind, body, and other faculties; it often signifies the individual self, which can either identify with the Self or retain a separate sense of "I."
29. For traditional discussions of the four states, see *Spanda Kārikā* 17 in Dyczkowski, *Stanzas on Vibration*, 94; and *Śiva Sūtra*s 1/8–1/10 in Mark S. G. Dyczkowski, trans., *The Aphorisms of Śiva: The Śiva Sūtra with Bhāskara's Commentary, the Vārttika*, translated with exposition and notes (Albany: SUNY Press, 1992), 28–35.
30. Flood, *Body and Cosmology*, 249. The *Śiva Sūtra*s similarly describe spiritual attainment as "unification with the great lake." See Kṣemarāja, *The Doctrine of Recognition: A Translation of Pratyabhijñāhṛdayam*, trans. Jaideva Singh (Albany: SUNY Press, 1990), 92–93.
31. Dyczkowski, *The Doctrine of Vibration*, 38.
32. Odin, *To the Other Shore*, 88.
33. Here her term for the true self is *tsitta atmase* (O 139). More basic and lasting than the empirical self (*pan*), the *ātman* is its lasting foundation, the center that shares the attributes of universal consciousness.
34. Grierson and Barnett, *Lallā-Vākhyāni*, 35.
35. *Vijñānabhairava Tantra* verse 120 states that "if one, after casting one's gaze on some object, withdraws it and slowly eliminates the knowledge of that object along with the thought and impression of it, he abides in the void." Jaideva Singh, *Vijñānabhairava or Divine Consciousness: A Treasury of 112 Types of Yoga* (Delhi: Motilal Banarsidass, 1979), 107.
36. Ian Whicher has made a similar argument about the goal of yogic practice in the Yoga Sūtras: *citta-vṛtti-nirodha*, the cessation of the turnings of thought, does not entail the absolute cessation of thought but is an epistemological practice to end one's misidentification with the various objects of consciousness. Ian Whicher, *The Integrity of the Yoga Darsana: A Reconsideration of Classical Yoga* (Albany: SUNY Press, 1998).
37. As Dyczkowski puts it, "Oneness is better understood as the coextensive unity (*ekarasa*) of both duality and unity. They are equally expressions of the absolute.... The two represent opposite polarities of a single reality." Dyczkowski, *The Doctrine of Vibration*, 37–38.
38. Odin, *To the Other Shore*, 78.
39. Jayant Lele, "Orientalism and the Social Sciences," in *Orientalism and the Postcolonial Predicament: Perspectives on South Asia*, ed. Carol A. Breckenridge and Peter van der Veer (Philadelphia: University of Pennsylvania Press, 1993), 45.
40. Bernard McGinn, *The Foundations of Mysticism: Origins to the Fifth Century* (New York: Crossroad, 1990), xvi.
41. Lady Love ranks among numerous female "emanations of the Divine, mediators between God and the cosmos, embodied universals, and . . . objects of identification and desire" in medieval Christian thought, which Barbara Newman has argued have the function of goddesses in the religious imagination.

Barbara Newman, *God and the Goddesses: Vision, Poetry, and Belief in the Middle Ages* (Philadelphia: University of Pennsylvania Press, 2003), 2–3.

42. Bernard McGinn, *The Flowering of Mysticism: Men and Women in the New Mysticism (1200–1350)* (New York: Crossroad, 1998), 235.
43. Margot Schmidt and Susan Johnson, trans., "'minne du gewaltige kellerin': On the Nature of *minne* in Mechthild of Magdeburg's *Fliessende Licht der Gottheit*," *Vox benedictina* 4 (1987): 102.
44. For other references to God's powerlessness see *FL* 1.22; 6.20; and the prologue. Hans Neumann comments that this powerlessness (*Unmacht*) does not contradict God's omnipotence (*Allmacht*) but should be understood as part of God's active potentiality (*potentia activa*). See Mechthild von Magdeburg, *Das fliessende Licht der Gottheit: Nach der Einsiedler Handschrift in kritischem Vergleich mit der gesamten Überlieferung*, ed. Hans Neumann, arranged by Gisela Vollman-Profe, vol. 2 (Munich: Artemis Verlag, 1993), 3–4.
45. Through Mary, the true nature of the human soul thus remains unsullied in the Trinity as salvation history proceeds. Cf. Barbara Newman, *From Virile Woman to Womanchrist* (Philadelphia: University of Pennsylvania Press, 1995), 150.
46. Jesus similarly compels the Trinity in *FL* 6.16; elsewhere Love plays this role (1.1).
47. See *FL* 4.16 and 7.47 for the nuances of this position.
48. For more on the eternal dynamic of desire, see Barbara Newman, "The Mozartian Moment: Reflections on Medieval Mysticism," in *Minding the Spirit: The Study of Christian Spirituality*, ed. Elizabeth A. Dreyer and Mark S. Burrows (Baltimore: Johns Hopkins University Press, 2005), 205.
49. McGinn, *The Flowering of Mysticism*, 169.
50. Amy Hollywood demonstrates that the will, and not the body, is the locus of sin for Mechthild. See Amy Hollywood, *The Soul as Virgin Wife: Mechthild of Magdeburg, Marguerite Porete, and Meister Eckhart* (Notre Dame, IN: University of Notre Dame Press, 1995), 78. For discussions of free will in Mechthild, see *FL* 3.9; 5.8; and 6.7; for the problem of self-will, see 2.1; 2.4; 2.23; 3.17; and 5.5.
51. See *FL* 2.4; 3.7; and 3.14.
52. Mechthild's most significant treatments of this theme occur in *FL* 1.22; 1.29; 3.2; 3.3; and 3.5. *Das ellende* is also the term for the breach in the heavenly hierarchy, now vacated by the fall of the angels (3.1).
53. The desert motif is territory where Mechthild and Eckhart share common ground. See Frank J. Tobin, "Mechthild of Magdeburg and Meister Eckhart: Points of Coincidence," in *Meister Eckhart and the Beguine Mystics: Hadewijch of Brabant, Mechthild of Magdeburg, and Marguerite Porete*, ed. Bernard McGinn (New York: Continuum, 1994), 48.
54. Richard summarizes this process in Richard of St. Victor, *Selected Writings on Contemplation*, trans. Clare Kirchberger (New York: Harper & Brothers, 1957), 232–33.
55. See William of St. Thierry, *The Nature and Dignity of Love*, trans. Thomas X. Davis (Kalamazoo, MI: Cistercian Publications, 1981), par. 26–27.
56. Newman, *From Virile Woman to Womanchrist*, 151.
57. See Margit Sinka, "Christological Mysticism in Mechthild von Magdeburg's *Das fliessende Licht der Gottheit*: A Journey of Wounds," *Germanic Review* 60, no. 4 (1985). Tobin argues that Sinka "does not misrepresent Mechthild's

thought; but she gives the false impression of structure where little is apparent." Tobin, *Mechthild von Magdeburg*, 102.
58. See, e.g., par. 45 in William of St. Thierry, *The Nature and Dignity of Love*. Ulrike Wiethaus stresses the simultaneity of Mechthild's frameworks in *Ecstatic Transformation: Transpersonal Psychology in the Work of Mechthild of Magdeburg* (Syracuse, NY: Syracuse University Press, 1996), 35–37.
59. Hollywood, *The Soul as Virgin Wife*, 177, emphasis added.
60. See *FL* 1.2; 1.7; 1.22; 3.10; 4.5; 4.15; 5.4; and 6.1.
61. Tobin, in Mechthild of Magdeburg, *Flowing Light*, 345 n. 18.
62. McGinn, *The Flowering of Mysticism*, 238.
63. Lakoff and Johnson, *Metaphors We Live By*.
64. Margot Schmidt sketches similarities between union through the Eucharist and the union of the Trinitarian persons in "'die spilende minnevluot': Der Eros als Sein und Wirkkraft in der Trinität bei Mechthild von Magdeburg," in *"Eine Höhe, über die nichts geht": Spezielle Glaubenserfahrung in der Frauenmystik?* ed. Margot Schmidt and Dieter R. Bauer (Stuttgart-Bad Cannstatt: Frommann-Holzboog, 1986), 75–76.
65. Franklin, *Mystical Transformations*, 95.
66. God's breath sustains the angels (*FL* 2.3; 4.14) and the blessed who *sweben* in heaven (3.1). It similarly invigorates the soul (5.6) and nourishes it through rapture and consolation (4.12). Also see 1.29; 5.32; and 6.13.
67. McGinn, *The Flowering of Mysticism*, 238.
68. References to the soul's adornment are ubiquitous (see *FL* 2.4; 2.19; 3.1; 4.24; 5.25; 5.28; and 7.1).
69. Jantzen, "Mysticism and Monism," 157.
70. Ibid.
71. Singh, *Vijñānabhairava or Divine Consciousness*, sūtra 92.

Chapter 3: Coming "Down" to Earth?

1. I have chosen to focus on the issue of continuity and difference between divinity and the world, but this is only one possible theological approach to ecology. For a typology of Christian positions, see James A. Gustafson, *A Sense of the Divine: The Natural Environment from a Theocentric Perspective* (Cleveland: Pilgrim Press, 1994), chap. 3.
2. Plumwood, *Feminism and the Mastery of Nature*, 60. Lynn White's now-classic article asserts the theme of domination of nature in Christianity: Lynn White Jr., "The Historical Roots of Our Ecological Crisis," *Science* 155 (1967).
3. Rosemary Radford Ruether, *Gaia and God: An Ecofeminist Theology of Earth Healing* (San Francisco: Harper San Francisco, 1992), 233.
4. Ibid., 234.
5. Heather Eaton, *Introducing Ecofeminist Theologies* (London: T&T Clark International, 2005), 97.
6. McFague, *Models of God*, 72. The author abandons the term monism for "panentheism" but develops the metaphor of the world as God's body in Sallie McFague, *The Body of God: An Ecological Theology* (Minneapolis: Fortress Press, 1993).
7. Grace Jantzen, *Becoming Divine: Toward a Feminist Philosophy of Religion* (Bloomington: Indiana University Press, 1999), 269. Also see Grace Jantzen, *God's World, God's Body*, for a philosophical defense of pantheism, using the categories of classical theism.

8. Catherine Keller, *Face of the Deep: A Theology of Becoming* (New York: Routledge, 2003), 218.
9. The Romantic idea that India offers a "harmonious connection between the human being and the natural world" has been both asserted positively in ecological conversations and criticized from a postcolonial angle. Laurie L. Patton, "Nature Romanticism and Sacrifice in Ṛgvedic Interpretation," in *Hinduism and Ecology: The Intersection of Earth, Sky, and Water*, ed. Christopher Key Chapple and Mary Evelyn Tucker (Cambridge, MA: Harvard University Press, 2000), 40.
10. For an overview of the Harvard conference and the ten volumes subsequently issued by Harvard University Press (1997–2003), see chap. 2 of Rosemary Radford Ruether, *Integrating Ecofeminism, Globalization, and World Religions* (Oxford: Rowman & Littlefield Publishers, 2005).
11. Odin, *To the Other Shore*, 60–62.
12. See Rita DasGupta Sherma, "Sacred Immanence: Reflections of Ecofeminism in Hindu Tantra," in Nelson, *Purifying the Earthly Body of God*, 95–101.
13. Rambachan, *The Advaita Worldview*, 79.
14. Sherma, "Sacred Immanence," 115, 123–27.
15. David L. Haberman, *River of Love in an Age of Pollution* (Berkeley: University of California Press, 2006). Also see Lina Gupta, "Ganga: Purity, Pollution, and Hinduism," in *Ecofeminism and the Sacred*, ed. Carol Adams (New York: Continuum, 1993), 99–116; and Kelly D. Alley, "Separate Domains: Hinduism, Politics, and Environmental Pollution," in Chapple and Tucker, *Hinduism and Ecology*, 355–88.
16. Kartikeya C. Patel, "Women, Earth, and the Goddess: A Shakta-Hindu Interpretation of Embodied Religion," *Hypatia* 9, no. 4 (1994).
17. Vandana Shiva, *Staying Alive: Women, Ecology and Development* (New Delhi: Kali for Women, 1988), chap. 3. The debate over the "feminist" function of goddesses in Hinduism—or lack thereof—is well represented in Alf Hiltebeitel and Kathleen M. Erndl, eds., *Is the Goddess a Feminist? The Politics of South Asian Goddesses* (2000; New Delhi: Oxford University Press, 2002).
18. Plumwood, *Feminism and the Mastery of Nature*, 67.
19. Ecofeminist theology is one arena where comparative or interreligious work is well under way. See Mary C. Grey, *Sacred Longings: Ecofeminist Theology and Globalization* (Minneapolis: Augsburg Fortress, 2004); Rita M. Gross and Rosemary Radford Ruether, *Religious Feminism and the Future of the Planet: A Christian-Buddhist Conversation* (New York: Continuum, 2001); and Ruether, *Integrating Ecofeminism, Globalization, and World Religions*.
20. Dyczkowski, *The Doctrine of Vibration*, 40.
21. Vrinda Dalmiya, "Loving Paradoxes: A Feminist Reclamation of the Goddess Kali," *Hypatia* 15, no. 1 (2000): 133.
22. *Śiva Sūtra* 1/15; in Dyczkowski, *The Aphorisms of Śiva*, 45.
23. This explanation of *Oṃ* derives from commentaries on *Spanda Kārikā* 3.42; summarized in Dyczkowski, *The Stanzas on Vibration*, 252–55.
24. Lalleśwarī similarly calls upon an alternative set of esoteric symbols for union, in K 122. For an explanation of other esoteric uses of language in Kashmir Śaivism, see Dyczkowski, *The Doctrine of Vibration*, 100–103; and Swami Lakshman Jee, *Kashmir Shaivism: The Secret Supreme* (Albany: SUNY Press; The Universal Shaiva Trust, 1988), 15–27.
25. Kṣemarāja, *The Doctrine of Recognition*, 100.

26. Kotru, *Lal Ded, Her Life and Sayings*, 85–86.
27. Although this standard information can be found in any introduction, in the following list of *tattva*s I follow Jaideva Singh, "Introduction," in Singh, *The Doctrine of Recognition*, 9–16.
28. Kotru, *Lal Ded, Her Life and Sayings*, 71.
29. Flood, *Body and Cosmology*, 92.
30. Dyczkowski, *The Doctrine of Vibration*, 194; cf. 165–66.
31. Isayeva, *From Early Vedanta to Kashmir Shaivism*, 147–48.
32. Flood, *Body and Cosmology*, 236. Flood details several rituals whose first step is the purification of the body. "The body, being a product of lower manifestation (of semen and blood), is impure in relation to higher levels, especially those above *māyā*. The body is therefore ritually destroyed, and thereby 'purified' in the imagination in order to transcend the lower, more restrictive layers of the universe" (272–73).
33. Odin, *To the Other Shore*, 90–91.
34. The reference to the "world" is indirect here: a literal reading would be "I am waiting for my breath to cut off."
35. Cf. sūtra 4 and commentary in Kṣemarāja, *The Doctrine of Recognition*, 52–55.
36. Flood, *Body and Cosmology*, 281.
37. Missing from the Kaul and Kotru collections, this verse appears not only in Odin but also in Shambhu Nath Bhatt and Janki Nath Bhan, "Lal Vakh," *Koshur Samachar*, 1970–71, #80; and B. N. Sopori, *Voice of Experience: Lal Ded and Her Vaakhs* (Sarwal Jammu: Kanti Offset Printing House, 1999), #55.
38. *Tantrāloka* 2/39; cited in Dyczkowski, *The Aphorisms of Śiva*, 8.
39. Tobin, "Introduction," 11.
40. Margot Schmidt, "'die spilende minnevluot,'" 81.
41. Bartholomaeus Anglicus, *De rerum proprietatibus* (1242–47; Frankfurt: Minerva, 1964), book 8.
42. Mechthild gives her reasons for the superiority of humans to angels in several passages, including FL 2.22; 3.1; 3.9; and 6.41. For a discussion of medieval Christian explanations for why Christ became human and not an angel, see Denys Turner, *The Darkness of God: Negativity in Christian Mysticism* (Cambridge: Cambridge University Press, 1995), 119.
43. As Thomas Aquinas explains the incorrigibility of the fallen angels, they cannot change their minds once they have chosen good or evil; because their will is purely intellectual and not appetitive, they will immovably. See Thomas Aquinas, *Summa theologica*, trans. Fathers of the English Dominican Province (New York: Benzinger Brothers, 1948), I, Q. 64, art. 2.
44. Petrus W. Tax, "Die grosse Himmelsschau Mechtilds von Magdeburg und ihre Höllenvision," *Zeitschrift für deutsches Altertum und deutsche Literatur* 108, no. 2 (1979), argues that much of what she reports may have been based on tradition and images she had seen.
45. Translators disagree about where Mary sits in relation to the Trinity. While Tobin, in Mechthild of Magdeburg, *Flowing Light*, places Mary upon the throne of the Trinity, "*an dem throne*" could be rendered "by" or "near the throne." Andersen, *The Voices of Mechthild of Magdeburg*, translates "by the throne stands Our Lady"; Galvani, in *The Flowing Light of the Godhead*, trans. Christiane Mesch Galvani (New York: Garland, 1991), posits a second throne: "at the throne of our lady."

46. Here I follow Tobin and Schmidt rather than Tax, who posits the desolation as a tenth choir of angels, in Tax, "Die grosse Himmelsschau," 117. See Tobin in Mechthild of Magdeburg's *Flowing Light*, 349 n. 8; and Schmidt in Mechthild of Magdeburg, *Das fliessende Licht der Gottheit*, trans. Margot Schmidt (Einsiedeln: Benziger, 1955), 366 n. 103.

47. Part of the "order" of hell consists in its consistent perversion of the goods of heaven, including a mockery of union with God as Bridegroom and a counterflow of wretchedness mirroring the goodness streaming from the other side of the cosmos (*FL* 3.21). Tax, "Die grosse Himmelsschau," 132.

48. See Andersen, *The Voices of Mechthild of Magdeburg*, 209–30.

49. See chap. 13 in Keller, *Face of the Deep*.

50. David Peter Lawrence, *Rediscovering God with Transcendental Argument: A Contemporary Interpretation of Monistic Kashmiri Śaiva Philosophy* (Albany: SUNY Press, 1999), 167–68. His term "dualistic" here merely indicates the existence of two and more closely resembles my use of the word "duality" than "dualism."

51. Ibid., 23; cf. 121.

52. Plumwood, *Feminism and the Mastery of Nature*, 60.

53. See the extensive survey and critique in McCulloch, *The Deconstruction of Dualism in Theology*.

54. Plumwood, *Feminism and the Mastery of Nature*, 67.

55. Ruether, *Integrating Ecofeminism, Globalization, and World Religions*, 46.

56. Harry Blair, "Appendix One," in Chapple and Tucker, *Hinduism and Ecology*, 531.

57. See Larry D. Shinn, "The Inner Logic of Gandhian Ecology," in Chapple and Tucker, *Hinduism and Ecology*, 213–41.

58. Vinay Lal, "Too Deep for Deep Ecology: Gandhi and the Ecological Vision of Life," in Chapple and Tucker, *Hinduism and Ecology*, 183–212.

59. This insight has emerged in Christian ecofeminist theology as well: Mary Grey, in *Sacred Longings*, chap. 9, reconsiders the positive value of "sacrifice" through Gandhian teachings; and Sallie McFague, in *A New Climate for Theology: God, the World, and Global Warming* (Minneapolis: Fortress Press, 2008), 135–38, proposes a "kenotic sensibility."

60. Shinn, "Inner Logic," 231–32.

61. For fine examples from feminist and mujerista standpoints in this burgeoning field, see Grey, *Sacred Longings*; and Ivone Gebara, *Longing for Running Water* (Minneapolis: Fortress Press, 1999).

Chapter 4: Body: Prison or Partner?

1. An earlier version of the argument of this chapter appeared in Michelle Voss Roberts, "Flowing and Crossing: The Somatic Theologies of Mechthild and Lalleśwarī," *Journal of the American Academy of Religion* 76, no. 3 (2008): 638–63.

2. Christiane Northrup, *Women's Bodies, Women's Wisdom: Creating Physical and Emotional Health and Healing*, rev. ed. (New York: Bantam, 1998), 30.

3. Scarborough, *Comparative Theories of Nonduality*, 94.

4. Luce Irigaray, *Between East and West: From Singularity to Community*, trans. Stephen Pluháček (New York: Columbia University Press, 2002), 61.

5. Caroline Walker Bynum, *Holy Feast and Holy Fast: The Religious Significance of Food to Medieval Women* (Berkeley: University of California Press, 1987), 6, with original emphasis.

6. Śiva Sūtra 1/14. Bhāskara comments on this verse: "Every physical body belongs to Him because the conscious nature (of every living being, various) according to its own particular type, is one." Dyczkowski, *The Aphorisms of Śiva*, 40.
7. For a fine treatment of this extensible concept of embodiment, see Flood, *Body and Cosmology*, chaps. 1 and 5.
8. Indian systems differ in their descriptions of the flow of energy through the *nāḍīs*. There have been various attempts to map Lalleśwarī's vocabulary onto these systems. She writes of cutting the six forests, after which the nectar of the moon begins to ooze (K 93). Kotru correlates this verse to the system of Kundalini yoga, which has seven chakras: Kotru, *Lal Ded, Her Life and Sayings*, 82. For a description of the full set of twelve chakras, see Singh, *Vijñānabhairava or Divine Consciousness*, 27.
9. Franklin, *Mystical Transformations*, 25.
10. In the Augustinian tradition, spirit and flesh are "primarily moral categories. The flesh, now subject to demeaning appetites and ultimately to death, and the soul, which cannot control its own divided will, are both carnal. Both will be made spiritual, for both must be redeemed." Paula Fredriksen, "Beyond the Body/Soul Dichotomy: Augustine on Paul against the Manichees and the Pelagians," *Recherches augustiniennes* 23 (1988): 111.
11. Kaul, *Lal Ded*, translates as "I knew only this body of mine always" (saying 129); Odin (O 22) has "I have always known only this body." One might even take the "one body" phrase to mean "I always saw myself and others as one" (my trans.).
12. Grierson and Barnett, *Lallā-Vākhāni*, 107. Odin, *To the Other Shore*, 74.
13. Some readers, however, view "shameful members" as the genitals, in order to claim that Mechthild saw gender differentiation and sexual procreation as results of the fall. See, e.g., David O'Dell Neville, "The Chalice of the Flesh: The Soteriology of the Body in Mechthild von Magdeburg's *Das fliessende Licht der Gottheit*," Ph.D. dissertation (Washington University in St. Louis, 2002), 16–17, 56; and Hildegard Elisabeth Keller, "'wan got geschuof inen nie schemeliche lide': Zur Geschichte der Sexualität und Scham im Spiegel des 'Fliessenden Lichts der Gottheit' der Mechthild von Magdeburg," in *Contemplata aliis trader: Studien zur Literatur und Spiritualität*, ed. Claudia Brinker, Urs Herzog, Niklaus Largier, and Paul Michel (Bern: Peter Lang, 1995), 19–45.
14. Kaul, *Lal Ded*, 1 n. 1.
15. Dyczkowski, *The Doctrine of Vibration*, 172–73. For examples of meditations on such moments of transition, see Dyczkowski, *The Stanzas on Vibration*, 100–102, 219–20, 275.
16. Cf. Flood, *Body and Cosmology*, 245–56, and see chapter 3, above.
17. Elsewhere, Lalleśwarī describes how the sun (in-breath), moon (out-breath), and all the senses dissolve (Kotru, 43):

> The sun sets, the moon begins to shine;
> the moon sets, the mind is left[,]
> the mind dissolved, nothing remains,
> The earth, the atmosphere and the sky,
> where have they all gone? [lit., are immersed]
> *(K 85)*

18. Dyczkowski, *The Aphorisms of Śiva*, xix.
19. Kotru, *Lal Ded, Her Life and Sayings*, xiii–xiv.

20. Dyczkowski, *Stanzas on Vibration*, 251.
21. Although the interiorization of worship has been a prominent theme since the Upaniṣads, Lalleśwarī in K 66–72 may be echoing the *Vijñānabhairava Tantra*: "The offerings with which worship is done, the objects with which the Highest Reality (*para*) together with His highest *śakti* (*parā*) is sought to be satisfied, and the worshippers are all (really speaking) one and the same. Whence then this worship?" (*Vijñānabhairava*, verse 153; cf. verses 141–43, 147).
22. Kotru, *Lal Ded, Her Life and Sayings*, x. This legend appears in two hagiographies of Nund Rishi, the seventeenth-century *Nūrnāma* and the nineteenth-century *Rishināma* (S. S. Toshkhani, personal correspondence, June 30, 2006).
23. For a survey of the concept of *jīvanmukti* across various Hindu traditions, see Andrew O. Fort and Patricia Y. Mumme, eds., *Living Liberation in Hindu Thought* (Albany: SUNY Press, 1996).
24. Andrew O. Fort, *Jīvanmukti in Transformation: Embodied Liberation in Advaita and Neo-Vedānta* (Albany: SUNY Press, 1998), 5. The concept of *jīvanmukti* spans the schools of Indian philosophy, but Lalleśwarī's Śaivism differs in a key respect from the Advaita (nondual) traditions that Fort discusses. The Advaitin denies the reality of the body in comparison with the ultimate nondual identity of *ātman* with *brahman*; for Lalleśwarī, liberation means knowing the phenomenal world of perceptions, diversity, and bodies itself to be Śiva's nature.
25. See Paul E. Muller-Ortega, "Aspects of *Jīvanmukti* in the Tantric Śaivism of Kashmir," in Fort and Mumme, *Living Liberation in Hindu Thought*, 187–217.
26. Lalleśwarī's words echo *Śiva Sūtras* 3/27, "The activity of the body is the vow"; and 3/28, "Common talk is . . . recitation of mantra." Dyczkowski, *The Aphorisms of Śiva*, 140–41.
27. Singh, *Vijñānabhairava or Divine Consciousness*, 106.
28. Dyczkowski, *Stanzas on Vibration*, 110, 117.
29. See Dyczkowski, *The Doctrine of Vibration*, 146.
30. See Michael J. Christensen and Jeffrey A. Wittung, eds., *Partakers of the Divine Nature: The History and Development of Deification in the Christian Traditions* (Grand Rapids: Baker Academic, 2007).
31. Notable examples of the bodily rewards Mechthild envisions in heaven can be found in *FL* 2.4; 3.1; 4.24; 5.25; and 7.1.
32. Mechthild prefers sight to express the purified sensorium (*FL* 2.3; 4.23; 6.29; 6.31; 7.37; 7.48); but she also enjoys God in terms of taste or smell (4.12; 6.1; 6.2; 7.47) and invokes all the five senses together (4.13; 7.15; 7.18; 7.38). God praises the soul in sensory terms in 1.16 and 3.2.
33. McGinn, *The Flowering of Mysticism*, 156.
34. Kotru, *Lal Ded, Her Life and Sayings*, 77.
35. In Amy Hollywood's reading, "the well-ordered soul" has the role "of tempering the oscillation between ecstasy and alienation experienced by the 'wounded soul.'" Hollywood, *The Soul as Virgin Wife*, 179.
36. Thomas P. Kasulis, "Introduction," in *Self as Body in Asian Theory and Practice*, ed. Thomas P. Kasulis, Roger T. Ames, and Wimal Dissanayake (Albany: SUNY Press, 1993), xiii.
37. Stephanie Paulsell, *Honoring the Body: Meditations on a Christian Practice* (San Francisco: Jossey-Bass, 2002).
38. Jackie Leach Scully, "When Embodiment Isn't Good," in *Theology and Sexuality* 9 (1998): 12, 23.

39. Doreen Freeman, "A Feminist Theology of Disability," *Feminist Theology* 29 (2002): 77. Freeman's response to feminist attitudes echoes in Elly Elshout et al., "Roundtable Discussion: Women with Disabilities: A Challenge to Feminist Theology," *Journal of Feminist Studies in Religion* 10, no. 2 (2006): 99–134.
40. Scully, "When Embodiment Isn't Good," 24.
41. Barbara A. B. Patterson, "Redeemed Bodies: Fullness of Life," in *Human Disability and the Service of God: Reassessing Religious Practice*, ed. Nancy L. Eiesland and Don E. Saliers (Nashville: Abingdon Press, 1998), 133.
42. Adele B. McCollum in Elshout et al., "Roundtable Discussion," 124.
43. Rita M. Gross, "Suffering, Feminist Theory, and Images of Goddess," *Anima* 13 (Fall 1986): 39.
44. Nancy L. Eiesland, *The Disabled God: Toward a Liberatory Theology of Disability* (Nashville: Abingdon Press, 1994), 31.

Chapter 5: Flowing Out to Others

1. Judith Butler, *Giving an Account of Oneself* (New York: Fordham University Press, 2005), 81.
2. Luce Irigaray writes beautifully of the twoness that attends not only birth but every relationship of love. Luce Irigaray, *To Be Two*, trans. Monique M. Rhodes and Marco F. Cocito-Monoc (New York: Routledge, 2001), 54–61.
3. See Butler, *Giving an Account of Oneself*, 71–78, for a discussion of psychologists who have theorized this primary impressionability.
4. Ibid., 100.
5. Plumwood, *Feminism and the Mastery of Nature*, 45.
6. Pamela Sue Anderson, *A Feminist Philosophy of Religion* (Oxford: Blackwell, 1998), 180, 166. Anderson's ethical imperative follows the standpoint theory developed in Sandra Harding, *Whose Science? Whose Knowledge? Thinking from Women's Lives* (Ithaca, NY: Cornell University Press, 1991).
7. Kotru, *Lal Ded, Her Life and Sayings*, vii. Parimoo goes as far as to detail what she must have learned through prolonged study "at the feet of her guru" in her father's home. Parimoo, *The Ascent of Self*, 56–60.
8. Kotru, *Lal Ded, Her Life and Sayings*, vii.
9. This tale derives from the seventeenth-century hagiography of Nund Rishi, the *Nūrnāma* (S. S. Toshkhani, personal correspondence, June 30, 2006). It is connected to a famous proverb attributed to Lalleśwarī: "They may kill a big sheep or a tender lamb, [but] Lalla will have her lump of stone all right." Kaul, *Lal Ded*, 10.
10. This is the earliest documented story about Lalleśwarī, in Bābā Dāwūd Mishkātī's "The Secrets of the Pious" (1654); cited in Kaul, *Lal Ded*, 2; and narrated again by Kotru, *Lal Ded, Her Life and Sayings*, vii–viii.
11. Kotru, *Lal Ded, Her Life and Sayings*, viii.
12. For this development, see Sanderson, "Śaivism and the Tantric Traditions," 159. Pandit attributes lack of monkhood to Kashmir's snowy climate, which "could not at all permit nudity and constant wandering for long winter months." Pandit, *Aspects of Kashmir Śaivism*, 197.
13. See Muller-Ortega, "Aspects of *Jīvanmukti* in the Tantric Śaivism of Kashmir," 195, 197; and Pandit, *Aspects of Kashmir Śaivism*, 119–20.
14. Flood, "The Śaiva Traditions," 200.
15. Abhinavagupta and Jayaratha agree that these partners could be "any female member of the siddha's family," to which Jayaratha adds the siddha's wife and a "beautiful friend." See Flood, *Body and Cosmology*, 292–93.

16. Kaul, *Lal Ded*, 3.
17. Flood, "The Śaiva Traditions," 216.
18. Kaul, *Lal Ded*, 12–13.
19. Koul, "Life Sketch of Laleshwari," 304.
20. These concessions to the viewer's modesty may be viewed at P. N. Razdan, "Gems of Kashmiri Literature and Kashmiriyat," http://www.koausa.org/KashmiriGems/LalDed.
21. Kotru, *Lal Ded, Her Life and Sayings*, viii.
22. Kaul, *Lal Ded*, 8. The first written appearance of this oral legend, to my knowledge, is in Koul, "Life Sketch of Laleshwari," 302–3.
23. Due to the lack of precise dates for Lalleśwarī, it is difficult to locate her with reference to the events of Kashmiri history; but see Kaul, *Lal Ded*, chap. 5; Odin, *To the Other Shore*, 10–19; and Shashi Shekhar Toshkhani, "Reconstructing and Reinterpreting Lal Ded," in *Lal Ded: The Great Kashmiri Saint-Poetess*, ed. S. S. Toshkhani (New Delhi: APH Publishing Corp., 2002), 39–66.
24. Flood, "The Śaiva Traditions," 202–3.
25. Dyczkowski, *The Aphorisms of Śiva*, 82.
26. See Kaul, *Lal Ded*, 14–15.
27. The spiritual genealogy of the last modern adept in the tradition, Swami Laksmanjoo (d. 1991), e.g., has been traced directly to Abhinavagupta, and thereby to one of the founders of Kashmir Śaivism, Somānanda. Hughes, *Self Realization in Kashmir Shaivism*, xxviii.
28. Kotru, *Lal Ded, Her Life and Sayings*, x–xi. His source for Lalleśwarī's spiritual genealogy may be from the early twentieth century: Koul, "Life Sketch of Laleshwari," 302.
29. Pandit, *Aspects of Kashmir Śaivism*, 44. Pandit mentions only the "worthy disciple Sheikh Nuruddin (Nund Reshi)" (238); while S. S. Toshkhani and others accept her instruction of this young Sufi saint, they vigorously deny the historical possibility of legends showing her being *influenced* by Muslim saints. For Toshkhani's refutation of any connection with other Muslim teachers, see his "Reconstructing and Reinterpreting Lal Ded," 40–45.
30. Sanderson, "Śaivism and the Tantric Traditions," 167. For a detailed discussion of the main branches of initiation of males in Śaiva traditions, see Flood, *Body and Cosmology*, 220–28.
31. This is the opinion of my Kashmiri teachers (personal conversations with Omkar Kaul, S. N. Bhatt, and S. S. Toshkhani, March–April 2006). The only possible support I have found for the unlikely idea that Lalleśwarī underwent the prolonged tutelage of the guru-disciple relationship lies in a *vaakh* where she recalls asking her guru repeatedly about the nature of the absolute (K 24).
32. Odin, *To the Other Shore*, 44–45.
33. Anderson, *A Feminist Philosophy of Religion*, 186, 188–89. Anderson does not query Mirabai's appropriation for contemporary class/caste concerns, but one might interrogate the power dynamics of this discourse as well.
34. Parita Mukta similarly demonstrates how Gandhi's reading of Mirabai as the paragon of wifely devotion obscures her embrace of low-caste, outsider-status, and the community solidarity she has inspired in modern low-caste devotees. Parita Mukta, *Upholding the Common Life: The Community of Mirabai* (Oxford: Oxford University Press, 1994), 186.
35. Odin, *To the Other Shore*, 37–38.

36. Ibid., 38.
37. Ibid., 25; cf. 38–39.
38. Ibid., 31.
39. Lalleśwarī repeatedly speaks of enemies and those who mock her: K 26, 38–43.
40. Kaul, *Lal Ded*, 17. The first written appearance of this oral legend is in Koul, "Life Sketch of Laleshwari" (1921), 306–7.
41. Odin, *To the Other Shore*, 92.
42. Neerja Mattoo, "Lal Ded—the Poet Who Gave a Voice to Women," in Toshkhani, *Lal Ded: The Great Mystic Saint-Poetess*, 72.
43. Odin, *To the Other Shore*, 53.
44. Ibid., 37. For studies that demonstrate the enduring social importance of renouncers in Indian communities, see Patrick Olivelle, *Rules and Regulations of Brahmanical Asceticism* (Albany: SUNY Press, 1995); and Meena Khandelwal, *Women in Ochre Robes: Gendering Hindu Renunciation* (Albany: SUNY Press, 2004).
45. Andersen, *The Voices of Mechthild of Magdeburg*, 80. For more on the councils leading to the Council of Vienne, see Grundmann, *Religious Movements in the Middle Ages*, 186.
46. Grundmann, *Religious Movements in the Middle Ages*, 176.
47. Mechthild of Magdeburg, *Das fliessende Licht der Gottheit*, ed. Neumann, 2:160, note on 7.47 in Mechthild's book. There were heretics in the Swabian Ries around same time whose expression of sexual union with God may have passed beyond allegory into claims of literal, physical consummation and pregnancy. The presence of this group may have encouraged Mechthild's Latin translators and editors to weaken her erotic language. See chap. 1 of Robert Lerner, *The Heresy of the Free Spirit in the Later Middle Ages* (Notre Dame: Notre Dame University Press, 1972).
48. Ibid., 143, 78.
49. Poor, *Mechthild of Magdeburg and Her Book*, 201.
50. Wendy Farley, "Mechthild of Magdeburg," in *Empire and the Christian Tradition: New Readings of Classical Theologians*, ed. Kwok Pui-Lan, Don H. Compier, and Joerg Rieger (Minneapolis: Fortress Press, 2007), 141.
51. See Sara S. Poor, "Mechthild von Magdeburg, Gender, and the 'Unlearned Tongue,'" *Journal of Medieval and Early Modern Studies* 31, no. 2 (2001): 213–50; and Poor, *Mechthild of Magdeburg and Her Book*, 18.
52. Farley, "Mechthild of Magdeburg," 146.
53. The "poor girl" of *FL* 2.4 is Mechthild's reference to herself. The statement at the end of the chapter, "Now the person to whom this happened is dead and gone beyond," was most likely added by a later editor of the text. See Tobin in Mechthild of Magdeburg's *Flowing Light*, 345 n. 16.
54. Newman, *From Virile Woman to Womanchrist*, 159.
55. Michelle Voss Roberts, "Retrieving Humility: Rhetoric, Authority, and Divinization in Mechthild of Magdeburg," *Feminist Theology* 18, no. 1 (2009): 55–80.
56. Poor, *Mechthild of Magdeburg and Her Book*, 59.
57. Other references to divine authorship of Mechthild's book occur in *FL* 3.1; 4.2; 4.19; 5.34; and 7.3. McGinn argues that Mechthild, like other medieval women authors, makes quasi-scriptural claims for her book, which can be seen in passages such as 3.20 and 5.12, in which she places herself in the lineage of five Old Testament prophets. See Bernard McGinn, "The Four Female Evangelists of the Thirteenth Century: The Invention of Authority,"

in *Deutsche Mystik im abendländischen Zusammenhang: Neu erschlossene Texte, neue methodische Ansätze, neue theoretische Konzepte,* ed. Walter Haug and Wolfram Schneider-Lastin (Tübingen: Max Niemeyer Verlag, 2000); as well as McGinn, *The Flowering of Mysticism,* 142, 223–25.

58. She similarly reinforces the gendered aspect of her submission to her earthly confessor in *FL* 5.12: "Master Heinrich, . . . ever since I, *sinful woman,* have been required to write, it has been a matter of great distress to me" (5.12, emphasis added).

59. Sermon 38.4, in Bernard of Clairvaux, *On the Song of Songs II,* trans. Kilian Walsh, Cistercian Fathers Series 7 (Kalamazoo, MI: Cistercian Publications, 1976), 189.

60. Wiethaus, *Ecstatic Transformation,* 92.

61. Keller, *From a Broken Web,* 3.

62. Ibid., 2. This strategy of the "male-identified" woman only compounds the problem of the separative and soluble selves: "She appends to her female emotional base the anxieties of the traditionally masculine separative self" (16).

63. Ibid., 3.

64. Ibid., 5. That these images are deeply connected with woman is evident in the mythic projection of gynophobia into sea monsters like Tiamat (73–88) and Freud's "oceanic feeling" (chap. 3). Also see Keller, *Face of the Deep,* where the author shifts from the web metaphor of the earlier book to explore the grammar of fluidity more fully.

65. Keller, *From a Broken Web,* 18.

66. Tobin, "Mechthild of Magdeburg and Meister Eckhart," 51.

67. Beverly J. Lanzetta, *Radical Wisdom: A Feminist Mystical Theology* (Minneapolis: Fortress Press, 2005), 133.

68. Ada María Isasi-Díaz, *Mujerista Theology* (Maryknoll, NY: Orbis Books, 1996), 21.

69. Anderson, *A Feminist Philosophy of Religion,* 178.

70. Ibid., 182.

71. See http://www.womensordination.org/.

72. For the journey of one such congregation, see Nibs Stroupe, *Where Once We Feared Enemies: Inclusive Membership, Prophetic Vision, and the American Church* (Lima, OH: CSS Publishing Co., 2005).

Chapter 6: Fluid Relations in a Dichotomous World

1. This insight is not entirely absent from feminist literature. Nancy Howell writes, "*Although it is not necessary that dualism create alienation,* the culture/nature dichotomy and the spirit/matter dichotomy *substantially support* the valuation of men over women and nature and ultimately endorse the exploitation of women and nature." Nancy R. Howell, *A Feminist Cosmology: Ecology, Solidarity, and Metaphysics* (Amherst, NY: Humanity Books, 2000), 41, with emphasis added.

2. Dyczkowski, *The Doctrine of Vibration,* 43, with emphasis added.

3. George Lakoff and Mark Turner, *More Than Cool Reason: A Field Guide to Poetic Metaphor* (Chicago: University of Chicago Press, 1989), 60–65.

4. Ibid., 85.

5. McFague, *Models of God,* 33.

6. *Pseudo-Dionysius: The Complete Works,* trans. Colm Luibhéid and Paul Rorem (New York: Paulist Press, 1987), 138–40.

7. On India's dams, see, e.g., William F. Fisher, "Sacred Rivers, Sacred Dams: Competing Visions of Social Justice and Sustainable Development along the Narmada," in Chapple and Tucker, *Hinduism and Ecology*, 401–22.
8. Lakoff and Mark Turner, *More Than Cool Reason*, 19.
9. Keller, *From a Broken Web*, 68, 163–99.
10. Laurel C. Schneider, *Beyond Monotheism: A Theology of Multiplicity* (New York: Routledge, 2007), 72.
11. Ibid., 74.
12. Ibid., 10.
13. Catherine Keller, *On the Mystery: Discerning Divinity in Process* (Minneapolis: Augsburg Fortress, 2008), 47.
14. Kristine A. Culp, "'A World Split Open'? Experience and Feminist Theologies," in *The Experience of God: A Postmodern Response*, ed. Kevin Hart and Barbara Wall (New York: Fordham University Press, 2005), 54.
15. Keller, *On the Mystery*, 116.
16. Ellen T. Armour, "Toward an Elemental Theology: A Constructive Proposal," in *Theology That Matters: Ecology, Economy, and God*, ed. Darby Kathleen Ray (Minneapolis: Augsburg Fortress, 2006), 53.
17. Ibid.; cf. Acts 17:28.
18. Elizabeth Royte, "Drugging Our Waters: How an Aging Population and Our Growing Addiction to Pharmaceuticals May Be Poisoning Our Rivers," *OnEarth* (Fall 2006): 26–31, http://www.onearth.org/article/drugging-our-waters.
19. For the most recent articulation of this argument, see McFague, *A New Climate for Theology*, chap. 4, esp. 72–79.
20. In "Separate Domains," Alley explains that the realms of sanitation and religious ritual do not overlap for worshipers of the Ganges, who insist that the goddess can never be polluted.
21. Vijaya Rettakudi Nagarajan, "The Earth as Goddess Bhū Devī: Toward a Theory of 'Embedded Ecologies' in Folk Hinduism," in Nelson, *Purifying the Earthly Body of God*, 278.
22. For a classic articulation of this argument, see Valerie Saiving, "The Human Situation: A Feminine View," in *Womanspirit Rising: A Feminist Reader in Religion*, ed. Carol P. Christ and Judith Plaskow (New York: Harper & Row, 1979), 25–42.
23. Keller, *From a Broken Web*, 134.
24. Ibid., 140.
25. Adrienne Rich, *Of Woman Born: Motherhood as Experience and Institution* (New York: W. W. Norton, 1986), 226.
26. Karen Baker-Fletcher, "The Strength of My Life," in *Embracing the Spirit: Womanist Perspectives on Hope, Salvation, and Transformation*, ed. Emilie M. Townes (Maryknoll, NY: Orbis Books, 1997), 124.
27. Wendy Farley, *The Wounding and Healing of Desire: Weaving Heaven and Earth* (Louisville: Westminster John Knox Press, 2005), 112.
28. *Julian of Norwich: Showings*, trans. Edmund Colledge and James Walsh (Mahwah, NJ: Paulist Press, 1978), 186.
29. Keller, *From a Broken Web*, 136.

Bibliography

Alley, Kelly D. "Separate Domains: Hinduism, Politics, and Environmental Pollution." In *Hinduism and Ecology: The Intersection of Earth, Sky, and Water*, edited by Christopher Key Chapple and Mary Evelyn Tucker, 355–88. Cambridge, MA: Harvard University Press, 2000.
Andersen, Elizabeth A. *The Voices of Mechthild of Magdeburg*. Oxford: Peter Lang, 2000.
Anderson, Pamela Sue. *A Feminist Philosophy of Religion*. Oxford: Blackwell, 1998.
Anglicus, Bartholomaeus. *De rerum proprietatibus*. 1242–47. Frankfurt: Minerva, 1964.
Aristotle. *Metaphysics*. In *The Basic Works of Aristotle*, edited by Richard McKeon. New York: Random House, 1941.
Armour, Ellen T. "Toward an Elemental Theology: A Constructive Proposal." In *Theology That Matters: Ecology, Economy, and God*, edited by Darby Kathleen Ray, 42–57. Minneapolis: Augsburg Fortress, 2006.
Baker-Fletcher, Karen. "The Strength of My Life." In *Embracing the Spirit: Womanist Perspectives on Hope, Salvation, and Transformation*, edited by Emilie M. Townes, 122–39. Maryknoll, NY: Orbis Books, 1997.
Balthasar, Hans Urs von. "Mechthilds kirchlicher Auftrag." In *Das fliessende Licht der Gottheit*, edited by Margot Schmidt, 19–45. Einsiedeln: Benziger, 1955.
Bernard of Clairvaux. *On the Song of Songs II*. Translated by Kilian Walsh. Cistercian Fathers Series 7. Kalamazoo, MI: Cistercian Publications, 1976.
Bhat, S. "Lal Ded: Her Spiritualism and Present Scientific World Order." In *Lal Ded: The Great Kashmiri Saint-Poetess*, edited by S. S. Toshkhani, 25–37. New Delhi: APH Publishing Corp., 2002.
Bhatt, Shambhu Nath, and Janki Nath Bhan. "Lal Vakh." *Koshur Samachar* (1970–71): 1–59.
Blair, Harry. "Appendix One." In *Hinduism and Ecology: The Intersection of Earth, Sky, and Water*, edited by Christopher Key Chapple and Mary Evelyn Tucker, 531–33. Cambridge, MA: Harvard University Press, 2000.
Butler, Judith. *Gender Trouble: Feminism and the Subversion of Identity*. New York: Routledge, 1990.
———. *Giving an Account of Oneself*. New York: Fordham University Press, 2005.
Bynum, Caroline Walker. *Fragmentation and Redemption: Essays on Gender and the Human Body in Medieval Religion*. New York: Zone Books, 1991.
———. *Holy Feast and Holy Fast: The Religious Significance of Food to Medieval Women*. Berkeley: University of California Press, 1987.
Chapple, Christopher Key. "Introduction." In *Hinduism and Ecology: The Intersection of Earth, Sky, and Water*, edited by Christopher Key Chapple and Mary Evelyn Tucker, xxxiii–xlix. Cambridge, MA: Harvard University Press, 2000.

Chatterji, J. C. *Kashmir Shaivaism*. Albany: SUNY Press, 1986.
Christ, Carol P. *Rebirth of the Goddess: Finding Meaning in Feminist Spirituality*. Reading, MA: Addison-Wesley, 1997.
Christensen, Michael J., and Jeffrey A. Wittung, eds. *Partakers of the Divine Nature: The History and Development of Deification in the Christian Traditions*. Grand Rapids: Baker Academic, 2007.
Clooney, Francis Xavier. *Divine Mother, Blessed Mother: Hindu Goddesses and the Virgin Mary*. Oxford: Oxford University Press, 2005.
———. *Hindu God, Christian God: How Reason Helps Break Down the Boundaries between Religions*. Oxford: Oxford University Press, 2001.
———. *Theology after Vedanta: An Experiment in Comparative Theology*. Albany: SUNY Press, 1993.
Coakley, Sarah. "Introduction: Religion and the Body." In *Religion and the Body*, edited by Sarah Coakley, 1–12. Cambridge: Cambridge University Press, 1997.
Collins, Patricia Hill. *Black Feminist Thought: Knowledge, Consciousness, and the Politics of Empowerment*. Perspectives on Gender Series 2. Boston: Unwin Hyman, 1990.
Culp, Kristine A. "'A World Split Open'? Experience and Feminist Theologies." In *The Experience of God: A Postmodern Response*, edited by Kevin Hart and Barbara Wall, 47–64. New York: Fordham University Press, 2005.
Dalmiya, Vrinda. "Loving Paradoxes: A Feminist Reclamation of the Goddess Kali." *Hypatia* 15, no. 1 (2000): 125–49.
Daly, Mary. *Beyond God the Father: Toward a Philosophy of Women's Liberation*. Boston: Beacon, 1973.
Doniger, Wendy. *The Implied Spider: Politics and Theology in Myth*. Lectures on the History of Religions, 16. New York: Columbia University Press, 1998.
Dyczkowski, Mark S. G., trans. *The Aphorisms of Śiva: The Śiva Sūtra with Bhāskara's Commentary, the Vārttika*. Translated with exposition and notes. Albany: SUNY Press, 1992.
———. *The Doctrine of Vibration: An Analysis of the Doctrines and Practices of Kashmir Shaivism*. Albany: SUNY Press, 1987.
———, trans. *The Stanzas on Vibration: The Spandakārikā with Four Commentaries. Translated with Introduction and Exposition*. Albany: SUNY Press, 1992.
Eaton, Heather. *Introducing Ecofeminist Theologies*. London: T&T Clark International, 2005.
Egge, James. "Theorizing Embodiment: Conceptual Metaphor Theory and the Comparative Study of Religion." In *Figuring Religions: Comparing Ideas, Images, and Activities*, ed. Shubha Pathak. Albany: SUNY Press, forthcoming.
Eiesland, Nancy L. *The Disabled God: Toward a Liberatory Theology of Disability*. Nashville: Abingdon Press, 1994.
Elshout, Elly, Dorothee Wilhelm, Carole R. Fontaine, Nancy L. Eiesland, Valerie C. Stiteler, Adele B. McCollum, and Margaret Moers Wenig. "Roundtable Discussion: Women with Disabilities: A Challenge to Feminist Theology." *Journal of Feminist Studies in Religion* 10, no. 2 (2006): 99–134.
Farley, Wendy. "Mechthild of Magdeburg." In *Empire and the Christian Tradition: New Readings of Classical Theologians*, edited by Kwok Pui-Lan, Don H. Compier, and Joerg Rieger, 139–51. Minneapolis: Fortress Press, 2007.
———. *The Wounding and Healing of Desire: Weaving Heaven and Earth*. Louisville, KY: Westminster John Knox Press, 2005.
Feldmeier, Peter. *Christianity Looks East: Comparing the Spiritualities of John of the Cross and Buddhaghosa*. New York: Paulist Press, 2006.

Fisher, William F. "Sacred Rivers, Sacred Dams: Competing Visions of Social Justice and Sustainable Development along the Narmada." In *Hinduism and Ecology: The Intersection of Earth, Sky, and Water*, edited by Christopher Key Chapple and Mary Evelyn Tucker, 401–22. Cambridge, MA: Harvard University Press, 2000.

Flood, Gavin D. *The Ascetic Self: Subjectivity, Memory and Tradition*. Cambridge: Cambridge University Press, 2004.

———. *Body and Cosmology in Kashmir Saivism*. San Francisco: Mellen Research University Press, 1993.

———. "The Śaiva Traditions." In *The Blackwell Companion to Hinduism*, edited by Gavin Flood, 200–228. Oxford: Blackwell, 2003.

Fort, Andrew O. *Jīvanmukti in Transformation: Embodied Liberation in Advaita and Neo-Vedānta*. Albany: SUNY Press, 1998.

———, and Patricia Y. Mumme, eds. *Living Liberation in Hindu Thought*. Albany: SUNY Press, 1996.

Franklin, James C. *Mystical Transformations: The Imagery of Liquids in the Work of Mechthild von Magdeburg*. London: Associated University Presses, 1978.

Fredriksen, Paula. "Beyond the Body/Soul Dichotomy: Augustine on Paul against the Manichees and the Pelagians." *Recherches augustiniennes* 23 (1988): 87–114.

Freeman, Doreen. "A Feminist Theology of Disability." *Feminist Theology* 29 (2002): 71–85.

Gebara, Ivone. *Longing for Running Water*. Minneapolis: Fortress Press, 1999.

Ghanananda, Swami, and Sir John Stewart-Wallace, eds. *Women Saints of the East and West*. Hollywood, CA: Vedanta Press, 1979.

Grant, Sara, RSCJ, *Śaṅkarācārya's Concept of Relation*. Delhi: Motilal Banarsidass, 1999.

Grey, Mary C. *Sacred Longings: Ecofeminist Theology and Globalization*. Minneapolis: Augsburg Fortress, 2004.

Grierson, Sir George, and Lionel D. Barnett. *Lallā-Vākhyāni: The Wise Sayings of Lal Dĕd, a Mystic Poetess of Ancient Kashmīr*. London: Royal Asiatic Society, 1920.

Gross, Rita M. "Feminist Theology as Theology of Religions." *Feminist Theology* 26 (2001): 83–101.

———. "Suffering, Feminist Theory, and Images of Goddess." *Anima* 13 (Fall 1986): 39–46.

Gross, Rita M., and Rosemary Radford Ruether. *Religious Feminism and the Future of the Planet: A Christian-Buddhist Conversation*. New York: Continuum, 2001.

Grundmann, Herbert. *Religious Movements in the Middle Ages: The Historical Links between Heresy, the Mendicant Orders, and the Women's Religious Movement in the Twelfth and Thirteenth Centuries, with the Historical Foundations of German Mysticism*. Translated by Steven Rowan. Notre Dame, IN: University of Notre Dame Press, 1995.

Gupta, Lina. "Ganga: Purity, Pollution, and Hinduism." In *Ecofeminism and the Sacred*, edited by Carol Adams, 99–116. New York: Continuum, 1993.

Gustafson, James A. *A Sense of the Divine: The Natural Environment from a Theocentric Perspective*. Cleveland: Pilgrim Press, 1994.

Haberman, David L. *River of Love in an Age of Pollution*. Berkeley: University of California Press, 2006.

Halbfass, Wilhelm. *India and Europe: An Essay in Understanding*. Albany: SUNY Press, 1988.

Harding, Sandra. *Whose Science? Whose Knowledge? Thinking from Women's Lives*. Ithaca, NY: Cornell University Press, 1991.

Hawley, John Stratton, and Mark Juergensmeyer. *Songs of the Saints of India*. New York: Oxford University Press, 1988.
Hiltebeitel, Alf, and Kathleen M. Erndl, eds. *Is the Goddess a Feminist? The Politics of South Asian Goddesses*. 2000. New Delhi: Oxford University Press, 2002.
Holdrege, Barbara A. *Veda and Torah: Transcending the Textuality of Scripture*. Albany: SUNY Press, 1995.
Hollywood, Amy. *The Soul as Virgin Wife: Mechthild of Magdeburg, Marguerite Porete, and Meister Eckhart*. Notre Dame, IN: University of Notre Dame Press, 1995.
Howell, Nancy R. *A Feminist Cosmology: Ecology, Solidarity, and Metaphysics*. Amherst, NY: Humanity Books, 2000.
Hughes, John. *Self Realization in Kashmir Shaivism: The Oral Teachings of Swami Lakshmanjoo*. Foreword by Lance Nelson. Albany: SUNY Press, 1994.
Inden, Ronald. *Imagining India*. Oxford: Basil Blackwell, 1990.
Irigaray, Luce. *Between East and West: From Singularity to Community*. Translated by Stephen Pluháček. New York: Columbia University Press, 2002.
———. *To Be Two*. Translated by Monique M. Rhodes and Marco F. Cocito-Monoc. New York: Routledge, 2001.
Isasi-Díaz, Ada María. *Mujerista Theology*. Maryknoll, NY: Orbis Books, 1996.
Isayeva, Natalia. *From Early Vedanta to Kashmir Shaivism: Gaudapada, Bhartrhari, and Abhinavagupta*. Albany: SUNY Press, 1995.
Isherwood, Lisa. "Sex and Body Politics: Issues for Feminist Theology." In *The Good News of the Body: Sexual Theology and Feminism*, edited by Lisa Isherwood, 20–34. New York: New York University Press, 2000.
Jantzen, Grace. *Becoming Divine: Toward a Feminist Philosophy of Religion*. Bloomington: Indiana University Press, 1999.
———. *God's World, God's Body*. Philadelphia: Westminster Press, 1984.
———. *Power, Gender and Christian Mysticism*. Cambridge: Cambridge University Press, 1995.
———. "'Where Two Are to Become One': Mysticism and Monism." In *The Philosophy in Christianity*, edited by Godfrey Vesey, 147–66. Cambridge: Cambridge University Press, 1990.
Jee, Swami Lakshman. *Kashmir Shaivism: The Secret Supreme*. Albany: SUNY Press; The Universal Shaiva Trust, 1988.
Julian of Norwich: Showings. Translated by Edmund Colledge and James Walsh. New York: Paulist Press, 1978.
Kasulis, Thomas P. "Introduction." In *Self as Body in Asian Theory and Practice*, edited by Thomas P. Kasulis, Roger T. Ames, and Wimal Dissanayake, ix–xx. Albany: SUNY Press, 1993.
Kaul, Jai Lal. *Lal Ded*. New Delhi: Sahitya Akademi, 1973.
Keller, Catherine. *Face of the Deep: A Theology of Becoming*. New York: Routledge, 2003.
———. *From a Broken Web: Separation, Sexism, and Self*. Boston: Beacon Press, 1986.
———. *On the Mystery: Discerning Divinity in Process*. Minneapolis: Augsburg Fortress, 2008.
Keller, Hildegard Elisabeth. "'wan got geschuof inen nie schemeliche lide': Zur Geschichte der Sexualität und Scham im Spiegel des 'Fliessenden Lichts der Gottheit' der Mechthild von Magdeburg." In *Contemplata aliis trader: Studien zur Literatur und Spiritualität*, edited by Claudia Brinker, Urs Herzog, Niklaus Largier, and Paul Michel, 19–45. Bern: Peter Lang, 1995.
Khandelwal, Meena. *Women in Ochre Robes: Gendering Hindu Renunciation*. Albany: SUNY Press, 2004.

King, Richard. *Orientalism and Religion: Postcolonial Theory, India and "the Mystic East."* London: Routledge, 1999.
Kinsley, David. "Devotion as an Alternative to Marriage in the Lives of Some Hindu Women Devotees." *Journal of Asian and African Studies* 15, nos. 1–2 (1980): 86–87.
Kipling, Rudyard. *Rudyard Kipling's Verse: Definitive Edition.* Garden City, NY: Doubleday, 1946.
Kotru, Nil Kanth. *Lal Ded, Her Life and Sayings.* Srinigar: Utpal Publications, 1989.
Koul, Anand. "Lalla-Vakyani." *Indian Antiquary* 60 (1931): 191–93.
———. "Lalla-Vakyani." *Indian Antiquary* 61 (1932): 13–16.
———. "Lalla-Vakyani." *Indian Antiquary* 62 (1933): 108–11.
———. "Life Sketch of Laleshwari—a Great Hermitess of Kashmir." *Indian Antiquary* 50 (1921): 302–8.
———. "Some Additions to the Lalla-Vakyani." *Indian Antiquary* 59 (1930): 108–13.
Kṣemarāja. *The Doctrine of Recognition: A Translation of Pratyabhijñāhṛdayam.* Translated by Jaideva Singh. Albany: SUNY Press, 1990.
Lakoff, George, and Mark Johnson. *Metaphors We Live By.* 1980. Chicago: University of Chicago Press, 2003.
Lakoff, George, and Mark Turner. *More Than Cool Reason: A Field Guide to Poetic Metaphor.* Chicago: University of Chicago Press, 1989.
Lal, Vinay. "Too Deep for Deep Ecology: Gandhi and the Ecological Vision of Life." In *Hinduism and Ecology: The Intersection of Earth, Sky, and Water,* edited by Christopher Key Chapple and Mary Evelyn Tucker, 183–212. Cambridge, MA: Harvard University Press, 2000.
Lalla. *Naked Song.* Translated by Coleman Barks. Athens, GA: Maypop Books, 1992.
Lanzetta, Beverly J. *Radical Wisdom: A Feminist Mystical Theology.* Minneapolis: Fortress Press, 2005.
Lawrence, David Peter. *Rediscovering God with Transcendental Argument: A Contemporary Interpretation of Monistic Kashmiri Śaiva Philosophy.* Albany: SUNY Press, 1999.
Lele, Jayant. "Orientalism and the Social Sciences." In *Orientalism and the Postcolonial Predicament: Perspectives on South Asia,* edited by Carol A. Breckenridge and Peter van der Veer. Philadelphia: University of Pennsylvania Press, 1993.
Lerner, Robert. *The Heresy of the Free Spirit in the Later Middle Ages.* Notre Dame: Notre Dame University Press, 1972.
Lewis, Reina. *Gendering Orientalism: Race, Femininity and Representation.* London: Routledge, 1996.
Mattoo, Neerja. "Lal Ded—the Poet Who Gave a Voice to Women." In *Lal Ded: The Great Mystic Saint-Poetess,* edited by S. S. Toshkhani, 67–80. New Delhi: APH Publishing Corp., 2002.
McCulloch, Gillian. *The Deconstruction of Dualism in Theology: With Special Reference to Ecofeminist Theology and New Age Spirituality.* Cumbria: Paternoster, 2002.
McFague, Sallie. *The Body of God: An Ecological Theology.* Minneapolis: Fortress Press, 1993.
———. *Models of God: Theology for an Ecological, Nuclear Age.* Philadelphia: Fortress Press, 1987.
———. *A New Climate for Theology: God, the World, and Global Warming.* Minneapolis: Fortress Press, 2008.
McGinn, Bernard. *The Flowering of Mysticism: Men and Women in the New Mysticism (1200–1350).* New York: Crossroad, 1998.
———. "The Four Female Evangelists of the Thirteenth Century: The Invention of Authority." In *Deutsche Mystik im abendländischen Zusammenhang: Neu*

erschlossene Texte, neue methodische Ansätze, neue theoretische Konzepte, edited by Walter Haug and Wolfram Schneider-Lastin, 175–94. Tübingen: Max Niemeyer Verlag, 2000.

———. "Introduction." In *Meister Eckhart and the Beguine Mystics: Hadewijch of Brabant, Mechthild of Magdeburg, and Marguerite Porete*, edited by Bernard McGinn, 1–14. New York: Continuum, 1994.

———. *Meister Eckhart and the Beguine Mystics: Hadewijch of Brabant, Mechthild of Magdeburg, and Marguerite Porete*. New York: Continuum, 1994.

———. *The Foundations of Mysticism: Origins to the Fifth Century*. New York: Crossroad, 1990.

Mechthild of Magdeburg. *Das fliessende Licht der Gottheit*. Translated by Margot Schmidt. Einsiedeln: Benziger, 1955.

———. *Das fliessende Licht der Gottheit: Nach der Einsiedler Handschrift in kritischem Vergleich mit der gesamten Überlieferung*. Edited by Hans Neumann. Arranged by Gisela Vollman-Profe. 2 vols. Munich: Artemis Verlag, 1990–93.

———. *The Flowing Light of the Godhead*. Translated by Christiane Mesch Galvani. New York: Garland, 1991.

———. *The Flowing Light of the Godhead*. Translated and introduced by Frank J. Tobin. New York: Paulist Press, 1998.

Meister Eckhart: The Essential Sermons, Commentaries, Treatises, and Defense. Translated by Edmund Colledge. New York: Paulist Press, 1981.

Miller, Barbara Stoler, trans. *The Bhagavad-Gita: Krishna's Counsel in Time of War*. New York: Bantam, 1986.

Miller, Jane. *Seductions: Studies in Reading and Culture*. Cambridge, MA: Harvard University Press, 1991.

Mukta, Parita. *Upholding the Common Life: The Community of Mirabai*. Oxford: Oxford University Press, 1994.

Muktananda, Swami. *Lalleshwari: Spiritual Poems by a Great Siddha Yogini*. Translated by Gurumayi. South Fallsburg, NY: SYDA Foundation, 1981.

Muller-Ortega, Paul E. "Aspects of *Jīvanmukti* in the Tantric Śaivism of Kashmir." In *Living Liberation in Hindu Thought*, edited by Andrew O. Fort and Patricia Y. Mumme, 187–217. Albany: SUNY Press, 1996.

Nagarajan, Vijaya Rettakudi. "The Earth as Goddess Bhū Devī: Toward a Theory of 'Embedded Ecologies' in Folk Hinduism." In *Purifying the Earthly Body of God: Religion and Ecology in Hindu India*, edited by Lance E. Nelson, 269–95. Albany: SUNY Press, 2000.

Nelson, Lance E. "The Dualism of Non-Dualism: Advaita Vedanta and the Irrelevance of Nature." In *Purifying the Earthly Body of God: Religion and Ecology in Hindu India*, edited by Lance E. Nelson, 61–88. Albany: SUNY Press, 1998.

———. "Foreword." In *Self Realization in Kashmir Shaivism: The Oral Teachings of Swami Lakshmanjoo*, edited by John Hughes, xi–xxxiv. Albany: SUNY Press, 1994.

———. "Reading the *Bhagavadgītā* from an Ecological Perspective." In *Hinduism and Ecology: The Intersection of Earth, Sky, and Water*, edited by Christopher Key Chapple and Mary Evelyn Tucker, 127–64. Cambridge, MA: Harvard University Press, 2000.

Neumann, Hans. "Mechthild von Magdeburg." In *Die deutsche Literatur des Mittelalters: Verfasserlexikon*, edited by Kurt Ruh, 260–70. Berlin: Walter de Gruyter, 1987.

Neville, David O'Dell. "The Chalice of the Flesh: The Soteriology of the Body in Mechthild von Magdeburg's *Das fliessende Licht der Gottheit*." Ph.D. dissertation, Washington University in St. Louis, 2002.

Newman, Barbara. *From Virile Woman to Womanchrist*. Philadelphia: University of Pennsylvania Press, 1995.

———. *God and the Goddesses: Vision, Poetry, and Belief in the Middle Ages*. Philadelphia: University of Pennsylvania Press, 2003.

———. "The Mozartian Moment: Reflections on Medieval Mysticism." In *Minding the Spirit: The Study of Christian Spirituality*, edited by Elizabeth A. Dreyer and Mark S. Burrows. Baltimore: Johns Hopkins University Press, 2005.

Nicholson, Hugh. "Comparative Theology after Liberalism." *Modern Theology* 23, no. 2 (2007): 229–51.

Northrup, Christiane. *Women's Bodies, Women's Wisdom: Creating Physical and Emotional Health and Healing*. Rev. ed. New York: Bantam, 1998.

Odin, Jaishree Kak. *To the Other Shore: Lalla's Life and Poetry*. New Delhi: Vitasta, 1999.

Olivelle, Patrick. *Rules and Regulations of Brahmanical Asceticism*. Albany: SUNY Press, 1995.

Otto, Rudolf. *Mysticism East and West: A Comparative Analysis of the Nature of Mysticism*. Translated by Bertha L. Bracey and Richenda C. Payne. New York: Collier Books, 1962.

Pandit, B. N. *Aspects of Kashmir Śaivism*. Srinagar: Utpal Publications, 1977.

Parimoo, B. N. *The Ascent of Self: A Reinterpretation of the Mystical Poetry of Lalla-Ded*. Delhi: Motilal Banarsidass, 1987.

Patel, Kartikeya C. "Women, Earth, and the Goddess: A Shakta-Hindu Interpretation of Embodied Religion." *Hypatia* 9, no. 4 (1994): 69–87.

Patil, Parimal G. "A Hindu Theologian's Response: A Prolegomenon to 'Christian God, Hindu God.'" In *Hindu God, Christian God: How Reason Helps Break Down the Boundaries between Religions*, edited by Francis Xavier Clooney, 185–95. Oxford: Oxford University Press, 2001.

Patterson, Barbara A. B. "Redeemed Bodies: Fullness of Life." In *Human Disability and the Service of God: Reassessing Religious Practice*, edited by Nancy L. Eiesland and Don E. Saliers, 123–43. Nashville: Abingdon Press, 1998.

Patton, Laurie L. "Nature Romanticism and Sacrifice in Ṛgvedic Interpretation." In *Hinduism and Ecology: The Intersection of Earth, Sky, and Water*, edited by Christopher Key Chapple and Mary Evelyn Tucker, 39–59. Cambridge, MA: Harvard University Press, 2000.

Paulsell, Stephanie. *Honoring the Body: Meditations on a Christian Practice*. San Francisco: Jossey-Bass, 2002.

Peters, Ursula. *Religiöse Erfahrung als literarisches Factum: Zur Vorgeschichte und Genese frauenmystischer Texte des 13. und 14. Jahrhunderts*. Tübingen: Niemeyer, 1988.

Plumwood, Val. *Feminism and the Mastery of Nature*. New York: Routledge, 1993.

Poor, Sara S. *Mechthild of Magdeburg and Her Book: Gender and the Making of Textual Authority*. Philadelphia: University of Pennsylvania Press, 2004.

———. "Mechthild von Magdeburg, Gender, and the 'Unlearned Tongue.'" *Journal of Medieval and Early Modern Studies* 31, no. 2 (2001): 213–50.

Porete, Marguerite. *The Mirror of Simple Souls*. Translated by Edmund Colledge. Notre Dame: University of Notre Dame Press, 1999.

Pseudo-Dionysius: The Complete Works. Translated by Colm Luibhéid and Paul Rorem. New York: Paulist Press, 1987.

Rambachan, Anantanand. *The Advaita Worldview: God, World, and Humanity*. Albany: SUNY Press, 2006.

Razdan, P. N. "Gems of Kashmiri Literature and Kashmiriyat." http://www.koausa.org/KashmiriGems/LalDed.html.
Rich, Adrienne. *Of Woman Born: Motherhood as Experience and Institution.* New York: W. W. Norton, 1986.
Richard of St. Victor. *Selected Writings on Contemplation.* Translated by Clare Kirchberger. New York: Harper & Brothers, 1957.
Rivera, Mayra. *The Touch of Transcendence: A Postcolonial Theology of God.* Louisville: Westminster John Knox Press, 2007.
Royte, Elizabeth. "Drugging Our Waters: How an Aging Population and Our Growing Addiction to Pharmaceuticals May Be Poisoning Our Rivers." *OnEarth* 28 (Fall 2006): 26–31. http://www.onearth.org/article/drugging-our-waters.
Ruether, Rosemary Radford. *Gaia and God: An Ecofeminist Theology of Earth Healing.* San Francisco: Harper San Francisco, 1992.
———. *Integrating Ecofeminism, Globalization, and World Religions.* Oxford: Rowman & Littlefield Publishers, 2005.
———. *New Woman, New Earth: Sexist Ideologies and Human Liberation.* New York: Seabury Press, 1975.
———. *Sexism and God-Talk: Toward a Feminist Theology.* Boston: Beacon Press, 1983.
Said, Edward W. *Orientalism.* New York: Vintage Books, 1978.
Saiving, Valerie. "The Human Situation: A Feminine View." In *Womanspirit Rising: A Feminist Reader in Religion,* edited by Carol P. Christ and Judith Plaskow, 25–42. New York: Harper & Row, 1979.
Sanderson, Alexis. "Śaivism and the Tantric Traditions." In *The World's Religions: The Religions of Asia,* edited by Friedhelm Hardy, 128–72. London: Routledge, 1988.
Sapru, Chaman Lal. "Lalleshwari and Kabir." In *Lal Ded: The Great Kashmiri Saint-Poetess,* edited by S. S. Toshkhani, 127–33. New Delhi: APH Publishing Corp., 2002.
Scarborough, Milton. *Comparative Theories of Nonduality: The Search for a Middle Way.* London: Continuum, 2009.
Schmidt, Margot. "Elemente der Schau bei Mechthild von Magdeburg und Mechthild von Hackeborn: Zur Bedeutung der geistlichen Sinne." In *Frauenmystik im Mittelalter,* edited by Peter Dinzelbacher and Dieter R. Bauer, 123–52. Ostfildern bei Stuttgart: Schwabenverlag, 1985.
———. "'die spilende minnevluot': Der Eros als Sein und Wirkkraft in der Trinität bei Mechthild von Magdeburg." In *"Eine Höhe, über die nichts geht": Spezielle Glaubenserfahrung in der Frauenmystik?* edited by Margot Schmidt and Dieter R. Bauer, 71–133. Stuttgart-Bad Cannstatt: Frommann-Holzboog, 1986.
Schmidt, Margot, and Susan Johnson, trans. "'minne du gewaltige kellerin': On the Nature of *minne* in Mechthild of Magdeburg's *Fliessende Licht der Gottheit,*" *Vox benedictina* 4 (1987): 100–125.
Schneider, Laurel C. *Beyond Monotheism: A Theology of Multiplicity.* New York: Routledge, 2007.
Scully, Jackie Leach. "When Embodiment Isn't Good." *Theology and Sexuality* 9 (1998): 10–28.
Sherma, Rita DasGupta. "Sacred Immanence: Reflections of Ecofeminism in Hindu Tantra." In *Purifying the Earthly Body of God: Religion and Ecology in Hindu India,* edited by Lance E. Nelson, 89–131. Albany: SUNY Press, 1998.
Shinn, Larry D. "The Inner Logic of Gandhian Ecology." In *Hinduism and Ecology: The Intersection of Earth, Sky, and Water,* edited by Christopher Key Chapple

and Mary Evelyn Tucker, 213–41. Cambridge, MA: Harvard University Press, 2000.
Shiva, Vandana. *Staying Alive: Women, Ecology and Development*. New Delhi: Kali for Women, 1988.
Singh, Jaideva. "Introduction." In *The Doctrine of Recognition: A Translation of Pratyabhijñāhṛdayam*, 3–39. Albany: SUNY Press, 1990.
———. *Vijñānabhairava or Divine Consciousness: A Treasury of 112 Types of Yoga*. Delhi: Motilal Banarsidass, 1979.
Sinha, Mrinalini. *Colonial Masculinity: The "Manly Englishman" and the "Effeminate Bengali" in the Late Nineteenth Century*. Manchester: Manchester University Press, 1995.
Siraisi, Nancy G. *Medieval and Renaissance Medicine: An Introduction to Knowledge and Practice*. Chicago: University of Chicago Press, 1990.
Slingerland, Edward. "Conceptual Metaphor Theory as Methodology for Comparative Religion." *Journal of the American Academy of Religion* 72, no. 1 (2004): 1–31.
Smith, Jonathan Z. "The 'End' of Comparison." In *A Magic Still Dwells: Comparative Religion in the Postmodern Age*, edited by Kimberley C. Patton and Benjamin C. Ray, 237–41. Berkeley: University of California Press, 2000.
———. "In Comparison a Magic Dwells." In *Imagining Religion: From Babylon to Jonestown*, 19–35. Chicago: University of Chicago Press, 1982.
Sopori, B. N. *Voice of Experience: Lal Ded and Her Vaakhs*. Sarwal Jammu: Kanti Offset Printing House, 1999.
Stroupe, Nibs. *Where Once We Feared Enemies: Inclusive Membership, Prophetic Vision, and the American Church*. Lima, OH: CSS Publishing Co., 2005.
Tax, Petrus W. "Die grosse Himmelsschau Mechtilds von Magdeburg und ihre Höllenvision." *Zeitschrift für deutsches Altertum und deutsche Literatur* 108, no. 2 (1979): 112–25.
Temple, Richard Carnac. *The Word of Lalla the Prophetess*. Cambridge: Cambridge University Press, 1924.
Thatamanil, John J. *The Immanent Divine: God, Creation, and the Human Predicament*. Minneapolis: Fortress Press, 2006.
Thomas Aquinas. *Summa theologica*. Translated by Fathers of the English Dominican Province. 5 vols. New York: Benzinger Brothers, 1948.
Tobin, Frank J. "Introduction." In Mechthild of Magdeburg, *The Flowing Light of the Godhead*, translated and introduced by Frank J. Tobin, 1–27. New York: Paulist Press, 1998.
———. *Mechthild von Magdeburg: A Medieval Mystic in Modern Eyes*. Columbia, SC: Camden House, 1995.
———. "Mechthild of Magdeburg and Meister Eckhart: Points of Coincidence." In *Meister Eckhart and the Beguine Mystics: Hadewijch of Brabant, Mechthild of Magdeburg, and Marguerite Porete*, edited by Bernard McGinn, 44–61. New York: Continuum, 1994.
Toshkhani, Shashi Shekhar, ed. *Lal Ded: The Great Kashmiri Saint-Poetess*. New Delhi: APH Publishing Corp., 2002.
———. "Reconstructing and Reinterpreting Lal Ded." In *Lal Ded: The Great Kashmiri Saint-Poetess*, edited by S. S. Toshkhani, 39–66. New Delhi: APH Publishing Corp., 2002.
Turner, Denys. *The Darkness of God: Negativity in Christian Mysticism*. Cambridge: Cambridge University Press, 1995.

Voss Roberts, Michelle. "Flowing and Crossing: The Somatic Theologies of Mechthild and Lalleśwarī." *Journal of the American Academy of Religion* 76, no. 3 (2008): 638–63.

———. "Gendering Comparative Theology." In *The New Comparative Theology: Voices from the Younger Generation*, ed. Francis X. Clooney. New York: Continuum, 2010.

———. "Retrieving Humility: Rhetoric, Authority, and Divinization in Mechthild of Magdeburg." *Feminist Theology* 18, no. 1 (2009): 55–80.

White, Lynn, Jr. "The Historical Roots of Our Ecological Crisis." *Science* 155 (1967): 1203–7.

Whicher, Ian. *The Integrity of the Yoga Darsana: A Reconsideration of Classical Yoga.* Albany: SUNY Press, 1998.

Wiethaus, Ulrike. *Ecstatic Transformation: Transpersonal Psychology in the Work of Mechthild of Magdeburg.* Syracuse, NY: Syracuse University Press, 1996.

William of St. Thierry. *The Nature and Dignity of Love.* Translated by Thomas X. Davis. Kalamazoo, MI: Cistercian Publications, 1981.

Women's Ordination Conference. http://www.womensordination.org.

Yearley, Lee H. *Mencius and Aquinas: Theories of Virtue and Conceptions of Courage.* Albany: SUNY Press, 1990.

Index of Names

Abhinavagupta, 67, 94, 168n15, 177n15
Anderson, Pamela Sue, 116, 123, 138, 143–44, 177n6, 178n33
Antal, 6
Aquinas. *See* Thomas Aquinas
Aristotle, xvii, xix–xx, 16, 153
Armour, Ellen, xii, 154
Augustine, 38, 71, 87, 153, 175n10

Baker-Fletcher, Karen, 158
Barnett, Lionel D., 89, 165n32, 166n43
Beatrice of Nazareth, 38
Bernard of Clairvaux, 7, 48, 50, 136
Bhāskara, 175n6
Blair, Harry, 79–80
Buddhaghosa, Bhadantacariya, 5
Butler, Judith, 115, 167n53, 177n3
Bynum, Caroline Walker, 84, 167n49

Clooney, Francis X., 4
Collins, Patricia Hill, 4

Dalmiya, Vrinda, 60

Descartes, René, xvii, xx, 56–57, 153, 163n2
Dyczkowski, Mark, 147, 168n15, 169n37, 172nn23, 24; 175n15

Eiesland, Nancy, 114
Elisabeth of Schönau, 130

Farley, Wendy, 130, 158
Feldmeier, Peter, 5
Franklin, James, 13, 87, 89–90
Freud, Sigmund, 180n64

Gandhi (Mahatma), 79–80, 174n59, 178n34
Grierson, George, 89, 165n32, 166n43

Hadewijch, 6, 38
Heinrich of Halle, 8
Hildegard of Bingen, 130
Hollywood, Amy, 46, 170n50, 176n35

Inden, Ronald, 6
Irigaray, Luce, 24, 84, 110, 154, 177n2

193

Isayeva, Natalia, 64

James, William, 166n44
Jantzen, Grace, 22, 50, 57, 76, 171n7
Jayaratha, 177n15
John of the Cross, St., 5, 43, 141
Johnson, Mark, x, 14–16, 47
Julian of Norwich, 159

Kasulis, Thomas, 109
Kaul, Jai Lal (J. L.), 9, 11, 33, 92, 119, 164n21, 166n42, 168n27, 173n37, 175n11, 177n10, 178n23
Keller, Catherine, xii, 57, 76, 153, 157
King, Richard, 17, 22, 168n19
Kotru, Nil Kanth, 11, 61, 89, 93, 117, 120, 122, 166n38, 168n26, 173n37, 175n8, 177n10, 178n28
Koul, Anand, 32, 165n32, 166n43, 168n27, 178nn22, 28; 179n40
Kṣemarāja, 94, 119, 169n30

Lakoff, George, x, 14–16, 47, 149–50, 152
Laksmanjoo, Swami, 178n27
Lalleśwarī. *See Index of Subjects*
Lanzetta, Beverly, 141
Lawrence, David, 76, 174n50

Madhva, xix
McFague, Sallie, xviii, 57, 155, 163n3, 171n6, 174n59, 181n19
McGinn, Bernard, 36, 47–48, 103, 165nn23, 26; 179n57
Mechthild of Hackeborn, 129
Mechthild of Magdeburg. *See Index of Subjects*
Meister Eckhart, 7, 19–20, 37, 46, 165n26, 170n53
Mirabai, 6, 123, 178nn33, 34

Mukta, Parita, 178n34
Muller-Ortega, Paul, 101

Nagarajan, Vijaya, 156
Nelson, Lance, 11, 163n6, 164n8
Newman, Barbara, 45, 169n41, 170nn45, 48
Nund Rishi, 100, 164n21, 165n32, 176n22, 177n9

Odin, Jaishree Kak, 24, 32, 35, 58, 63–64, 89, 95, 124–5, 166nn38, 39; 173n37, 175n11, 178n23
Otto, Rudolf, 19–20

Pandit, B. N., 177n12, 178n29
Paul, St. 87, 97
Plato, xvii, 57, 78, 163n2
Plumwood, Val, 2, 59, 77, 116, 163n2 (intro.), 163n2 (chap. 1)
Poor, Sara, 9, 129–30, 132–33, 179n51
Porete, Marguerite, 8, 19, 37–38, 45, 46, 128, 167n6
Pseudo-Dionysius, 38, 71, 150, 166n47

Rājānaka Rāma, 168n25
Rambachan, Anantanand, 58, 167n2
Rich, Adrienne, 157
Richard of St. Victor, 44–45

Said, Edward, 22, 36, 168n16
Sanderson, Alexis, 122, 166n40, 177n12
Śaṅkara, x, xiii, 5, 17–18, 20–21, 58, 167n2
Scarborough, Milton, xix, 1
Schneider, Laurel, xii, 153
Scully, Jackie Leach, 110
Sherma, Rita, 58, 76, 172n12

Shinn, Larry, 80, 174n57
Smith, Jonathan Z., 3–4, 164nn10, 11
Somānanda, 178n27

Teresa of Avila, 6
Tertullian, xvii
Thatamanil, John, xix, 20, 167n5
Thomas Aquinas, xvii, 5, 153, 173n43

Tobin, Frank, 8, 47, 141, 170nn53, 57; 173n45, 179n53
Toshkhani, Sashi Shekhar, 165n32, 178n29
Turner, Mark, 149–50, 152

Vasugupta, 122

William of St. Thierry, 44–46, 48

Index of Subjects

abhiṣeka, 159
absence, divine. *See* separation
abuse, 115, 117, 123, 126–27, 140–42
Adam, 70, 89
adhikāra, 11. *See also* authority
adornment, 49, 171n68. *See also* reward
Advaita Vedānta, xix, 17–18, 21, 32, 36, 51, 58, 167n2, 176n24
air, xxii, 13–15, 48, 51, 55, 67, 73, 81, 100, 149–51, 154–55, 161
āṇavamala, 25, 33
angels, 50, 51, 69, 72, 89, 99, 102, 135, 170n52, 171n66, 173nn42, 43, 46
antinomianism, 37, 67, 129
apophatic theology, 19, 32, 150
asceticism, 30, 58, 72, 75, 79–81, 84, 89, 95–97, 99, 102–3, 109, 149
ātman, 17–18, 20, 32, 169nn28, 33; 176n24
attachment, 26–28, 42, 52, 73, 79, 95, 168n24. *See also* desire; nonattachment
authority, 11–12, 37, 127, 130, 131–35, 140, 166n44, 180n58

authorship, female, 9, 11, 128–30, 135, 179n57

baptism, 158, 159
beguines, 6, 7, 9, 81, 128–36, 143–44, 164n22, 165n28
Bhagavad-Gita, 163n6, 168n24
bhakti, 6, 10, 166n38
bodily fluids, 13, 15, 99, 115, 150, 153, 154, 158, 167n49
body, xx–xxi, 14–15, 48–49, 69, 71–72, 73, 83–114, 119, 120, 136, 142, 149, 157–58, 161, 170n50, 173n32, 175nn11, 13; 176n26
  in the afterlife, 49, 77, 102, 104–5 (*see also* reward)
  capacities of, 99, 100–105, 109
  as divine, 93–94, 102, 113
  limitations of, 90–91, 97–98, 103, 109, 111
  as microcosm, 60, 85–86, 92–94, 96, 109, 112
  as partner, 84, 88, 91, 104–5
  as prison, 83–84, 91, 104
  and taboos, 154, 159

brahman, xii, xix, 17–18, 20, 21, 32, 58–59, 86, 176n24
breastfeeding. *See* nursing
breath, 48, 84–86, 92–94, 105–6, 108, 110–12, 149, 155
  divine, 48, 112, 148, 161, 171n66
  as microcosm, 92–93, 111–12
buddhi, 62, 85
Buddhism, xix, 21, 58, 120

Cartesian dualism, xvii, x, xx, 50, 56–57, 78, 83–84, 108–10, 113
caste, xix, 3, 10, 11, 118, 140, 159, 178nn33, 34
chakras, 85, 175n8
Christ, wounds of, 99, 103, 158
Christianity
  as dualistic, xviii, 77
  medieval, 5–6, 8, 37, 44, 50, 68–69, 81, 84, 109, 113, 131, 132, 135–36, 164n22, 165n26, 167n49, 169n41, 173n42, 179n57
church, 7, 8, 9, 71, 128–29, 131, 133–35, 143, 144, 158
class, xxi, 4, 116, 118–21, 127–28, 136. *See also* poverty; renunciation
clergy, criticism of, 9, 129, 134
colonialism, x, 3, 17, 22, 51. *See also* Orientalism; postcolonial theory
community, xxi, 7–8, 71, 80, 97, 121, 126–27, 131–32, 134–36, 140, 143–45, 158
comparative theology, ix–xiii, xix, 3–5, 18
  and metaphor, 13–16
  and outsiders, 5, 11–12
comparison, 84, 164n11
  of Mechthild and Lalleśwarī, 51–53, 73–78, 99–100, 105–8, 110–14, 139–45, 147–49, 157
conceptual metaphor theory, x, 14–16, 149

confession (sacrament), 8, 98, 134, 135
consciousness, 24–36, 51–53, 59–68, 75–77, 85–86, 91–96, 101–2, 107–113, 121–22, 125, 140–43, 148–51
  states of, 30–31, 35
container metaphor, 15, 150–53
cosmology, 57, 59–78, 147
Council of Vienne (1311–12), 9, 128, 179n45
courtly tropes, 7–8, 38–39, 41, 91, 98, 130, 132
creation, 60–63, 68–69, 153
  pure and impure, 61–64, 77
Crusades, 130

dams, 152, 181n7
dark night
  of the feminine, 141–42
  of the senses, 43, 141–42
  of the soul, 43, 141–42
*darśana*s, 12, 164n7, 166n45
De proprietatibus rerum, 69
desire, 26, 27–28, 36, 40–42, 44, 48, 52, 62, 64–65, 72–75, 79, 86–87, 95, 107, 111–13, 143, 170n48
  for God, 27–28, 40, 41, 52, 65, 68, 73, 74, 77, 106, 127, 139, 161
  God's, 38–41, 48, 130, 161
detachment, 75, 125–26
dialogues, in *The Flowing Light of the Godhead*, 38, 72, 87, 90–91, 104–5
difference, xvii–xxi, 52–53, 79, 116, 127, 139, 142, 147, 157
  of Creator and creature, 37, 59, 72
  within divinity, 23–24, 37–39
  of God and world, 75–78
  as necessary for relation, 34–35, 121
  in relation to others, 140, 159
dīkṣā. *See* initiation

Index of Subjects

disabilities studies, 110–11, 114, 176n39
discipline. *See* asceticism
dissent, female, 123, 129–30, 144
diversity, xviii, xix, xx, 12, 18, 21, 24–25, 34, 53, 59, 78, 111, 126, 140, 148, 176n24. *See also* difference; duality
divinization, 20, 40, 42, 47, 100, 102–5, 111, 113, 128–30
Dominicans, 8–9, 81, 128, 130, 134
dualism, xi–xii, 108–9, 147, 152–53, 154, 156, 163n2 (chap. 1)
   between body and mind, 83–84, 96, 109, 144
   critiques of, xvii
   defined, xviii, 1–2, 147
   between East and West, 18, 23, 148
   Hindu, xix, 21, 64
   between men and women, 23
   as more than two, 16, 114
   as not inevitably linked, xx, 3, 116, 180n1
   perpetuated in critique, 3, 84
   positive evaluation of, xviii
   between self and other, xxi, 116
duality, xix, 1
   of *ātman* and *brahman*, 17, 20
   as distinct from dualism xiii, xviii, 1, 76, 147
   of God and self, 17–20, 32, 49, 147
   of God and world, 74, 82, 147
   as necessary for relation, 41, 49, 131, 177n2
   of self and other, 53, 101, 115–16, 119–21, 126–27, 138–39, 145, 147
   of subject and object, 19, 24, 53, 61, 101, 125, 148
   and oppression, 16

Earth. *See* ecology; materiality; microcosm
East, the, stereotype as monistic, x, xx, 18, 33, 35, 51, 56, 76, 78
ecofeminism, xviii, 172n19, 174n59
ecology, 55–59, 78, 79–81, 154–56, 171nn1, 2; 172n9
   models of, 79–80
ecstasy, 46, 49, 72, 89–90, 97–98, 103, 107, 158, 171n66, 176n35
elemental theology, xxii, 13, 51, 62, 68, 73–75, 85, 154–56
ellende, das, 42–44, 170n52
emanation cosmology, 62–63, 67, 74, 92, 148
emotions. *See* passions
empowered means, 92–94
environment. *See* ecology
Environmental Protection Agency, 155
epistemology, 34, 64, 66, 74–75, 78, 169n36
equality, 2, 37, 39, 119–21, 123, 135, 140, 143
erotic metaphors, 28, 35, 48–49, 129, 130, 179n47
Eucharist, 47, 69, 88, 98, 103, 134, 171n64
Eve, 89, 136
experience, 112, 116, 154, 156
   bodily, as basis for comparison, xi, 14, 51, 105, 149

fall, the, 69, 89–90, 170n52, 173n43, 175n13
feminine, the, 21–23. *See also* women
feminism, xi, xvii, 132, 142, 163n6, 176n39, 180n1
   and Hinduism, 58, 172n17
feminist theology, ix, xii, xviii, xx, 14, 110, 137, 141, 153, 172n19, 174nn59, 61, 176n39
flesh, 87–88, 103, 136, 175n10

fluidity, x, xii, xxi, 13, 15, 30, 36, 38, 46–48, 50, 51, 59, 73–75, 78, 84, 93–94, 98, 99, 103, 105–8, 110, 111, 113, 116, 122, 130–31, 135, 136–39, 143–45, 148–54, 156–61, 167n49

Ganges River, 160, 181n20
gender, xvii–xx, 89, 115, 119, 121, 123–25, 133, 135–37, 141, 180n58
genre, x, 8, 13, 15, 23
German, 6–7, 9, 50, 88, 129–130
global warming, 55, 155
God
  as Bridegroom, 7, 39, 43, 48, 53, 174n47
  nonpersonal images of, 35, 52, 154, 160
  triadic conceptions of, 76 (*see also* Trinity)
guru, 11, 120, 121–23, 140, 141, 144, 177n7, 178n31

heaven, 57, 68–73, 74, 77, 79, 97, 102, 103, 104, 135, 149, 170n52, 171n66, 176n31
Helfta, convent at, 8, 128, 133
hell, 43, 68–71, 70, 73, 77, 88, 97, 134, 149, 174n47
heresy, 7–9, 19, 128–29, 164n22, 179n47
heterosexism, xxi, 2, 140, 142, 144, 152
hierarchy, xii, xvii–xviii, 2, 16, 34, 56, 58–59, 108, 154
  cosmic, 63–64, 69–71, 73–75, 78, 79, 170n52
  as distinct from dualism, 121–23, 139–41, 147
  fluid, 122, 131–35, 137, 140
  social, xxi, 125–26, 130–31, 135, 144, 152
Hindu theology, 166n46

Hinduism, xix–xx, 3–6, 12, 18, 20, 58–59, 79, 95, 120–21, 155, 159, 166n46, 168n19, 172n17, 176n23
  as dualistic, xix
  and feminism, 58, 172n17
  six orthodox schools of, 3, 21
Holy Spirit. *See* Trinity
human nature, 29–30, 41, 50–53, 85–88, 151. *See also* pluralist anthropology
humility, 19, 40, 45, 103, 107–8, 129, 130, 131, 132–35, 137, 142, 147, 150

idolatry, 18, 37
illusion, xii, xix–xx, 20, 21, 25, 56, 58, 50, 62–63, 89, 167n2. *See also māyā*
imitation of Christ, 45, 69, 87, 98, 111, 132
immanence, xx, 24, 32, 34–36, 52, 55–56, 58, 73, 76, 93, 105, 138–39
impurity, xi, 1, 24–28, 33, 61, 63–64, 67, 77, 113, 122, 159, 173n32. *See also mala*s
incarnation, 19, 37–39, 49, 69, 73, 87–88, 99, 102–3, 105, 113, 154, 158, 173n42
individual means, 92–94
influence, 115, 154, 158
initiation, 118, 122–23, 178n30
Islam, 18, 37, 120–21, 178n29

jīvanmukti, 100–2, 107, 125–26, 139, 140, 177nn23, 24
John the Baptist, 70, 128–29
Judaism, 18, 37, 70, 166n47
Judas, 136

Kabbalah, 37
karma, 25–26, 28, 64, 66, 101, 148
karmamala, 25–26

Index of Subjects

Kashmir Śaivism, xx, 10, 21, 25, 30, 34, 36, 52, 60–64, 66, 76, 85, 91–92, 94, 95, 111, 113, 117, 122–25, 151, 168n13, 172n24, 176n24, 178nn27, 30
  and householders, 11, 117–18, 140
  Kaula school, 118
  Trika school, 10, 31, 166n39, 168n28
Kashmir, medieval, 66, 120
Kaula school. *See* Kashmir Śaivism
Koshur Samachar, 32

Lady Love, 38, 90, 130, 169n41
Lady Soul, 48, 90. *See also* soul
Lalleśwarī
  biography of, 9–11, 23–24, 122, 165n32, 166n42, 177n7, 178n23
  critique of, 32–33, 64, 89, 124
  as guru, 11, 117, 122, 127, 140
  opposition to, 124–27, 140, 142, 143
  sayings of, 11, 32, 33, 117, 166n43
Latin, 6, 7, 8, 9, 129–30, 133, 179n47
liberation theology, 137
licham, 87–88. *See also* body
limbo, 70, 88
lip (*libe*), 87–88. *See also* body
logic
  dualistic, 2, 56, 116
  of fluidity, 116, 148
  of metaphors, x–xi, 116
  of the One, 153
love
  and knowledge, 52–53
  nature of God and soul as, 75
  that flows downhill, 108, 131, 133, 137, 139–40, 159
  See also minne
Lucifer, 70, 132

Lux divinitatis, 9. *See also The Flowing Light of the Godhead*

Magdeburg Synod (1261), 8, 128
*mala*s, 24–27, 113, 148, 168n22
manas. *See* mind
mantra, 31, 92–93, 101, 123, 176n26
marginality, 4–5, 14, 116, 127–30, 131, 133, 138, 139–44, 159. *See also* outsider within
Mary (mother of Jesus), 39, 70, 87, 98, 102, 170n45, 173n45
materiality, xx, 42, 57, 63–64, 69, 74, 76–77, 82, 108
māyā, 20, 25–26, 58, 61, 65–67, 86, 173n32. *See also* illusion
māyīyamala, 25, 66
Mechthild of Magdeburg
  biography of, 7–9, 43, 134
  critique of, 104, 142
  opposition to, 8, 127–29, 134, 140, 142, 143
medieval period, 5–6
meditation, 28–30, 34, 52, 60, 63, 94, 169n35, 175n15
mendicant orders, 81, 128, 131, 136. *See also* Dominicans
metaphor, 13, 47–48, 111, 130, 139, 148–52
  as basis for comparison, x–xi, 14, 105, 149
microcosm
  body as, 60, 91
  breath as, 92–93
  desire as, 28, 75, 95
  Earth as, 71, 134
  individual consciousness as, 28–30, 86, 101, 151, 168n28
mind, xx, 31, 62, 65, 83, 86, 93–94, 102, 109, 113, 127
minne, 38, 40, 75
missionaries, Christian, 3, 17–18, 130, 168n19

moderation, 42, 73, 75, 80–81, 95–96, 97, 101, 109
modernity, 56, 84, 108, 113
monism, xii–xiii, 20, 21–23, 24, 33, 50, 51, 57, 59, 167n3, 168n13
mujerista theology, 142, 174n61
mutuality, xxi, 2, 13, 38–40, 57, 68, 130, 132, 136, 139, 140, 145, 153
mysticism, 12, 21–23, 36–37, 50, 52, 166n44

nāḍīs, 85–86, 92, 105, 149, 175n8
nakedness, 48–49, 101, 118–20, 125, 130
narratives
  of the body, 88–91, 100–5, 109
  of dualism, xvii, 163n2 (intro.)
  of female dissent, 109
nature
  divine, 29–30, 68
  human, 29–30, 57, 69, 73, 121, 125, 128 (*see also* pluralist anthropology; *sahaj*)
  of the soul, 41, 50, 51 (*see also* soul)
  of the world, 76–78 (*see also* ecology)
Neoplatonism, 57, 76
nonattachment, 126, 141–42, 168n24
nondualism, xii–xiii, xix, 3, 18–20, 21, 51, 58–59
nursing, 99, 100, 144, 151

old age, 45, 72, 100, 102, 110
Oṃ, 60, 94, 101, 172n23
orality, 7, 9, 11–12, 23, 36, 123, 165n32, 178n20, 179n40
order, 70, 73, 102, 174n47. *See also* hierarchy
Orientalism, x, 22, 36, 168n16
otherworldliness, x, 56, 71–72, 73, 80, 81, 113

outsider within, 4–5, 11–12, 142, 144, 164n16. *See also* marginality

pain, 1, 42, 44–46, 70, 85, 88, 90, 97–98, 102, 104, 105, 107–8, 110, 111–13, 131, 141, 158. *See also* suffering
panentheism, 20, 57, 59, 76, 171n6
pantheism, 18, 20, 57, 59, 76, 167n3, 171n7
paradise, twofold, 71. *See also* heaven
passions, 27, 96, 127
past lives, 61, 120
patriarchy, xii, xviii, xix, 3, 22–23, 117–19, 123, 124–25, 129, 132, 136, 137, 153
Pelagianism, 110–11
penance, 70–71, 81, 88, 97–98, 102
pervasion cosmology, 62–63, 67, 74, 92
play, 38–40, 67, 74–75, 131
pluralist anthropology, 84–88, 96, 113. *See also* human nature
postcolonial theory, ix, 22, 51, 172n9
poststructuralism, x, xvii, xxi, 2, 4, 14
poverty, 81, 128, 131, 136–37, 142
power, 4–5, 64, 126, 132, 137, 140, 143
powerlessness, divine, 39–40, 130, 170n44
practical dualism, xix, 3, 56, 58, 74, 89, 105, 156
practices, religious, 33, 91–100, 105, 111
  See also asceticism; meditation; yoga
prakṛti, 58–59, 62
prāṇa. See breath
pregnancy, 102–3, 115, 119, 157–58, 179n47
premodernity, xx, 84, 110–13, 116

Presbyterian Church (U.S.A.), 144, 180n72
process theology, xiii, xvii, xviii, 2, 20
procession and return, 40, 53, 113, 148, 166n47
psychology, 2, 66, 115, 136, 157, 177n3
purgatory, 70–71, 77, 88, 97, 134
puruṣa, 58, 62

racism, xxi, 2, 115, 142, 144, 152
rapture. *See* ecstasy
rebirth, 26, 120, 124, 139
relation, xviii, xx–xxii, 2–3, 34, 76, 115, 161
  with divinity, 34, 39–41, 48, 52–53, 72–75, 97, 112–13
  of the one and the many, 21
  with the other, 127, 157–59
  rooted in divinity, 13, 37–39, 58, 68
  and the self, 15–16
renunciation, 67, 79–80, 117–18, 125, 127, 140, 179n44
revelation, 12, 133–34, 136, 140, 158, 166n47
reward, 9, 70–71, 77, 88, 103, 104–5, 108, 135, 149, 176n31. *See also* adornment
risk, 53, 107, 115, 130, 135, 143–44
rivers, 13, 58, 151–52, 155, 160–61
  as Goddesses, 59, 155–56, 160, 181n20
Romanticism, 18, 79–80, 171n9

sacraments, 71. *See also* baptism; confession; Eucharist
sahaj, 29–30, 51, 92, 94–95, 101, 112, 118, 168nn26, 27
Śaiva Siddhanta, xix, 21
Śakti, 13, 24, 52, 58, 59–61, 66, 76, 94, 169n28
saṃsāra, 26, 101
  as ocean, 30, 65–66, 105
  See also past lives; rebirth
Sanskrit, 6, 11, 18, 166n42
satkaryavāda. *See* theories of causation
self
  connective, 138
  as obstacle, 41–42, 143
  separative, xxi, 116, 124–25, 138–40, 144, 157, 180n62
  soluble, 138–39, 157, 180n62
  true identity in the divine Self, 18, 23, 25–26, 29–35, 51, 52–53, 67, 86, 92, 94–96, 102, 109, 120, 143
senses
  embodied, 62, 87, 90, 93, 102–4, 107, 109, 112–13, 176n32
  (*see also* spiritual sensorium)
  interpretive, spiritual vs. fleshly, 129
sensible transcendentals, 154
separation, from God, 20, 30, 40–44, 46, 49, 63, 73, 98, 107, 141
service, 41, 128, 131, 136–37, 139
Siddha Śrikantha, 10, 122
sin, 13, 18, 56, 70, 88, 90, 110, 136, 148
Śiva, 21, 33, 61
  as consciousness, 24, 29, 52, 60, 148 (*see also* consciousness)
  five activities of, 29, 60, 93
  and Śakti, 13, 24, 59, 76, 94
Śiva Sūtras, 92, 126, 169n30, 176n26
Song of Songs, 41, 48–49, 103
soul, xx, 52, 72, 87, 103–4, 108, 109, 168n28, 170n45
  as Bride, 7, 39, 44–45, 48, 53, 136 (*see also* Lady Soul)
  as image of Trinity, 39–40, 112
Spanda Kārikās, 102, 169n28, 169n29, 172n23
spanda, 102
spirit, 87
spiritual sensorium, 103–4, 109, 176n32

stages of the Christian life, 44–46
Sufism, 37, 122, 178n29. *See also* Islam
suffering, 44–46, 71, 85, 88, 97–98, 106–8, 110–13, 141
symbol. *See* metaphor
systematic theology, ix, xiii

taboo, 154, 159
tantra, 11, 21, 59, 91, 123, 166n39
   practices of, 31, 60, 67, 101, 117, 177n15
*tattva*s, 61–63, 66, 68, 74, 77, 85–86, 101, 121, 140, 172n27, 173n32
The Flowing Light of the Godhead, 8, 68, 129, 133
theodicy, 81
theories of causation, 62–63
theōsis, 102. *See also* divinization
third space, 24, 125
Tiamat, 153, 180n64
touch, 1, 24, 62, 158
tradition, 12
tragedy, 127, 139–42
transcendence, 24, 32–37, 52, 55–56, 58, 66–67, 73, 76–77, 96, 124–25, 138–39, 151–52
   and the body, xx, 89, 91, 93–94, 102, 158, 173n32
   of suffering, 106–7, 111–12
transition, moments of, 34, 92, 175n15
   See also void, the
Trika School. *See* Kashmir Śaivism
Trinity, 37–39, 45, 47, 51–52, 68, 70, 72, 87, 90, 102, 129, 131, 139, 148, 153, 156, 161, 170nn45–46; 171n64, 173n45
tsyeth, 86. *See also* consciousness

union, 18, 46–50, 51, 158, 172n24
   in differentiation, 20, 50, 51

unity-in-difference, 125, 143
Upaniṣads, 17–18, 176n21

vernacular, the, 6–7, 9–10, 23, 118, 129–30, 165n26
Vijñānabhairava Tantra, 52, 85, 101, 166n39, 169n35, 176n21
visions, 7–8, 36, 38, 68, 70–71, 74, 77, 78, 98, 99, 102–4, 107, 128–29, 134, 173n44, 176n31
vivartavāda, *See* theories of causation
void, the, 31–32, 33–34, 60–61, 66, 75, 77, 92, 153, 156, 157, 169n35
vulnerability, 115–116, 119, 128, 133, 157–58

Waldensians, 128
water, xxii, 10, 13, 14–15, 30–31, 46, 51, 55, 62–63, 67, 68, 73, 75, 93, 95, 100, 105–6, 108, 117–18, 130, 149, 150–51, 153–55, 157–61. *See also* fluidity
West, the, stereotype as dualistic, x, xx, 18, 36, 50, 51, 56, 76–78
will, 20, 25, 41–42, 50, 126, 170n50
womanist theology, 141, 158
women, x, 5–6, 12, 22, 58, 108
Women's Ordination Conference, 144
world, xi, 64–65, 76, 124–25
   as deluding, 18, 25, 56, 65–66, 74, 167n2
   as God's body, 57, 66–67, 155, 171nn6, 7

yoga, 10, 64, 85, 91, 94, 105, 107, 111, 169, 164n7, 166n39, 175n8
   as resource for the West, 84, 110
yogic powers, 23, 102, 117, 120–21, 122